D1563666

Hidden in the Home

SUNY Series in Women and Work

Joan Smith, Editor

Hidden in the Home

The Role of Waged Homework in the Modern World-Economy

Jamie Faricellia Dangler

State University of New York Press

331.4
D18h

Published by
State University of New York Press, Albany

© 1994 State University of New York

Printed in the United States of America

Marketing by Theresa Abad Swierzowski
Production by Laura Starrett

For information, address State University of New York Press,
State University Plaza, Albany, New York 12246

Library of Congress Cataloging-in-Publication Data

Dangler, Jamie Faricellia, 1958–
    Hidden in the home : the role of waged homework in the modern
world economy / Jamie Faricellia Dangler.
        p. cm.
    Includes bibliographical references and index.
    ISBN 0-7914-2129-5 : $49.50.—ISBN 0-7914-2130-9 (pbk.) : $16.95
    1. Women electronic industry workers—New York (State)
    2. Cottage industries—New York (State) 3. Sexual division of labor—
New York (State) 4. Home labor—New York (State) I. Title.
    HD6073.E372U653 1994
    331.4'4'0973—dc20   94-282
                                                                    CIP

10 9 8 7 6 5 4 3 2 1

Contents

7

List of Tables

Acknowledgments

I have many people to thank for helping me during the years it took to see this project through from start to finish. At the top of the list is my husband, Steve, whose support is always generously given, and my son, Luke, who makes all that I work for worthwhile.

I owe a great deal to Frank Hearn, who opened an intellectual door for me that has influenced the course of my entire life. If I am fortunate enough to make some contribution to sociology, through this book or subsequent work, it will be in no small measure the result of my association with Frank.

The initial research, including my field study of electronics industry homeworkers in central New York, was done during my years of graduate work in sociology at SUNY Binghamton. I am most grateful for the help I received from Robert Bach. In addition to his sharp critique of my work during its early development, he projected an excitement about the project and its potential merits that was truly inspirational. Others at SUNY Binghamton who offered intellectual and emotional support during those earlier years include Giovanni Arrighi, Beverly Silver, Terry Hopkins, Joan Smith, Jane Collins, Rita Argiros, Anna Davin, Mark Beittel, Nicole Grant, Jim Matsen, and Mark Selden. I was privileged to have been able to present my work in its early stages to my associates in the Research Working Group on World Labor at the Fernand Braudel Center and to have been given an opportunity by Immanual Wallerstein to participate in the Second International Forum on the History of the Labor Movement and of the Working Class. The criticisms and suggestions I received through these avenues were crucial to the development of my analysis.

During the last few years, as I struggled to refine my work for publication, I have benefited greatly from the support and encouragement given by my colleagues at SUNY College at Cortland. Among them are Lisi Krall, Julie Gricar Beshers, Craig Little, Herb Haines, Stuart Traub, Howard Botwinick, Bill Lane, Gretchen Herrmann, and Dev Kennedy. I am also deeply grateful for the painstaking review of an earlier draft of my manuscript by Eileen Boris and three anonymous reviewers from SUNY Press. Though they are not responsible for the shortcomings of my work, their criticisms undoubtedly helped me make it better.

I am grateful to the Business and Professional Women's Foundation for the grant that helped support my field study. I am also indebted to Joyce Durgerian of the New York State Department of Labor for her help during my visits to the DOL and Bill Dennison of the ILGWU for giving me access to the network of electronics industry homeworkers in central New York.

As always, Gilda Haines came through to help me overcome the traumas of manuscript preparation at every stage. Because of her there are no problems that can't be solved and no deadlines that can't be met.

For my parents, John and Lucille Faricellia; my sister, Sarina; and my brother Michael and his family

Preface

My interest in home-based work was sparked in the early 1980s by my observation of women in central New York doing industrial homework for electronics firms.[1] While I was aware of the long and troubled history of homework in industries such as artificial flower- and garment-making, I was surprised to find home-based work flourishing in what I had assumed to be a "modern" industry characterized by centralized production and moderate to high wage rates. As I began to study this particular group of workers I became increasingly aware of the fact that researchers in the United States were observing and documenting the existence of other nontraditional types of paid work in the home. Not only was homework continuing to flourish in the needlework trades (Hosenball 1981; Rauch 1981), it was also being used in the Silicon Valley electonics industry (Carey and Malone 1980; Katz and Kemnitzer 1983; Morales 1983), and by a wide range of businesses for clerical and computer work (Sleeper 1982; Scott 1982). The growing literature on various types of home-based work in the United States, complemented by a corresponding body of research in other developed countries such as Britain and Italy (Hakim 1980; Mattera 1980; Wilkinson 1981) as well as in the Developing World (*Newsletter of International Labour Studies* 1984) raised a key theoretical question. Were the pockets of homework discovered in the late 1970s and 1980s simply anomalies in the modern world-economy, or were they an integral and growing part of contemporary capitalist production?

The starting point in my attempt to answer these questions was a study of homework in the electronics industry in the central part of New York State. I began the project in the midst of a well-publicized legal battle between the State Labor Department and homework distributors. The state's discovery in the early 1980s of electronics industry homework in rural areas surrounding the city of Syracuse coincided with a mounting national concern about illegal homework in the face of the Reagan Administration's attempt to roll back 40 years of federal homework regulation.[2] Against a backdrop of national debate over the legitimacy of provisions under the Fair Labor Standards Act, which prohibited homework in needlework industries such as knitted outerwear and women's apparel, New York State Labor Department officials became embroiled in a controversy over the meaning and intent of state anti-homework statutes.

While Article 13 of the State's Labor Law expressly prohibits or closely regulates homework in certain industries (men's and boy's outer clothing, men's and boy's neckwear, artificial flowers and feathers, gloves, and operations involving "inserting, collating, and similar work") the application of the law to industries not specifically mentioned is left to the discretion of the industrial commissioner. When, beginning in 1981, the Labor Department began citing homework distributors in the electronics industry for violation of the state's homework law, the distributors challenged the legitimacy of these charges in court, arguing that the law was "not intended to cover the situations we're dealing with in central New York" and that the commissioner, by taking the law as a mandate to prohibit industrial homework across the board was "misreading the law."[3] The controversy over homework in central New York added a new dimension to the national debate on this issue. Not only were specific regulations covering traditional homework industries under attack, but the applicability of general homework statutes to "new" industries was challenged.

After following the controversy on both the state and federal levels for almost two years, I happened to stumble upon some information that would lead me into the network of "illegal" electronics homeworkers in central New York. In 1983 a union organizer gave me a small list of homeworkers he had met during the course of his work in the area. Given the possibility of learning about this group of people and their work firsthand I was compelled to follow this timely lead.

My ability to gain access to those involved in illegal homework was enhanced by the fact that their work had already been exposed and covered extensively in the local press. Rather than desiring anonymity, most of those I interviewed felt that "telling their story" would elicit further support for their cause. This applied to both homeworkers and their employers. I was able to conduct in depth interviews with 39 homeworkers (36 women and 3 men).[4] I also interviewed all five of the major homework distributors in the area (who served as middlemen between home-workers and the firms they worked for), three company managers, from two of the three major homework firms[5], two attorneys representing homework distributors in court cases against the Labor Department, the chief attorneys representing the State Labor Department and the Industrial Board of Appeals[6], the director of the Labor Department's Division of Labor Standards, and a senior Labor Standards investigator. All interviews took place between October 1983 and August 1986.

My original goal in undertaking this research was to tell the story of a group of homeworkers in central New York. From the outset I saw them as "nontraditional" homeworkers because of their class and ethnic backgrounds (white, European descent, working- and middle-class), their geographic location (rural), and the industry for which they work (electronics). In another sense, however, they are "traditional" because, like most other home-based workers, they are predominantly women. On a personal level, I was motivated by a desire to reveal the actual struggles these women face on a daily basis—the struggle to earn a living, coordinate paid work with childcare and household responsibilities, and maintain some degree of stability and happiness in their marital relationships. As a resident of a relatively poor county in central New York, I have been acutely aware of the multifaceted strategies employed by the poor to meet economic and personal needs. I saw homework as an important part of the survival strategy adopted by many. I became interested in analyzing the reality of their lives in terms of both objective conditions and their personal perceptions and concerns.

My work was also influenced by theoretical issues. In particular, I sought to understand the role of homework in modern capitalism and to make sense of the experiences of central New York homeworkers in light of prevailing theories about homework and other "informal productive structures" (Pinnaro and Pugliese 1985). Accordingly, my personal and theoretical interests converged in an effort to examine how the particular experiences of the workers I studied could shed light on prominent conceptions about home-based work. On a practical level, I have discovered that an in depth look at the lives of these people reveals the inherent limitations of conventional policy proposals offered by the key actors—capital (working through the political right) and organized labor—in the recent political debates about homework. Proposed solutions to the "homework problem" fail to confront

the inherent contradictions of most home-based work—the conflict between production and reproduction and waged and nonwaged work—and thus fail to speak to the real needs and dilem-
mas of homeworkers.

The situation in central New York provides a unique opportunity to explore the realities of contemporary homework from
multiple perspectives. The relations between capital, labor, and
the state are revealed in lucid form as each one tries to secure its
interests and disclose its view of the meaning and impact of
homework. In the chapters that follow, I will tell their stories and
analyze their situation in view of a broader historical and economic perspective that can clarify the meaning of contemporary
home-based work.

Introduction

"What's wrong with working in my home?" asked a woman I interviewed in 1986 as she sat at her kitchen table winding thin, colored wires through a small core to make transformers for a central New York electronics firm. Her question arose in the context of our discussion of the State Labor Department's depiction of her job as exploitative, substandard work. Though I was well acquainted with the history of the exploitative conditions associated with industrial homework in the United States, I could not give her an unequivocal answer. In fact, I was becoming more confused about this question as I talked to homeworkers who emphasized the benefits working at home brought them and their disdain for those who sought to protect them from exploitation: "People's impression of homeworkers is that we're all dummies because we're exploited. But people doing homework are capable of doing many other jobs. People think those doing homework can't hold another job or don't know any better. If you're saying a person is exploited, you're saying they're dumb" (Interview 23).

These comments were made in the context of electronics assemblers' desperate fight to keep their homework jobs in the face of a New York State Labor Department effort to apply its anti-homework laws to their work. The point of view they express was echoed by others around the country whose previously hidden work was brought to the public eye in the midst of controversy over the Reagan Administration's attempt to repeal federal home-work statutes.[1] Despite the positive publicity given to work-at-home programs for white-collar workers and professionals, which presented home-based work as a gender-neutral option that could provide a reasonable income and a flexible work arrangement for men or women, homework opponents recognized the fact that the overwhelming majority of homeworkers are now, and always have

been, women—most of whom are in low-wage service and industrial occupations with the potential to be denied basic worker
rights such as the legal minimum wage.

The debate that took place through the popular press and at
congressional hearings brought forth the voices of homeworkers,
prohomework and anti-homework employers, labor unions, public officials, journalists, and academics, and revealed the complex
and contradictory realities of the homework issue. How could it
be that working from home was perceived simultaneously as
exploitative and liberating, as an expression of worker choice and
a reflection of the lack of choice, as a creative strategy for combining family and work and the embodiment of women's "double
burden," as a worker's right and a worker's denial of rights?

Since the beginning of my endeavor to explore the realities of
contemporary home-based work, I have struggled to reconcile
homeworkers' perceptions of their work with a broader understanding of its contradictory effects in their lives and its role in
eroding wage rates and working conditions for other workers. For
many women homework is a practical and desirable option given
their household responsibilities and labor market position. But,
as Boris (1987) has argued, while the ability to work at home may
be relatively beneficial for some, for the most part homework
helps to maintain the subordinate position women, as a group,
hold at home and on the labor market. What is most problematic
about the "homework system," as it has operated in the past and
continues to operate for most homeworkers, is that it has helped
to create and sustain a gender division of labor that not only
guarantees the permanence of women's "double burden," but also
prevents the development of a healthier integration of family and
work life for both sexes. Furthermore, homework has historically
undercut factory and office work by cheapening the cost of labor
and overhead for employers. Thus, in homework we see the
confluence of household and labor market dynamics, each conditioned by the traditional gender division of labor.

But there is a huge gap between analysis of the exploitative
nature of most home-based work and a clear agenda for transforming household and labor market relations in a way that would
improve conditions for homeworkers. The voices we heard in the
public debates of the 1980s revealed that there is often a disjunc-
tion between the reality of people's everyday lives, which often
forces them to "choose" homework from a limited and poor set of
employment options (and to fight for the right to make that
"choice") and a broader vision of better working conditions for

all workers, which would include the end of exploitative home-work. This rift is readily visible in the contemporary politics surrounding the issue. While the political right attempts to re-move restrictions on home-based work across the board, oppo-nents of homework, particularly labor unions, fight to prohibit it entirely.[2] In this debate, which places the issue in an either-or framework (the absence of all restrictions on homework versus complete elimination of homework), neither position speaks to the needs of most homeworkers. While the latter have tended to support conservatives in their effort to keep homework legal, they do so out of the need to preserve their incomes. The conservative agenda, however, is to maintain homework as a cheap, flexible production option for industry, which guarantees the continued exploitation of most homeworkers. This is certainly not in their best interests. At the other end of the spectrum, a desire to eliminate the exploitative conditions associated with home-based work is the crux of liberal efforts to ban all homework. While homeworkers would benefit from an end to these conditions (subminimum wages and the absence of worker rights and protec-tions such as social security insurance, health and safety provi-sions, overtime pay, and so on), they do not support the outright prohibition of home-based work. To do so would fly in the face of their struggle for economic survival.

The controversy over homework brings together two broader, interconnected struggles—the fight to improve wages and working conditions for all workers and the effort to develop a better and more equitable way for men and women to combine work and family life. In many ways, homework is the embodiment of the obstacles that have prevented us from accomplishing these goals in the past, for it is the fullest expression of the traditional gender division of labor as it simultaneously affects the household and labor market. But the contemporary politics of homework does not allow for the fact that efforts to attain these goals must be joint ones. They require renegotiation of gender roles in the home, worker organization to strengthen labor's position vis-à-vis capi-tal, the strengthening of workers' efforts to transform the organi-zation of work in a way that makes it more compatible with family needs, and public policies to support people's ability to satisfy both workplace and family demands without compromising ei-ther. The agents of such change will include workers as well as policy-makers and the organized groups that can influence them most. The polarized politics of homework has so far prevented us from proceeding to bridge the gap between these naturally interconnected, yet artificially separated, terrains of struggle. But how can we get beyond this impasse?

This book is an attempt to propose a modest, yet important, starting point. In simple terms, its purpose is to clarify the role and significance of homework in the modern economy, to move beyond viewing it simply as an anomalous vehicle for worker exploitation occasionally imposed by capitalists. Instead, an understanding of the full dimensions of the homework dilemma requires its analysis from two points of view: as a creative strategy adopted by women workers whose employment options are limited by the gender division of labor in the household and the external labor market, and as a production option used by capital to lower labor costs and increase flexibility.

This dual perspective is necessary if we are to move beyond simplistic analyses that lead to reliance on "solutions" that leave the root of the homework problem intact. For example, liberal proposals to strengthen and extend homework regulation, while important, will not by themselves transform the conditions that foster the spread of exploitative home-based work. In fact, the focus on banning all homework has clearly separated those working for an end to exploitative homework from homeworkers themselves. It seems to me that those who have fought hardest for regulatory action (most notably, labor unions) implicitly underestimate the significance of the worker-led impetus for homework, which springs from the gender division of labor within households. While they understand the impetus for homework that comes from capital, and thus focus their efforts on blocking employers' ability to utilize this production option, they have not come to terms with the immediate impact of their actions on those they seek to protect. While homework opponents have a longer-term, more comprehensive view of the potential benefits to all workers of ending exploitative homework, their strategy for reaching this goal seems to deny the importance of homeworkers themselves as agents of change.

In order to overcome the conceptual and practical barriers that keep apart those who should be allies in the fight to end exploitative homework, we must recognize the impact of the social, as well as the economic, relations that underlie and support the "homework system." This means that gender must be placed at the center of our analytical framework. It also means that we must move beyond the past tendency to see homework as a marginal form of work that can be stamped out with appropriate regulatory action. Instead, it is important to acknowledge that homework has served as a relatively permanent vehicle for the incorporation of a significant portion of the female labor force into the capitalist production process and that deep-rooted social forces support its continuance. Homework derives from the confluence of women's contradictory role as laborers in the sphere of paid production and unpaid workers in the sphere of reproduction. Any attempt to eliminate exploitative homework must focus equal attention on transforming women's position in both spheres.[3] It must bring together struggles in the home with struggles in the workplace. Concretely, women homeworkers must be able to pursue an alternative model for combining family and work responsibilities—one that would be free of the power inequities that currently characterize their home and work lives. Such a model might very well include home-based work, but under a fundamentally new set of social and economic conditions.

With this in mind, we can propose an analytical framework that allows for a multidimensional approach to an analysis of the homework system. On one level, the study of homework must involve an understanding of how the gender division of labor simultaneously affects household and labor market relations. At the same time, we must consider how those social relations affect and are affected by economic forces. Accordingly, my approach is to combine analysis of processes that occur on a microlevel (in households) with those that occur on a macrolevel; to place the analysis of homework in a global economic and historical context that allows us to see the relationship between local, regional, and global patterns of economic development and the strategies for survival pursued by workers whose actions are conditioned by a variety of social and economic forces (gender division of labor, cultural practices, economic conditions, for example).

Accordingly, I have come to view the study of homework, first and foremost, as the study of the interaction of capital and labor— of the forces and dynamics of capitalist development and of human agency as it responds to and helps shape those forces and dynamics. But in addition to understanding how capital and labor interact to affect economic development and foster the proliferation of particular forms of work such as homework, we need to consider how the state fits into the picture. Underlying the analysis that runs through my work is the assumption that the homework system has been forged through the interaction of all three actors: capital, labor, and the state. It is on this point that I hope to move beyond the predominant focus on capital and labor in much of the homework literature. An understanding of the relationship between capital and labor, and each one's ability to realize its particular interests with regard to homework, depends on our ability to recognize the state's role as an *active* mediator—one that injects its own interests into the arena of class conflict it actuates. Accordingly, while the actions of capital, labor, and the state reflect specific interests, all three, in combination, have played an important role in the development of homework as a structural feature of the modern economy.

Key Issues in the Investigation of Homework

Chapter 2 presents a picture of the lives of homeworkers as revealed to me by those I interviewed. I examine their labor market position, household organization, family economy, and strategies for coping with rural poverty. My research adds substance to the collection of available case studies from advanced industrial countries because it covers a nontraditional group of industrial homeworkers and helps broaden our conception of the people involved in this type of work. While most historical and contemporary case studies in the United States focus on legal and illegal immigrants in urban areas, my study reveals the use of rural, nonimmigrant, working- and middle-class women in homework operations.[4] Thus, it challenges the myth that homework is simply a past chapter in the history of American workers' fight for decent employment—a chapter thought to be revisited only in isolated and unusual circumstances, such as those associated with large-scale immigration.

My study also provides an interesting perspective on the impetus behind the spread of homework in recent decades. In this case, an enclave of homework production was created in the 1960s not simply as a result of its imposition by employers seeking a cheap source of labor, but also through women's efforts to forge work alternatives in the context of a depressed local economy, the physical isolation imposed by rural life, and household and childcare responsibilities. Homework in central New York developed in the context of community networks of family and friends, which linked rural women to urban-based national and multinational electronics firms. It came to be perceived on all sides as a production option that could be mutually beneficial to the companies and the communities they operated around. This case can, therefore, shed light on the importance of worker agency in shaping economic development—a factor highlighted in recent analyses of industrial restructuring, such as Benton's insightful study of the informal economy and industrial development in Spain (1990), and Mingione's analysis of the importance of both economic and social factors in forging work alternatives in societies around the world-economy (1991). My case study, though a modest contribution, may provide further support for the analytical framework suggested in these pathbreaking works.

In chapter 3 I examine the conditions under which homework becomes a viable production option for modern enterprise as well as its relationship to current strategies employed in the global restructuring of capitalist production. Many of the questions that shaped my research agenda have been asked by others who have sought to examine the role of homework in the world-economy with peripheral and semi-peripheral countries as their starting point. For example, in their study of homeworkers in Mexico City, Beneria and Roldan (1987) shed light on the close articulation between formal and underground (legal and illegal) productive activities and their relation to the production networks of multinational corporations. More recently, Benton's (1990) analysis of "productive decentralization" in Spain seeks to explain how unregulated forms of production, including homework, are part of complex and varying patterns of industrial restructuring, and, thus, central to modern capitalism. The information I obtained about the production strategies of three electronics firms in central New York is presented and analyzed in view of more general patterns of industrial restructuring across the world-economy. One of my objectives is to shed light on the social and economic processes that link women in core, semiperipheral, and peripheral countries through a global production system, while at the same time recognizing the different patterns of industrial organization and employment that emerge in different places at different times.

While analyses of current patterns of industrial restructuring allow us to see how unregulated or "casualized" forms of production have expanded under crisis conditions, it is important to see beyond the crisis and analyze homework from a broader historical and theoretical perspective. While past and contemporary studies have recognized homework as a distinctive vehicle for the exploitation of women, ironically, the association of this form of production with women has, at the same time, obscured its significance in analyses of capitalist development. For the most part, it has been presented as a conjunctural phenomenon (tied to economic crisis), a transitional phenomenom, or an antiquated survival of a past stage in capitalist development. These views follow, in part, from our inability to get past the artificial separation between work and home, productive and reproductive spheres. Because of women's conceptual relegation to the latter, the significance of their work for capitalist production has often been obscured. This is certainly true with regard to waged homework. Despite its occasional splash of visibility in urban centers (where it can be readily identified as a source of super-exploitation of the most powerless women, such as immigrants) homework has remained hidden in the home—integrated with unpaid, reproductive activities. The task at hand is to open the doors and windows to get a glimpse of what Marx called the "outside department of the factory" (and in today's economy, the office).

Accordingly, the underlying thesis of chapters 4 and 5 is that homework is a structural rather than a conjunctural feature of modern capitalism. In chapter 4 I trace the historical origin of industrial homework, highlighting its emergence as a form of production in the mid-nineteenth century and its relationship to other types of domestic production such as the putting-out system. I argue that by the nineteenth century putting-out became transformed into a new "system of industry," industrial homework, characterized by a fundamentally different set of relations between capital and capitalist-controlled domestic labor. Through reassessment of conventional views, which see centralized production as the optimal and inevitable tendency in capitalist development, (those of labor process theorists such as Braverman [1974] and Marglin [1971]), I demonstrate how industrial homework "fits in" with modern capitalism.

After opening the theoretical space for an understanding of homework's place in the modern economy, I turn to the task of uncovering the economic and social factors that have supported its use over the last century. The insights offered in recent analyses of the role of informal productive activities, often referred to as the informal sector, have guided my work. For example, Mingione (1991) emphasizes the interplay of social and economic factors in creating heterogeneous forms of work across the world-economy. He identifies the global economic and organizational trends that support the continued expansion of informal activities (economic downturn and slow growth, vertical disintegration of firms, automation, tertiarization, for example) but emphasizes the simultaneous importance of social factors in determining patterns of work. In his view, an understanding of the "social economy," that is, "socio-economic phenomena such as informal activities, self-provisioning, the economic role of the family and ethnic relationships and the variety of household work strategies" (1), must replace an analysis of informal activities that focuses only on their "macroeconomic origins and impact." The importance of Mingione's perspective for my work is that it supports the incorporation of gender into an analysis of capitalist development. Concretely, it allows us to move beyond simply seeing gender relations as creating a group of workers particularly susceptible to exploitation—as a passive variable in the process of capitalist development. Instead, gender can be brought to the center stage by extending the logic of Mingione's perspective. The task at hand is to understand the ways in which gender relations condition the development of the "social economy." Homework provides a unique opportunity for such understanding. Similarities in the social relations that underlie it cut across cultures and regions of the world.

Chapter 5 expands on the conceptual framework laid out in chapter 4 by considering how the gender division of labor in capitalist society simultaneously conditions the development of the production process and guarantees the availability of a female labor force whose paid work is conceptualized differently from men's, with substantial consequences for wages, working conditions, and terms of employment. A critique of dual labor market theory serves as a point of departure for my analysis. While the former provides a useful description of divisions in the labor market (for example, the concentration of women in low-status, low-paying jobs), it does not explain how those divisions develop historically. It simply takes for granted what needs to be explained. More specifically, while dual labor market theorists focus on the role played by technological, market, and control factors in the emergence of different forms of work (how these factors present particular options to capitalists), understanding how patterns of labor force participation develop over time requires consideration of how ideology, culture, labor-capital conflict, and conflict among different groups in the labor force affect the incorporation of groups divided along gender, racial, and ethnic lines. An analysis of homework provides an important point from which to uncover the limitations of dual labor market theory and construct an alternative approach that allows us to see how the sexual division of labor in the home affects the development of the capitalist production process (as opposed to simply fitting into it) and helps create segmented labor markets.

In this chapter I argue that gender ideology has created an artificial distinction between men's and women's work, which brings the latter to the labor market saddled with the weight of assumptions about the conditional nature of their paid work. In homework we see the full expression of the dual effect of this ideology. First, the availability of a labor force assumed to be composed of supplementary wage earners with a marginal commitment to paid work and a primary commitment to household and childcare responsibilities conditions the development of the production process: home-based work emerges as a possible option for capitalists precisely because of the unique circumstances of a segment of the labor force. At the same time, assumptions about the conditional nature of women's paid work set up barriers that limit their points of entry to the labor market. This, in turn, makes homework a practical work option for women, given their relatively limited set of job possibilities. Thus, a vicious cycle is set in motion.

While chapters 2 through 5 focus on different dimensions of the labor-capital relation and the confluence of household and labor market dynamics, in chapter 6 I attempt to clarify the ways in which state action affects and is affected by both. Here I insert the last piece of a conceptual puzzle that recognizes the interaction of all three "actors"—capital, labor, and the state—in the forging of the homework system. I focus on state policy in the United States and how it has shaped the organization of homework in this country over the course of the twentieth century. I argue that state policy has affected the pattern of homework's use in at least four ways. First, protective labor legislation has played a role in creating conditions fostering the expansion of homework during certain periods. For example, in the early part of the century, the passage of laws that regulated the hours and conditions of women's and children's employment encouraged the decentralization of work in some traditional female occupations and the consequent proliferation of homework. Second, variation in state-level homework regulation has led to the concentration of homework in states without, or with weak, homework laws. Furthermore, regional variation in enforcement efforts has affected the spatial distribution of homework across states and within states (between rural and urban areas). Third, the uneven application of state and federal homework laws across industries has created a split between legal and illegal homework operations. In prohibited industries homework has been pushed underground and characterized by wages and working conditions below those set by legal statute. At the same time, some homework carried out in accordance with prevailing labor standards has existed in nonprohibited industries and under permit procedures established by state and federal regulations. Finally, the fact that state legislation has helped shape the organization of production in homework operations is revealed in the outcomes of worker and employer responses to homework laws. Reliance on the contractor or middleman as an organizational mechanism to mediate between firms and the homeworkers they hire developed as employers sought ways to insulate themselves from liability under homework laws. Moreover, the "conspiracy of silence" upheld by many homeworkers in an effort to prevent government involvement that could lead to the elimination of their jobs has helped sustain the exploitative nature of most homework operations.

In addition to documenting the contradictory outcomes of state homework policy, my aim in chapter 6 is to expound on my critique of the contemporary politics of homework in the United States—to move beyond the narrow perspective in recent debates, which sees legislative reform as the solution (whether it be the conservative call to eliminate restrictions on homework in order to bring it out from underground or the liberal strategy to ban all homework outright). The focus on legislative reform misunderstands the contradictory nature of state action and the complex role of the state as an actor in the development of the homework system. Since the generally exploitative character of waged homework is rooted in the gender division of labor and the nature of the labor-capital relation, the state alone cannot be the source of its transformation or elimination. On the contrary, the state often helps to perpetuate the conditions that support exploitative homework. A close examination of the contradictory interests and actions of state agencies in the development of homework regulation since the turn of the century allows us to analyze the nature of the capitalist state and how it relates and responds to the demands of capital and labor with regard to homework.

Finally, in the concluding chapter, I discuss the limitations of policy suggestions that have emerged in the United States from conventional debate between the political right and anti-homework liberals over the problem of exploitative homework. I consider more innovative policy proposals and propose directions for future research that might help uncover the deep-rooted obstacles that so far have blocked the structural transformations required to improve the lot of today's homeworkers.

Different Types of Home-Based Work

Before moving on it is necessary to distinguish between various types of home-based work in order to clarify the difference between waged homework, historically characterized by highly exploitative conditions, and the home-based work of professionals and the truly self-employed. Each is characterized by fundamentally different working conditions, production and market relations, and wage and benefit levels. In both scholarly and popular debates about home-based work there has been a tendency to confound these vastly different categories. The confusion that results has significant implications for policy proposals, and has helped foster the dichotomous politics that leads people to take inherently contradictory general positions (completely prohomework versus completely anti-homework).

In the introduction to their edited collection of articles on homework, Boris and Daniels elucidate a key issue in the current debate over the spread of paid work in the home: "The issue posed by the current controversy is stark: will such labor encourage new forms of sweated industry which reinforce the existing sexual and racial divisions of labor and stymie worker self-organization, or can it serve as a basis for an alternative to mass production, a new organization of work which integrates home and workplace in a more organic, autonomous synthesis?"

As I hope to make clear in the chapters ahead, there is no simple answer to this question. The exploitative potential of paid work in the home varies with the particular characteristics of the work arrangements specific to different types of home-based work. While current proponents of homework tend to ignore the glaring differences between professional telecommuters and garment industry pieceworkers in their calls for the deregulation of homework, more serious analysts recognize that the experiences of different groups of home-based workers can be disparate. With varying wages, levels of job security, amounts of bargaining power, positions in the labor market, and working conditions, home-based workers may experience their work as more or less exploitative or accommodating (Gerson 1993; Christensen 1993). As a starting point in my analysis, therefore, it is important to define and distinguish between three general categories of home-based workers: the self-employed, waged homeworkers, and salaried professionals.

My purpose in delineating these categories is to identify waged workers who depend on their employers for the opportunity to do work and whose weak position in the labor market influences their decision to work at home. Distinguishing this group from home-based workers who are independent producers (the truly self-employed) or who choose to work at home from a position of strength on the labor market (salaried professionals) is important for an analysis of the implications of the spread of different types of paid work in the home.[5] Those in the former group are subjected to increasingly exploitative work arrangements while those in the latter may indeed have the potential to enjoy a more autonomous and flexible work experience.

Home-based self-employment appears to be on the rise, particularly among women. Since the early 1970s self-employment has increased steadily, reversing the pattern of steady decline that characterized the years between 1948 and 1972 (Fain 1980). This increase can be attributed, in part, to the dynamism of small-scale entrepreneurial activity in expanding service and information-processing industries—a dynamism fueled largely by a surge in business start-ups by women working out of their homes. Although self-employed men continue to outnumber their female counterparts, between 1975 and 1985 the number of self-employed women grew six times faster than the number of self-employed men. Almost half of the new businesses started by women in recent years (more than 300,000) are operated from the home (Silver 1989, 107).

In analyzing the implications of increasing self-employment from the home, it is important to recognize the gender gap that may exist with regard to earnings and prospects for employment stability. While men are concentrated in the goods-producing industries that saw a growth in self-employment through the 1970s, such as construction, self-employed women are concentrated in the trade and service industries and have a greater likelihood of operating from the home. Although the growth of home-based industries has been portrayed in the popular media as the key to economic success for women (Greengard 1984), a number of features commonly associated with such businesses indicate their heightened vulnerability to failure when compared with male businesses and with female businesses not operated from the home. According to Silver (1989), most women's businesses have annual receipts of under $5000. In addition, when compared to their female counterparts whose businesses are not operated from the home, "home-based businesswomen are more likely to start their own businesses without partners, use smaller start-up capital, have lower expenses, employ fewer people, and earn lower profits." Thus, the "precarious nature of many small businesses not only suggests that the contemporary surge in entrepreneurial homework is cyclical but also makes ambiguous the employment status of many who regard themselves as independent producers or contractors" (Silver 1989, 107).

Official data as well as recent analyses of self-employment trends fail to distinguish between the "true self-employed" and the "disguised self-employed" (Fain 1980; Kraut and Grambsch 1987). This distinction is particularly important when assessing the work experiences of self-employed homeworkers. Workers who are truly self-employed have direct contact with the market for their products and direct control over all aspects of their work.[6] Others, who may be designated officially as self-employed, participate in a classic employer-employee relationship with their opportunity to work dependent on a particular firm. The latter are typically subcontractors who supply goods at the behest of a single firm and whose operations are completely dependent on the demand of that firm. For example, many home-based assemblers in the electronics industry are officially classified as self-employed even though all aspects of their work (availability of work, control over work, setting of wages and hours) mirror those of an employee.[7]

Making the distinction between these two types of self-employed workers is important for an analysis of homework since their working conditions, standard of living, and life chances can be quite different. Furthermore, support for the deregulation of homework is based in large part on the assumption that homeworkers are independent, self-employed workers who do not require the same legal protections guaranteed to factory or office workers. But "disguised self-employed" homeworkers have more in common with factory and office workers than with workers who are truly self-employed. In fact, for analytical purposes, it is more appropriate to categorize them in the second group of home-based work: waged homework.

Waged homework is work performed on domestic premises for a specific employer. It is defined by the following characteristics. First, an employer or his contractor provides the opportunity to work and supplies raw materials needed in production. Second, the labor process is not directly supervised by the employer or contractor. Supervision and control by the employer does exist, however, in an indirect form. For example, while workers generally determine the pace, pattern, and method of their work, they usually have no control over what is produced, what wage rates are, and where and how products are marketed. Third, the product of the homeworker's labor is not for household consumption. Fourth, a contractor or employer is responsible for marketing and selling the final product. Fifth, payment is typically made on a piece rate basis and thus directly related to output. Sixth, labor for homework can be purchased in discrete or variable amounts and production usually involves skills that are generally available in the labor force, are easily learned, or are already possessed by potential homeworkers. Finally, most waged homeworkers, historically and in the present, are women and children (Dangler 1986, 258–59; 274, n.3).

Within the general category of waged homework we can distinguish between industrial homework and service homework. Industrial homework includes labor-intensive processes and assembly work in manufacturing industries. The industries known to employ homeworkers range from garment-making to automobiles to electronics. Service homework includes specialist typing, routine clerical work (much of which is now done via home computers), and packing and packaging (sorting, labeling, stapling, and sealing) (Allen 1983, 652).

Finally, the third type of home-based worker is the salaried professional who chooses to work at home from a position of strength on the labor market. A list of success stories presented in the magazine *Personal Computing* is typical of the popular press's lauding of experiments by professionals in home-based work. Eager to escape the daily stress of long commutes and traffic delays, suburban professionals such as a Louisville television producer/director and a Los Angeles moonlighter, who earns $10,000 a year as an administrative and communications freelancer, are spotlighted by the magazine as typical of a new breed of home-based worker (Schwartz 1987).

The terms on which the current debate over homework is being waged illustrate the importance of drawing the distinctions outlined above. Those who support the deregulation of homework in the United States on the basis of "personal freedom" and "entrepreneurship" portray homeworkers as a homogeneous group of people with equal chances for a lucrative and fulfilling work experience. The tendency to confound home-based clerical workers and salaried professionals who utilize new computer technologies into a single category—telecommuters—is a case in point. One of my primary objectives is to expose the fallacies that follow from indiscriminate analyses of home-based work. I distinguish between those types of home-based work arrangements whose expansion promises to worsen working conditions and lower living standards for workers and those which offer participants a more accommodating work experience. Similarly, recognizing that home-based work is not a single, homogeneous category is important for an understanding of the role of different forms of home-based work in global economic restructuring.

2

Electronics Industry Homeworkers in Central New York

When I was growing up my mother was out to work. I would come home from school and be alone. I want to be there for my kids (Interview 4).

It doesn't pay to work outside [of the home] because of travel and overwork. People making minimium wage are taken advantage of. When you're home you don't need to make minimum because you don't have expenses for gas, lunches, and clothes (Interview 16).

I had difficulty getting an outside job because of my polio. I have to walk with a cane (Interview 20).

I'm not career-oriented. I want to take care of my kids and home but I need to bring in an income (Interview 21).

It's cheaper for me to work at home because we heat with wood and I can keep the stove going (Interview 24).

We have a dairy farm plus my husband has an outside job. I need to make some money on my own and be there to oversee the farm. My son has gotten hurt twice [working on the farm]. I need to be there (Interview 29).

This sample of comments taken from interviews I did with electronics industry homeworkers in central New York reveals the circumstances that often converge to support women's "choice" to work at home instead of seeking outside jobs. Like most women bound by traditional gender roles they confronted the difficult task of combining paid work with unpaid labor to meet household and childcare needs. Moreover, their task was made especially

difficult by their position in the labor market, the stagnant economies of the rural communities they lived in, and other hardships
imposed by rural poverty. In this context, homework emerged as
a viable income-producing strategy. It took root in their communities in the late 1960s when a few employees of electronics firms
in the Syracuse area began taking work home from the factory. As
employers realized the benefits this work option could bring
them, word of the availability of homework jobs spread through
networks of friends and neighbors. Thus, employers' efforts to
obtain a relatively cheap and flexible workforce for labor-intensive
assembly operations combined with workers' initiatives to carve
out practical work options. The result was an enclave of homework operations that played an important role in the regional
economy for more than 10 years.

A glimpse into the lives of homeworkers in central New York
reveals the difficulties faced by poor and working class families
struggling to make ends meet. It also gives us an important vantage
point from which to see how waged homework, as a structural
feature of the modern economy, arises out of women's efforts to
control their lives as household members within the set of limitations imposed on them by the gender division of labor in the
home and on the labor market.

Research Method and Characteristics
of the Sample

A snowball sampling technique was used to identify potential
interviewees for my study of homeworkers. Snowball sampling
involves using "informants to introduce [the researcher] to other
members of their group" (Burgess 1982, 77). It is particularly
useful when the size and characteristics of the population from
which the sample is to be drawn are unknown or if it is extremely
difficult to gain access to group members. In this study a snowball
sampling technique was required because industrial homework is
illegal in New York State. Special homework permits are available
only to the elderly, the disabled, or those required to care for the
disabled. The majority of homeworkers in the electronics industry
do not operate with such permits and there were no readily
available records from employers from which a representative
sample could be drawn. I obtained a small list of electronics
industry homeworkers from a union organizer and conducted
interviews with members of this initial group.[1] Each was asked to

supply the names of other homeworkers. A similar strategy was used with each new respondent. A primary problem with snowball sampling is the lack of random selection of respondents. Generalizations about a larger population based on the characteristics and experiences of a sample are largely dependent on each individual in the population having an equal chance of being selected for an interview. Snowball sampling increases the probability of some individuals being selected who are part of the network in which the original contacts were established. The result is that the use of this technique tends to select a group with homogeneous characteristics (Hakim 1980).

Snowball sampling has several advantages, however. As mentioned previously, the illegality of homework makes this the only sampling technique that could be used under existing circumstances. It also closely reflects the way in which homework activities are organized. Through use of this technique, I was able to draw out the importance of the networks of family and friends that served as a foundation for the flourishing of this type of employment for more than ten years in central New York. The expansion of homework in this region can be attributed in large part not only to active recruiting on the part of employers, but also to the importance of its visibility in the community. Using these networks to find new respondents also provided the trust people facing economic hardships and working in illegal activities needed to share their experiences with an outsider.

Another limitation of this sampling technique is that it did not allow me to determine accurately the size of the population of homeworkers. I have tried to approximate the number of homeworkers employed during the time of the study and in previous years by relying on information provided by those who took part in distributing such work. According to distributors interviewed, hundreds of workers, mainly women, assembled basic components such as transformers, coils, and circuit boards in their homes for both national and multinational electronics firms between 1969 and 1981. One distributor reported that she trained and employed about 300 people during her three years of organizing homework operations. Another, who was in business for 12 years, claimed to have had between 150 and 200 people working for her at any one time. A third made a similar claim, while a fourth had 42 homeworkers working for her when her operations were closed down in 1981. The distributor who had been in business the longest estimated that the electronics industry in central New York employed about 800 homeworkers at a time on a steady basis during the 1970s and into the '80s. After 1981 the number of homeworkers decreased substantially because of a New York State Labor Department effort to vigorously enforce its anti-homework law in the electronics industry.

Of the 39 homeworkers in the sample, only seven were still doing homework at the time of the interviews. Thirty had been forced to stop because the operations of their distributors were halted by the State Labor Department. Two had stopped voluntarily. Interviews with homeworkers averaged 69 minutes in length, with the longest lasting for three hours and the shortest for 20 minutes. Twenty-eight respondents were interviewed in their homes, two were interviewed at their current places of work, and nine were interviewed over the telephone. The substance and average length of the interviews were consistent regardless of whether they were conducted in person or by phone. In the case of the latter, however, the quality of the interview experience suffered somewhat from my inability to record personal observations regarding their places of residence and general living conditions. Interviews were conducted by phone only if the respondent specifically requested it or if scheduling conflicts did not allow me ample travel time to reach respondents' homes. In two cases, after unsuccessfully trying to locate respondents' remote residences, I settled for telephone interviews to avoid inconveniencing them further by having to set up another interview time.

In 11 of the interviews conducted in respondents' homes, spouses who were not homeworkers and/or children were present. In four cases homeworkers' spouses actively participated in the interview. In two cases, the husbands of female homeworkers were present for the interview and displayed annoyance at my presence. Other homeworkers were interviewed at home when their spouses were out at work and their children were at school.

Demographic Profile of Homeworkers

Of the 39 homeworkers in my sample, 36 were women and three were men. The average age of respondents was 37, with the youngest at 21 and the oldest at 61. The majority were in their thirties. All were white and American-born except for two Korean immigrants. All were married, with most having two, three, or four dependent children. One had eight children, four had children grown and living away from home, and only two had none. Just over half of the respondents were high school graduates or had completed a high school equivalency program. Twelve did not finish high school, while one graduated from college and another completed some college courses. All but four of the homeworkers were long-term residents of central New York. The four more recent residents included the two Korean immigrants, one woman originally from downstate New York, and one from out of state.

All respondents lived within a 40-mile radius of the city of Syracuse. While three resided in cities (two in Cortland and one in Utica) and four lived in suburban areas around Syracuse, the rest of the sample was split almost evenly between small towns and rural areas. As discussed more fully below, the physical isolation of the homeworkers residing in small towns and rural areas was a significant factor in the spread of homework in central New York. A stagnant rural economy and considerable distance from urban centers of employment made homework an attractive employment option for many. Fourteen of the homeworkers live in small towns whose populations range from just over 200, such as Bouckville and South Otselic, to over 5,000, such as Cazenovia and Eaton.[2] Spread across four counties (Chenango, Cortland, Madison, and Onondaga) most of these towns are located off connecting highways, separated by at least five miles from other small towns. The sparsely populated expanses between these towns are the rural areas where the remaining 18 in the sample live.

Household Composition

All of the respondents live in a traditional nuclear family structure. One family had a grandmother living with them on a temporary basis. Of the 36 who had dependent children, three had only high school–aged children, three had only preschool–aged children, and the rest had a mixture of preschool, grammar school, and high school children. Thus, the majority of homeworkers, who were in their thirties, were in the middle of their child rearing years.

All but five of the homeworkers (two women and the three men) said they had primary responsibility for household duties such as shopping, cooking, cleaning, and child rearing. Most indicated that they received negligible help with such tasks from their husbands or children. Given this situation, the majority of those interviewed saw homework as an employment option that would allow them more time to meet household responsibilities compared to working outside the home. In general, homework was seen as allowing more time for household chores than an outside job because of the flexibility it affords in arranging time for different tasks and the elimination of considerable travel time to work because of their remote residences. Only one respondent indicated that she had less time for household tasks with homework compared to outside work because she found it difficult to organize her time efficiently as a homeworker.

Overall Economic Status of Homeworkers

The generally low economic status of most homeworkers in the sample is confirmed upon examination of household income data, including both homework and nonhomework earnings. Because of sensitivity to questions concerning husband's income, only 26 of the 39 respondents provided me with such information.[3] The discussion that follows is based on data from those 26.[4] My observations of those who refused to answer questions regarding their husbands' earnings, particularly of their residences and overall living standards, leads me to conclude that they also fit the general patterns revealed below. In fact, my impression at the time of the interviews was that most of those who refused to report income data did so out of pride. They did not wish to disclose the low-paying, low-status jobs held by their husbands.

Among the 26 for whom income data were available, average family earnings, including homework and nonhomework wages, was $19,336. As moderate as this average level seems, the presence of a few relatively high incomes skewed the result. Closer examination of the data reveal that the majority of families had earnings well below this average. In only ten cases (38.5 percent) was family income at or above this average. Among the remaining 16 families, average income was $11,989, with four households falling below official poverty levels for their family size.

The extent of poverty among those in my sample is also revealed by comparing their earnings to state and countywide income levels. For example, the average yearly income figure for my sample ($19,336) translates into weekly family earnings of approximately $372. Table 2.1 shows the average weekly earnings of employees covered by unemployment insurance for the state as a whole and the five counties from which my sample was drawn. Comparing the average weekly earnings *per family* in my sample with average earnings *per employee* in the central New York region reveals the relatively poor economic position of my respondents. (Keep in mind that my figure for average family earnings includes income from both husbands and wives, from homework and outside work.)

Four respondents reported receiving some form of public assistance during their years as homeworkers, including assistance from the Women's, Infants', and Children's program (WIC), food stamps, cash assistance, and fuel supplements. Three others reported that they needed and received public assistance only after losing their homework jobs. A few others claimed to have been eligible for public assistance but because of their pride did not apply. One such woman, who had applied for food stamps in the past, expressed her disdain for that experience. "I'll never apply again," she said. "They make you feel like you're crawling."

The importance of homework earnings to most of the families in the sample becomes clear when we examine income levels from nonhomework jobs alone. Most of the nonhomework income was provided by homeworkers' spouses, although five homeworkers earned additional income in second jobs such as housecleaning, apple picking, home sewing, and cafeteria work. Average family income from nonhomework sources was $15,349, with only eight families earning at or above this level. Without the addition of earnings from homework, six families would have fallen below official poverty levels. In these cases, homework was essential in keeping households from dropping below the poverty line. (See Table 2.2.)

While measuring income in relation to official poverty levels gives us a quantitative assessment of poverty, it falls short of providing a true picture of the lives of these workers and the importance of homework earnings to their family budgets. For example, while only four families are officially designated as poor when all household income is taken into account, the low earn-

Table 2.1　Average Weekly Earnings of Employees (Excluding Government Employees) Covered by Unemployment Insurance.

	New York State	Cortland County	Chenango County	Madison County	Oneida County	Onondaga County
1983	$377.57	256.00	292.65	239.65	283.76	339.21
1984	396.86	264.04	302.84	250.16	295.35	355.97
1985	419.76	275.03	315.08	264.66	308.06	367.18
1986	444.46	286.82	338.52	270.59	319.59	381.31

Source: New York State Statistical Yearbook, the Nelson A. Rockefeller Institute of Government, 1980–90.

Table 2.2 Income Categories

	NUMBER OF HOMEWORKERS	% OF SAMPLE
Household income above poverty level, with or without income from homework	16	62
Total household income above poverty level, but below poverty level without homework*	6	23
Total household income below poverty level, with or without homework income	4	15

*This category includes the two respondents for whom homework was the sole source of income.

ings and related financial hardships of most of the other families indicates that there is a severe discrepancy between "official" poverty and true poverty. It is obvious that families with children who earned below $15,000 in the 1980s, as did many in the sample, although not officially designated as poor, were destined to have a difficult time making ends meet. Among those who evaded the poverty label were a family of four living on $12,000 a year and a family of two living on $9,600 at the time of the interviews.

The character of the residences I visited reflects the overall economic status of the homeworkers in the sample. Of the 27 homes I saw I would describe only four (three suburban and one rural) as well-maintained in the sense of needing few visible repairs to the house itself or its furnishings. The three suburban homes, all located in residential developments, fit the typical middle-class image of a modern (all were built after 1960) well-furnished home with neatly kept lawns and shrubbery. The rural home in this category was an old country house that had been restored by its owners, complete with beautiful woodwork and wood floors.

Most of the other homes were old and in need of either structural or cosmetic repairs. Furniture was typically old and worn. The following examples illustrate the types of homes I observed. One suburban house clearly stood apart from other houses in its neighborhood for its worn appearance. In need of painting both inside and outside, it was furnished with old furniture and kitchen appliances. A small town home was in need of repair both inside and outside, as evidenced by its peeling shingles, unfinished, bare wood floors, peeling wallpaper, and sparse old furniture. A rural home in general disrepair, with peeling outside paint, cracked plaster walls, and old, worn furniture and rugs, had been expanded in piecemeal fashion, giving it a ramshackle appearance. Most of the respondents who lived in such homes revealed their inability to maintain their houses as they would have liked given a lack of funds.

My overall impression was that the useful life of household articles and the structures that contained them was typically extended beyond desirable limits. A few of the houses stood out for the severity of their disrepair. For example, one rural home was in such decay it seemed to warrant condemnation for failing to meet structural as well as health standards. The linoleum on the floor was so worn and frayed I thought it was simply a dirt floor on first glance. The plasterboard walls, which were peeling, had never been painted. Broken windows, worn and broken furniture, and leaky faucets were readily apparent.

Of the 39 respondents 26 owned their own homes and ten rented houses or apartments. Three had rent-to-own arrangements whereby they paid rent, part of which was set aside by the owner as a future downpayment toward purchase of the house. In all three of these cases, this arrangement was arrived at to benefit both parties—the owner who was unable to sell and the future buyer who had no downpayment and could not qualify for a bank loan. Of the 26 who owned their homes, six had no mortgage payments since they inherited houses that had been in their families for two or more generations. Such houses tended to be old farm houses in rural areas in need of constant maintenance and repair.

It is clear that the majority of the 39 families studied can be characterized as being among the working poor. As previously mentioned, I am confident that this characterization holds true even for those whose exact incomes were not disclosed. Examination of the lifestyles and hardships common among the majority of families reveals the true scope of their poverty. In considering the following indicators of poverty, keep in mind that there were two wage earners in every household, though in a few the non-homeworker was temporarily out of work due to layoff or illness.[5]

A major problem faced by many of those in the sample is the high cost of medical and dental care and their lack of sufficient insurance to cover such services. Of the 39 families, 20 had wage earners who received some form of health insurance through their employers, though many had only partial coverage and had to pay for some medical services themselves. One homeworker, whose insurance through her husband's employer covered only hospitalization, said she has to avoid doctors' visits for her eight children unless "absolutely necessary." In addition, since she cannot afford regular dental checkups for them they only see a dentist "if they have a toothache." Fourteen indicated that they pay for their own health insurance, which constitutes a significant drain on their family budget. One self-insured homeworker reported that she paid $1600 in 1985 for Blue Cross from an income of less than $10,000 a year. Finally, four reported that their families had no health insurance at all, while a fifth, an elderly woman, said she could not afford proper health care for herself since she wasn't insured, even though her husband received Medicare/Medicaid.

The lives of the working poor are often marked by the constant struggle to maintain a stable existence. When asked to assess their family income in relation to the cost of living, only four felt that their earnings had increased in relation to their expenses during the years prior to our interview. The majority reported that their purchasing power had remained stable or declined during the years of their marriage. Compounding their vulnerability to new financial demands was a general insufficiency or lack of savings to fall back on in the event of an emergency. Most of those in the sample reported that it was difficult to save extra money, with eight reporting that they had absolutely no savings at all.

Typically confined to low-paying and unstable jobs, sudden financial pressures caused by accidents, illnesses, replacement of essential household items such as major appliances, or vehicle repair can quickly drag a family deeper into poverty. A number of families in the sample experienced such incidents around the time of their involvement with homework. One woman explained that her family's income "managed to keep up with the cost of living" until a series of doctor bills incurred as the result of minor illnesses among her children "set [them] back for a few years." Another, whose husband had been unable to keep a steady job because of severe rheumatoid arthritis, trying 14 different jobs during the seven years of their marriage, summed up her family's situation with the simple statement, "We go without a lot." A third, whose husband experienced intermittent layoffs from a local factory, explained how her family, because they had no medical insurance, "got behind in [its] bills" after her two children were hospitalized for viral infections.

For others, economic survival involves supplementing income with household production of goods and services normally purchased on the market (Gershuny 1983). One homeworker with eight children and a family income of less than $20,000 a year grows and cans all her own vegetables (600 quarts a year). In addition, she and her husband raise beef cattle, which they sell one by one when they are in need of money. A young couple whose combined income was less than $10,000 also reported growing all of their own vegetables, while many others had garden plots of various sizes used to grow vegetables for freezing and canning. In a number of households heat is provided by woodburning stoves, with the wood harvested by family members. In addition, most families reported doing their own household repairs rather than purchasing repair services on the market. Finally, in many households purchase of goods takes place at secondhand stores and garage sales. Thus, among the poorest of the sample, most clothes and furniture are bought used. As one homeworker explained, "We couldn't get by if we had to shop in regular stores."

Among the homeworkers whose income fell in the middle ranges of the sample (between $15,000 and $25,000), there was generally less need to provide goods and services domestically or shop at secondhand stores. While the six homeworkers who fall into this category tended to see their incomes as barely sufficient to keep up with the cost of living, their hardships took a different and less immediate form. For example, one homeworker explained that her family had no money for extras such as "taking the kids to the movies." For another, her family budget did not allow expenditures for holiday festivities, particularly Christmas presents. While such deprivations are by no means critical to the survival of these families their impact is significant in view of the middle-class standards and expectations to which such families subscribe.

Homework Earnings and Family Budgets

The importance of income earned through homework to the survival of many families in the sample is illustrated by the contribution it makes to family budgets for essential expenditures on food, clothing, and regular household bills. When asked how important homework earnings were to the household budget, two reported it as the major income, 25 as one of two supplementary incomes with both being equally essential, and 12 as marginal (to earn extra money).[6] The 27 homeworkers in the first two categories recognized the essential contribution they made to their

family budgets and typically reported that their homework income was used on a regular basis for expenditures on food,
clothes, and major bills such as household utilities. In contrast,
there is some discrepancy between the reported labeling and
objective use of homework income among those in the third
category. Many of the 12 respondents who reported that their
homework income was marginal also listed basic expenditures as
commonly covered by the money they earned as homeworkers.
As Table 3 illustrates, half of them (six respondents) used their
wages from homework for essential expenditures such as groceries, transportation, and miscellaneous bills. For example, one
woman stated that even though she considered her earnings to be
"extra," they were earmarked for groceries. Another used her
"extra" money to make car payments. The other six who described their earnings as marginal explained that their money was
used for personal expenditures such as clothes for themselves,
recreational activities for their children, or education costs.[7] Only
one earmarked her money for vacations. Thus, while some women
viewed their addition to family earnings as marginal, it is clear
that they often used "their money" for the same kind of expenditures as those who recognized their indispensable contribution
to the household budget.[8]

A further illustration of the significance of homework as a
source of income for most of the families studied is the long-term
pattern of its use among a majority of respondents. The average
duration of employment as a homeworker for the sample group
was 5.5 years, with the shortest at less than a year and the longest
at 14 years. In addition, those who worked as homeworkers the
longest tended to work more hours per week at their jobs than
those who did homework for shorter periods. There was a clear
pattern among the former to engage in homework as a full-time
job. Seven homeworkers stayed with their jobs for less than two
years and all of them worked less than 20 hours a week on average.
Of the remaining 32 homeworkers, who did homework for more
than two years (the average duration among this group was 6.8
years with a range from three to 13 years), all but two worked
more than 20 hours per week on average, with seven working 40
or more hours. It is clear that for a majority of those in the sample,
homework was viewed as a long-term occupation done on or close
to a full-time basis.

Finally, the importance of homework earnings is starkly illustrated in two particular cases. One woman who contributed almost half of her family's $17,440 yearly income through home-

Table 2.3 Most Frequently Reported Use of Homework Income by Reported Labeling of Homework Income for Entire Sample of 39

Respondents' Labeling of Homework Income	N	Groceries	Mortgage or Rent	Household Repairs	Misc. Bills	Personal Expenditures*	Car Payments	Household Utilities	All Expenditures
Major or sole source of income	2								2
One of two supplementary incomes—both essential	25	9	3	2	4	2		5	
Marginal—to earn extra money	12	3			2	6	1		
Totals	39	12(31%)	3(8%)	2(5%)	6(15%)	8(20%)	1(3%)	5(13%)	2(5%)

*Personal expenditures include money spent on clothing for the respondents themselves, recreational activities, children's schooling, and miscellaneous spending money. One respondent in this category used her homework income specifically for vacations.

work was forced to seek public assistance (food stamps, cash assistance, and medicaid) after losing her job due to state enforcement of homework laws. An elderly woman, whose homework earnings amounted to an average of $90 a month not only needed to seek public assistance, but also lost ownership of a recently purchased mobile home because she couldn't meet the mortgage payments after loss of this income.

Conditions of Employment

The main job of central New York homeworkers in the electronics industry was to build transformers, a basic component used in a variety of electronic devices. Homeworkers were employed to wind fine coated wires around small metal cores. The transformers differed according to the size of the core, the number of times the wire had to be wound around the core, and the number of wires used. Workers were paid a piece rate for each completed transformer. This rate, which ranged from two to fifteen cents for the homeworkers in the sample, varied according to the degree of difficulty assigned each type of transformer. Most homeworkers in the sample reported earning between three and five cents for most of the transformers they worked on.

The ability of a central New York homeworker to make minimum wage or above depended on how fast she was able to work. Of those interviewed, roughly half claimed that it was very difficult, if not impossible, for them to make minimum wage. The other half seemed to have developed sufficient skill to increase their speed in order to earn more. The lowest average wage reported by a homeworker was $1.20 an hour while the highest was $8.35 an hour. While all of the homeworkers reported that they decided how much work to do in a given week and that there was no pressure put on them by distributors to complete specified quantities within a certain amount of time, most of them felt self-imposed pressure inherent in the piece rate system.[9] Accordingly, their pace of work was determined by their wage goals. Some homeworkers expressed the belief that it took "a special kind of person," someone who could adapt well to "boring and tedious work," to be able to earn good wages doing homework. They spoke of the need to develop a "rhythm" in order to keep up the pace required to wind enough cores in one hour to earn minimum wage. "If you were very fast, you could almost make minimum wage, but mostly you would come up short of the minimum," explained an eleven-year veteran of electronics homework. Others felt they had no problem making minimum wage or above if they worked steadily at a fast, even pace.[10]

The ability of respondents to earn wages they considered sufficient seemed to depend on their success in integrating homework with their household responsibilities and childcare. About half of those interviewed conformed to set schedules dividing homework time from time used for household responsibilities and childminding. The workers in this group said they set their work hours around their children's school and nap schedules. Thus, it was typical for a homeworker with preschool children to work during nap times and then again in the evenings and one with school-aged children to work in the mornings and afternoons. Despite the delineation of their day into specific homework and housework times, many of these women said they frequently took breaks from the former to "squeeze" in cooking and cleaning.

The other half of the sample consisted of homeworkers who had no set schedule for homework but would fit it in between household tasks and childminding during the day and after their children were in bed at night. Many of these workers said they became so adept at their work they could "wind wires without looking at them" and were able to do their work and "keep an eye on the kids" at the same time. A number of these respondents also reported doing homework at night while watching television. The complete integration of home life and work life is clearly illustrated by the experiences of these workers. A few women reported that they could take their homework anywhere and "did the wires" every chance they got. For example, homeworkers reported working on transformers when visiting friends, waiting at the doctor's office, playing bingo, and riding in the car with their husbands. One woman who worked as a volunteer at the local ambulance corp took her work when on duty there. For many, who had friends and relatives who also did homework, the tedium of building transformers could be broken by having "friends come over to have tea and work."

Most of those in the sample reported that they had no set workspace in their homes. The most frequently reported places of work were the kitchen table and the living room (on the couch or a comfortable chair with a small table or tray to set the components on). Only two respondents reported having a special table set up on a regular basis in a quiet room specifically for their work.

Distributors and Social Networks among Homeworkers

Thirty-six of the 39 respondents in the sample became aware of the availability of homework jobs through relatives and friends. In fact, most knew more than one other person who worked as a homeworker. Only three learned of this job opportunity through newspaper ads placed by distributors. The strength of the social networks around which homework is organized became apparent as I uncovered the complex of interrelationships among homeworkers and between homeworkers and distributors.

Four of the five distributors (all women) were former homeworkers who decided to try and earn more money by becoming distributors. Each of them started their distributing operations by employing people they knew who were in need of work. Two of them also placed a few want ads for homeworkers in local newspapers. The fifth distributor, a man, was never a homeworker. All of the distributors claimed that they did not have to actively recruit workers, but instead received ample requests for work as people found out about homework from relatives, neighbors, and friends. This claim was substantiated by most of the homeworkers interviewed. The general perception among those in the sample was that there were more than enough people willing to take a homework job. Once a distributor set up operations in a community, word spread quickly through networks of family and friends and a ready pool of available labor was tapped.

The relationship between homeworkers and their distributors can be described, in general, as very congenial. The latter were seen as peers in the community, often socially connected to homeworkers through direct friendships or friendships in common with others. All of the homeworkers felt their distributors were fair and reasonable in their business relationships, and many saw them as extremely compassionate in their dealings with homeworkers who faced particular hardships. For example, one distributor sometimes agreed to pick up and deliver components to workers when transportation problems arose, despite the fact that this was generally the homeworker's responsibility. Another was known to make every effort to divide work evenly among homeworkers during slack times rather than "lay off" anyone. I was also given accounts of instances where distributors paid people for faulty work and redid incorrectly wound transformers themselves in order to spare homeworkers from the loss of needed

income. In general, homeworkers spoke highly of their distributors and the way they conducted their business. A few spoke of
stories they had heard about one of the distributors not paying
wages on time and treating people unfairly. In fact, the State
Labor Department's investigation of electronics industry homework in central New York was initiated on such a complaint. I was
never able, however, to substantiate these accusations through the
interviews I did.[11]

Comparison of Central New York Homeworkers and More "Traditional" Homeworkers

The established use of homework in central New York challenges
the typical characterization of this type of production as an urban
phenomenon that relies mainly on the use of immigrant labor.
Instead, this particular case study lends support to the claim that
homework can flourish with the use of rural or suburban, nonimmigrant, working- and middle-class women. Understanding the
similarities and differences between the work experiences of
different types of homeworkers in the United States is important
for an analysis of the implications of the spread of homework to
new segments of the labor force.

The main difference between the workers I studied and the
urban-based, immigrant workers typically associated with this
type of work is the absence among the former of some of the most
salient abuses the homework system has created. For example,
while studies of urban homeworkers in garment-making and electronics have found child labor to be an important factor in workers' ability to increase their earnings, only eight of those I interviewed reported having family members help with their work.[12]
One explained that her children sometimes helped her sort wires
according to size and color, while the other seven reported that
their husbands helped occasionally (usually to count and trim
wires). For the most part, child labor did not appear to be a
significant part of these homework operations.[13]

In addition to the relative absence of child labor, the experiences of central New York homeworkers seemed qualitatively
better than that of their urban, immigrant counterparts in a number of other ways. For example, the payment of kickbacks to
homework employers for the "privilege" of receiving a homework
job and the vulnerability to abuses such as sexual harassment,

nonpayment of wages, and payment of phony "taxes" to employers do not appear to be a part of the experiences of those I interviewed.[14] Furthermore, electronics homework in central New York did not involve the use of toxic chemicals, as is frequently the case in Silicon Valley; nor were women forced to complete quotas dictated by their employers.[15]

Despite such differences between the experiences of women from central New York and immigrant and urban-based homeworkers, the conditions under which they work are very similar. As discussed earlier, the situation faced by the homeworkers I studied by no means reflects the autonomy, economic prosperity, and contentment that proponents of homework associate with modern-day "cottage industry." Instead, the homework jobs found in central New York are typically a cut below the standard minimum waged jobs available to women in the larger labor market, and while homeworkers support efforts to allow them to continue their work, they do so more out of absolute necessity (a lack of alternative employment that fits their specific needs) than out of a genuine desire to do homework.

As with garment industry homeworkers in cities like New York and Los Angeles and electronics industry homeworkers in the Silicon Valley, the ability of a central New York homeworker to make minimum wage or above depended on how fast she was able to work. Thus, pressure to increase the pace and intensity of work is a normal part of trying to earn decent wages under the piecework system, and seems to be an underlying feature of homework regardless of the characteristics of the workers or the industry for which the work is done. In addition, the strong association between homework and poverty documented in studies of urban homeworkers extends to nontraditional groups. As indicated above, for many of the homeworkers I studied, earnings from homework were an essential component of family income, often allowing families to maintain a stable existence, even if hovering at poverty levels. The importance of the income from this work to the maintenance of adequate living standards for central New York homeworkers demonstrates the extent to which current depictions of "cottage industry" as a new source of pin money for well-off women seeking constructive uses for their time is mistaken. As one homeworker put it, "It's not a fun job. People who do it do it because they need the money."

Important similarities can be found between the income needs, labor market position, and domestic responsibilities facing homeworkers, regardless of ethnicity, geographic location, or legal status. The common links underlying homework are related specifically to gender. In case studies researchers typically try to isolate the key factors that lead women to accept homework jobs. A superficial reading of the homework literature might lead one to conclude that lack of childcare is the single most important motivation for homeworkers. But while some studies focus almost exclusively on this factor (Beach 1989), others draw out the complexity of circumstances that affect the options open to women in the household and external labor market. In fact, Allen (1983), Christensen (1988), and Walsh (1987) point out the incompatibility of homework with childcare and consider the combination of circumstances that lead women to accept homework instead of work outside the home. For women in developing as well as in developed countries, lack of employment alternatives (Rao and Hussain 1984), discrimination in the workplace (Morales 1983), social or religious restrictions on women accepting outside work (Mitter 1984; Van Luijken 1984), and ideological convictions, which give primacy to the role of women as wives and mothers (Allen 1983), combine to constrain women's choices for paid work.

Although improved childcare provisions would do much to increase options for paid work available to women, it would not, by itself, eliminate the full scope of the double burden women face. In fact, Allen (1982) argues that the structure of the labor market and domestic ideology combine to limit the options available to women as a group. Thus the situation homeworkers face is no different, on the whole, from the situation faced by women who work outside the home. In her view there is

> no clear dividing line between those who do homework and those who work on the labour market, either in terms of economic need, or other characteristics. In fact, some do both simultaneously and our evidence indicates that homework labour is most adequately viewed as one of a number of poor options open to women within the structure of the labour market and the continued expectations of the dominant familial ideologies. These operate both on a level of personal relations and are embedded in social and economic policies of the state and voluntary organizations, including employers and trade union organizations. What does differentiate between women's paid work in households and that done in the factory or office are the terms and conditions on which they sell their labour. (394)

The convergence of ideological and labor market constraints on paid work was evident in the lives of the women I interviewed. While 17 of the 39 respondents stated that childcare was the main reason they took a homework job, none of them described this need as stemming from a lack of childcare alternatives and only three pointed to the high cost of childcare as an obstacle to working outside of the home. Instead, traditional views of family and women's roles and consideration of their limitations on the job market conditioned these women's choice to stay at home for their children. Eight specifically mentioned their "preference" or "desire" to adhere to traditional family roles and values. Comments such as "I believe a mother should be at home with her kids," and "I'd rather be a housewife and mother than go to work outside," were indicative of the sentiments expressed by this group.

The other nine respondents who gave childcare as their main reason for taking a homework job qualified their responses by citing the additional factors that made staying at home with their children imperative. Flexibility to meet domestic and paid work demands, the low pay they were likely to receive in outside jobs, and the costs of working outside (transportation and clothes) were given as factors that combined with childcare needs to make work at home desirable.

As Table 2.4 shows, the main reasons for taking a homework job given by the remaining 22 respondents were physical problems that made working out of the home difficult (two respondents), inability to get an outside job (three), the need to stay at home for other reasons such as farming or tending a wood stove (two), the high travel and/or clothing expenses of working outside (three), a personal preference for working at home (two), and the desire for flexible work time (one). Three of the respondents, two of whom were men, did homework in addition to their regular outside jobs and gave the need for extra income as their main reason for working at home. Four others could not isolate a single motivating factor, but mentioned a combination of circumstances drawing from the range presented above. Finally, the third man in the sample did homework because he felt it fit in well with his lifestyle, which revolved around small-scale farming and seasonal work as a farm hand. In short, the reality of the female homeworkers' lives was such that a set of material and ideological constraints converged to cause them to seek the most reasonable solution to the problem of their double burden.

Table 2.4 Main Reason for Taking a Homework Job by Income Category

	Children	Prefer Homework to Outside Work	More Money from Homework—Fewer Expenses	Physical Problems; Can't Work Outside Home	Extra Income on Top of Regular Job	Difficulty Getting Outside Job	Need to be Home for Other Reasons	Flexibility of Homework	Other/ Ambiguous
Total Sample (39)	17(43%)	2(5%)	3(8%)	2(5%)	3(8%)	3(8%)	2(5%)	1(3%)	5(15%)
Above poverty level with or without homework	9	1			2	1	1		2
Total household income above poverty level but below poverty level without homework	2	1	1			1	1		
Total household income below poverty level with or without homework income	2			1				1	
No household income figures given	4		2	1	1	1			4

Variation Among Homeworkers in
Central New York

I have argued elsewhere (Dangler 1989) that homeworkers in the central New York electronics industry constitute an identifiable group with some characteristics that distinguish them from more traditional homeworkers in the United States, namely, urban immigrants in the needlework industries. While the homeworkers I studied have much in common in terms of class background, income needs, rural lifestyle, and household composition, there is still significant variation among them. In what follows I will highlight six specific cases that represent "ideal types" within the group. My aim is to reveal the primary forms of variation within my sample and to identify the life circumstances that affect women's decisions to do paid work in their homes.

CASE 1—THE LARGE FAMILY COMBINING PAID WORK WITH SUBSISTENCE
FARMING

Lucy Morse[16] represents the type of homeworker whose family's survival depends on combining paid work with subsistence farming. At age 37, married for 18 years at the time of the interview, Lucy lived in an old farmhouse with her husband and eight children (who ranged in age from three to 18 at the time of the interview). During her last year as a homeworker, Lucy's husband's job as a school bus driver in a small rural community paid approximately $12,000. Lucy's addition of $6,720 from homework brought their annual income up to $18,720, which was below the official poverty level of $19,968 for their family size. In order to feed their family, the Morses grow most of their own vegetables, canning about 600 quarts each year. They also raise a few beef cattle for meat and, on occasion, have had to sell a cow in order to obtain needed cash. The Morses receive aid from WIC but were told they did not qualify for food stamps.

The farmhouse Lucy and her family live in is old and worn. It is obvious that the original house was made larger by a series of additions that appear to have been simply "tacked on." There is an old barn in back to house the cattle and a large garden plot beyond. The Morses own their house and the 30 acres surrounding it. At the time of the interview they had been on this property for 14 years and had paid for it in full. Even with no rent or mortgage payments they found it difficult to meet their expenses.

According to Lucy, their cash income and subsistence farming allowed them to live a comfortable life until set back by the accumulation of unpaid medical bills, incurred mainly as a result of illnesses that typically plague small children. Since her husband's insurance only covers hospitalization, the cost of doctor visits for regular pediatric care, for immunizations, and for recurrent childhood problems such as ear infections soon went beyond their means. As a result, the family has been forced to cut back on visits to the doctor "unless absolutely necessary" and has eliminated dental care almost completely. In Lucy's words, "we go to the dentist if one of our children has a bad toothache."

In addition to cutting back on medical and dental services, the Morses have used other strategies to lower their need for cash income. For example, they put in a wood furnace to replace their oil furnace, and harvest their own wood for fuel. They also have the ability to expand their vegetable garden to increase food production. The major problem with the latter is the extra work it brings Lucy, particularly in canning the produce. Subject to recurrent anemia, she finds it difficult to meet all of the physical demands placed on her. Even though she receives help from her older children, Lucy is clearly overtaxed, emotionally and physically, by her effort to meet the demands of childcare, food production, food processing, and other household maintenance tasks. She explained that doing homework was one way to cut the amount of strenuous labor she had to do. By increasing her cash income through homework, she could reduce the amount of produce the family needed to grow and process. Assembling transformers, though time-consuming and tedious, was much less physically taxing than harvesting and canning large quantities of vegetables.

After three years of working at home for the electronics industry, Lucy lost her homework job in 1981. Since then she has tried to supplement her husband's income by selling toy animals she crochets at home. At the time of the interview, she had plans to set up a small gift shop in her house, where items she made could be sold. It seems, however, that the likelihood of success in this endeavor is severely limited by the physical isolation of her home. While Lucy had done babysitting in her home before taking the homework job, the attention needed by her own children made this an unacceptable alternative.

In sum, the Morses represent a type of family common in poor rural farming communities in upstate New York. The husband, who was a farmer most of his life, needed outside employment to supplement his farming activities. The jobs available to him, however, were relatively low paying. (Prior to his employment as a bus driver, a job he had been in for eight years, he worked for a time at a factory in the nearest city and then in a warehouse loading and unloading trucks). The wife, whose employment before marriage consisted of assembly line jobs in local factories, found her employment options limited with the birth of her children. In Lucy's case, having such a large family, with each child born within two years of the previous one, made working outside the home impossible. Within the set of home-based work options available to her, electronics subassembly proved most practical.

CASE 2—THE ELDERLY POOR

Ida and George Hanson, both in their sixties, spent most of their lives living and working in central New York. Through the 1940s, '50s, and '60s Ida worked in local factories as a sewer in the garment industry and an assembler at a typewriter plant. In the early '70s she began to do domestic work—cleaning in other people's homes and taking in ironing. For a short time she worked as a cleaner in a local factory. Since the mid-1960s, George has been a self-employed piano tuner. Though his income has fluctuated over the years, he and Ida maintained a comfortable standard of living until old age and illness sapped their earning power.

Stricken with cancer, George has had to limit his working hours considerably. In order to compensate for his lost income, in 1980 Ida began combining electronics subassembly in her home with housecleaning outside the home. Their combined income from outside work was less than $10,000 in 1986, while Ida earned an additional $1,080 that year from homework. While this was enough to keep them above the official poverty level, it did not allow them to meet regular expenses for food, housing, and medical bills.

Through the 1980s, poverty crept up on the Hansons, slowly eroding their living standards and security. First of all, while George's medical expenses are covered by medicare/medicaid, Ida has no insurance coverage at all. She explained that she cannot afford proper health care for herself and is unable to see a doctor for the chronic bursitis that forces her to limit her work to about 20 hours per week. In addition, as their income dropped, the Hansons found themselves unable to afford their mortgage payments and lost the mobile home they purchased in 1975. Since the home was "taken back" by the company that owns the trailor park they live in, they have been allowed to continue living there and now pay rent. Ida expressed concern about their security in this situation, commenting that the owners "would like to have us out of here."

Unable to meet expenses with their limited earnings, the Hansons depend on food stamps and emergency heat aid from the government. With no savings or equity and steadily diminishing earning power, they face a frightening and uncertain future.

CASE 3—THE WORKING POOR

The term "working poor" came to take on special significance in the 1980s. It refers to a growing segment of the poor who work for wages insufficient to support their families or who desperately seek work but cannot find it (Harrington 1984). Some work part-time, others work full-time, and many are unemployed because they cannot find work or have been laid off from their jobs. Many of the homeworkers I visited fall into this category. Among them is Tammy Benton, a 27-year-old mother of three.

The Bentons constant struggle to rise above poverty has been set back frequently by Mr. Bentons intermittent layoffs from a series of skilled blue-collar jobs. At the time of the interview in 1986, he was earning about $17,000 a year as a molder in the machine tool industry, a job he had held for close to a year. The jobs he had had before that carried similar pay scales. During the nine years of his marriage, Mr. Benton experienced two layoffs that lasted for long periods—one for two years and another for just under a year. During the latter, homework provided the family's sole income, with both husband and wife working to assemble transformers.

Throughout their marriage, Tammy combined homework with part-time work at a school cafeteria to supplement her husband's income. She started to do homework while still in high school and continued after marriage until she lost the job in 1985. For Tammy, her 12 years as a homeworker allowed her to raise her earning power beyond the limitations imposed by the local labor market. The outside jobs she held as a teacher's aide and a cafeteria worker were part-time and low-paying. Thus, doing paid work at home helped her compensate for her underemployment on the labor market. Homework allowed her the flexibility to keep an outside job and to limit her need for childcare.

With no more than a high school education both Tammy and her husband have found limited job opportunities in their rural community. Mr. Benton is likely to remain in blue-collar jobs that are relatively low paid and subject to seasonal or cyclical layoffs. Tammy sees part-time service work as her only possibility for outside employment. With the loss of homework, the family has had to seek public assistance (mainly food stamps) in order to supplement an income insufficient to support a family of five.

CASE 4—THE WORKING POOR, WITH PHYSICAL DISABILITIES

While many among the working poor must live with income fluctuations due to frequent layoffs or continual job changes, others can be hampered by physical disabilities that make it difficult to find or retain work. Patty Bates's family is a case in point. Stricken with rheumatoid arthritis at an early age, Patty's husband Mike has lost job after job, either forced to quit because he was unable to meet job demands or "let go" by employers unsympathetic to his physical condition. At the time of the interview, they had been married for seven years and Mr. Bates (aged 33) had tried 14 different jobs during that period.

With no education or training beyond high school, both Patty and Mike have limited options on the job market. These options were narrowed further for Mike by his physical disability and for Patty by the birth of their three children within a six-year period. During her first pregnancy, Patty was forced to quit her assembly line job at a local factory. It was then that she took a job as an electronics subassembler in her home. Her decision to take a homework job stemmed from her limited opportunities on the job market and inability to afford daycare for her children. She worked at home assembling transformers from 1980 to 1986, when she lost her job as a result of the State Labor Department's actions against her distributor.

During her last year as a homeworker, Patty's husband worked for a vending machine company, earning about $7,000 for the year, while she contributed $3,120 to the family budget from her homework job. Even with both incomes, the Bateses earned below the official poverty level for their family size. Patty explained that even with both of them working, the family had to rely on food stamps, WIC, and fuel supplements from the Department of Housing and Urban Development (HUD) in order to survive. When asked if her husband was eligible for disability benefits, Patty explained that he wanted to continue working as long as he could since "doctors say he'll be in a wheelchair before long."

By the time of our interview, Patty had been without her

homework job for three months. With the loss of her income the family's immediate strategy was to rely more heavily on public assistance and wait until their youngest child started school before Patty searched for outside work. In the meantime, she was exploring other alternatives for home-based work, such as upholstering and making crafts that could be sold in the community.

CASE 5—THE FARM FAMILY IN NEED OF SUPPLEMENTARY INCOME

In many ways the Ryans are a classic farm family struggling to survive in the midst of an economy hostile to the family farm. In their late twenties at the time of the interview, Nancy and Jim Ryan had lived all their lives in the farming community of central New York. After taking over Jim's family's farm, they hoped that agriculture would allow them to support their three children and preserve the way of life they had come to know best. Like many other small farmers, however, Jim is unable to earn an income sufficient to support his family. In 1986, he earned approximately $12,000 by selling his farm products.

In order to supplement these earnings, Nancy has had to work and has held both outside and home-based jobs during the nine years of their marriage. She had been employed as a homeworker for two years when she lost her job and, since then, has had to rely on the small cake decorating business she operates from her home to supplement the family's income from the farm. Although she earned less than $3,000 per year as a homeworker, that income was crucial in keeping the family above the official poverty level for those two years.

Nancy saw homework as the best alternative for paid employment available to her. Outside jobs she had held in the past included department store clerk, cashier, and pieceworker at an electronics assembly plant. In her view, it "didn't pay" to get another outside job because of the low wages she was likely to receive, the distance she would have to travel for work, and the wages she would have to pay someone to look after her children (aged 14 months, 4, and 5 at the time of the interview). Nancy explained that after losing her income from homework her family "just had to adjust. We have a lot of broke days and live from paycheck to paycheck."

CASE 6—HOMEWORK INCOME MARGINAL TO FAMILY BUDGET

While income from homework was an essential component of family budgets for the majority of households in my sample, there were a few cases in which its contribution was marginal, or not essential for the family's survival. For example, this was the situation in the four households whose nonhomework income was $30,000 or more per year. Marian Richman is indicative of the homeworkers in this group. For her homework is a way to earn "extra spending money" and "get work experience," while remaining at home to care for her children.

At age 37, with work experience at a photo print shop and in retail sales, Marian decided to stop working in order to care for her home and two children (aged 10 and 13 at the time of the interview). With no financial pressure to earn money, she decided to take a homework job when the opportunity "fell into her lap." Her neighbor, a manager at a large electronics firm, decided to branch off and start his own small company. With insufficient plant and equipment for an in-house workforce, he began recruiting homeworkers from among friends and neighbors to assemble components for his products.

For Marian, homework became a way to earn extra money and "help out a friend." Once her neighbor expanded his in-house operations and phased out his use of homeworkers, she no longer worked for wages. Although Marian plans to reenter the workforce when her children are older, she places primary importance on her role as wife and mother during this period of her life.

Conclusion

While the majority of homeworkers in my sample have similar economic and social profiles, there is variation in the particular circumstances that caused each to choose homework instead of work outside the home. For the women I interviewed, a combination of factors relating to economic need, limited labor market options, and gender roles within the home affected their "choice" to become homeworkers. As with other groups of homeworkers, the struggle to combine paid work with unpaid labor in the household led these women to adopt home-based work as an income-producing strategy.

While the specific reasons each woman chose electronics assembly as opposed to other types of home-based work vary, two generalizations emerge from the sample as a whole. First, many had done other types of home-based work, such as babysitting, sewing, upholstering, and crafts. Electronics homework provided steadier income since markets for these alternative types of work were quite small and unstable in the areas where most homeworkers live. In the case of babysitting, many homeworkers live in places too remote to provide a convenient location for working parents to bring their children. Similarly, the demand for goods and services such as homemade crafts, sewing, and upholstering is small in poor, sparsely populated rural areas.

Second, in some cases, the decision to do electronics work was based simply on personal preference. For instance, three women mentioned that they chose to assemble transformers as opposed to babysitting because they did not feel that caring for children as an occupation suited their personalities. These women also recognized that there were few other lucrative opportunities for home-based work.

Finally, six of the homeworkers combined electronics work with one or more other home-based jobs because none provided enough of an income by itself. The other jobs were babysitting, cake decorating, homemade crafts, upholstering, newspaper delivery, and care of foster children. One woman grew bean sprouts in her home for sale to local oriental restaurants.

3

Restructuring of Global Capital: An Impetus for the Spread of Homework

In contemporary accounts of the spread of homework, journalists and scholars alike often question who holds responsibility for initiating work-at-home programs. Is it employers seeking to lower labor costs and increase flexibility or is it workers themselves demanding an alternative to the more rigidly structured environment of the office or factory? The answer to this question is complex and extremely important for an understanding of the implications of waged homework for the future of the American workforce.

While it is widely acknowledged by those on all points of the political spectrum that capitalists benefit from transforming office-based or factory-based production operations into homework, the exploitative nature of this type of work has been largely overshadowed in the popular media by an emphasis on the alleged convenience and flexibility it affords workers. Some of the most widely publicized accounts of industrial homework and telecommuting have focused on benefits to employees. In fact, workers have actively sought to eliminate government regulations that prevent them from choosing homework as an employment option (Cawthorn 1983; Clark 1981; *Newsweek* 1981).

While some of the impetus behind the recent spread of homework has undoubtedly come from workers, we must also examine the extent to which homework is an employer-initiated form of production tied to current strategies of capital restructuring. In fact, it is problematic to view homework as either exclusively motivated by capital or exclusively motivated by labor. Instead, its expansion in recent decades can be explained by certain features of the contemporary world economy that have given rise to conditions that make homework an attractive work option for both capital and labor. The accumulation processes that have operated during the recent capitalist crisis have created conditions that have spurred capital to seek cheaper and more flexible production options. In this context, homework has emerged as a particular form of decentralized production that meets industry needs. At the same time, capital's response to the accumulation crisis (especially the increasing "casualization" of employment and the transfer of production from developed to developing countries) has constrained choices available to workers in the labor market and in the home. In this context, homework becomes an increasingly attractive option to those women faced with a combination of limited job opportunities, cuts in social service provisions, and household and childcare responsibilities. In short, the very set of accumulation processes that operate during crisis creates home-based wage labor and creates the need for women to accept it.[1] While in chapter 2 we examined one side of this process (women's initiatives to develop more accommodating work options through homework), this chapter focuses on the extent to which homework is an employer-initiated form of production.

Homeworkers: Employees or Self-Employed?

There are two separate and distinct organizational mechanisms employers have used to establish homework operations. First, homeworkers can be "contracted" as "self-employed" individuals and become indirectly linked to the firm their work originates from, often through multiple layers of subcontractors or middlemen. For most of these workers self-employment is a nominal designation that hides the fact that they are waged homeworkers: they are dependent for work on a single employer; they lack contact with the market for their product; they have minimal control over the terms and conditions of their work. The expansion of this type of homework arrangement is part of a broader trend toward decentralization of production and will be examined in light of this trend. The second method for establishing homework operations is through the direct hiring of home-based workers by a firm. This type of employment relationship is more likely to occur in industries and occupations where homework has not been regulated by the state or where permit procedures allow firms to hire homeworkers under exceptional circumstances.[2] The direct hiring of homeworkers as employees will be discussed as one aspect of the trend toward more "casualized" employment. While these two types of homework appear to be different in some respects (for example, the relationship between employer and employee in each case bears a different legal status), they are linked in that they impart common advantages to employers and disadvantages to workers, and are similarly tied to current strategies of capital restructuring.[3]

Decentralization of Production: Econonomic Restructuring and Incentives for Using "Self-Employed" Homeworkers

In her discussion of the 1983 Garment Strike in Canada, Lipsig-Mumme refers to homework as a "gender-specific tactic of economic restructuring" (1987, 44). As such, it is one of a number of production options whose increase over the last two decades is tied to new accumulation strategies pursued by global capital. In the context of increased competition, a changing international division of labor, and continued stagnation and economic crisis in the developed world, national and multinational firms have sought to decentralize production in order to lower labor costs, increase flexibility, and minimize investment risks. Recent increases in various forms of decentralized activity, namely subcontracting, franchising, and self-employment, are part of this broad trend. Examination of the proliferation of such work arrangements in recent years reveals the significance of decentralization as a key strategy in the restructuring of global capital and allows us to see the overall context within which homework has flourished.

The 1960s ushered in a new era of competition and crisis for global capital. As Developing countries began their ascent in the world economy, competitive pressures mounted. As labor militancy increased in certain core countries, labor costs rose. As the relatively stable economic position of the United States and others in the developed world was shaken by growing instability, sustained crisis replaced the postwar prosperity enjoyed for almost 20 years. In this context of intense competition and uncertainty, decentralization of economic activity, including decentralization of production, marketing, sales, and business services, emerged as a key strategy on the part of capital to cheapen and reestablish control over labor and to reduce new risks imposed by economic uncertainty (Berger 1980a; Brusco and Sabel 1981; Lipsig-Mumme 1987; Russell 1984).

The economic incentives underlying decentralization of production were complemented by technological and political changes that began in the mid-1960s to make this new strategy possible on a large scale for the first time. These included technological developments that made the logistics of overseas subcontracting much easier and allowed for the de-skilling of the production process in many industries. The development of air freight facilities and advances in telecommunications solved logistical problems while de-skilling and the development of compact, versatile components allowed formerly integrated production operations to be split and spread across the globe. In addition, the rise of new labor-intensive industries such as electronics, which adopted decentralized production almost from the start, is significant in this regard. Finally, the rejection of import substitution as a method of industrialization and consequent shift toward export-oriented policies in the developing nations signalled the readiness of these nations to make themselves available for international subcontracting. Government regulations in core countries, such as U.S. Tariff Items 806.70 and 807.00, which permit low effective tariffs on further processing abroad of semi-manufactures produced in developed countries, increased the attractiveness of offshore production for many firms.

Within core countries such as the United States, one result of this progressive "loosening" of the economy is the proliferation of individualized and small-scale economic activities in the form of self-employment, franchising, and subcontracting. The link between these three types of employment is illustrated in Figure 1. Most franchisees and subcontractors are classified as self-

Figure 1

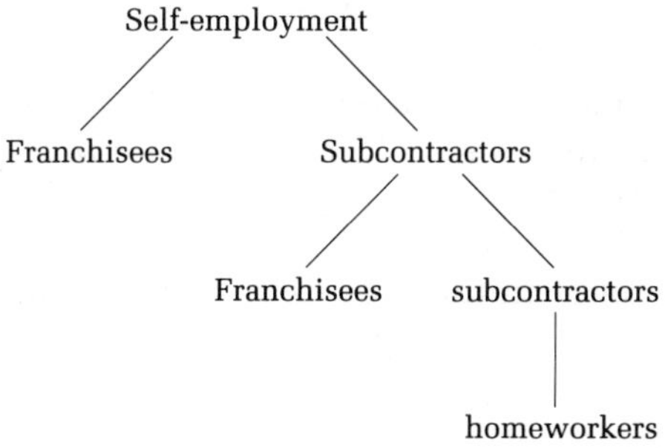

employed and thus constitute subsets of the latter category. Furthermore, subcontractors can further decentralize activities by using subcontractors themselves or by franchising their operations. Finally, as the subcontracting chain is expanded, homework sometimes emerges as the final link. Thus, examination of recent trends in self-employment sheds light on the expansion of homework.[4]

After decades of steady decline, self-employment began to increase in the early 1970s. Aronson (1991) points out that while it has been difficult to accurately measure self-employment because of "inadequate demographic and labor market counting schemes" and "ambiguity in the definition of self-employment itself," data from principal sources, including the Census, Bureau of Labor Statistics, and Internal Revenue Service, reveal the same trend.[5] For example, Bureau of Labor Statistics data show that the number of self-employed Americans in the nonagricultural workforce grew from approximately 5.2 million in 1970 to 8.7 million in 1988 (U.S. Dept. of Labor, Employment and Earnings, monthly reports). Furthermore, Fain (1980) points out that these figures are underestimates since they do not include self-employed individuals whose businesses are incorporated or those self-employed in second jobs.[6] Focusing on relative rates of increase in the postwar period, Aronson uses Social Security data to show that for the period from 1955 to 1986 self-employment increased by 53 percent, which is about half the rate of increase in wage and salary employment (Aronson 1991, 3).

Aronson recognizes that a variety of factors has likely converged to affect self-employment trends in the United States. After a brief examination of "structural influences" ("changes in the rate of economic growth and in the organization of production, the growth of service industries, and advances in technlogy") and institutional changes (franchising, the organization and delivery of health services, and increases in the minimum wage), he is unable to single out a primary factor in the growth of self-employment. He adds that changes in factors "less accessible to measurement, such as shifts in attitudes toward autonomy, flexibility in working hours, willingness to accept economic risk, and even work itself," as well as the increased participation of women in self-employment "suggests the probability of the importance of nonpecuniary factors" (40–41). Keeping in mind Aronson's caution against overemphasizing any single factor in an analysis of self-employment trends, it is useful to examine the potential importance changes in the organization of production have had for such trends. For example, Russell (1984) concludes that the recent growth in self-employment in the United States reflects, in part, employers' increasing preference for dealing with self-employed individuals instead of hiring their own employees. Although it is difficult to separate those individuals whose self-employment was created through the divestiture of certain operations by large firms, from those who create new businesses not directly tied to specific companies (through dependence on contracts), it is possible to attribute a portion of the increase in self-employment to decentralization of economic activities for large firms. Increases in self-employment through franchising and independent contracting reflect, in part, employers' efforts to divest themselves of operations that would otherwise be handled by employees.

The U.S. Department of Commerce reports that between 1980 and 1990 the number of franchisee-owned franchised establishments grew from approximately 357,000 to 424,000—an increase of almost 16 percent. Company-owned franchised establishments also increased, from approximately 85,000 to 97,000 (*Statistical Abstracts of the United States* 1992, 770). Most of the growth in franchising, dating back to the 1950s, can be attributed to increases in a particular type of franchise—the "business format franchise." This type is characterized by "an ongoing business relationship between franchisor and franchisee that includes not only the product, service, and trademark, but the entire business format itself—a marketing strategy and plan, operating manuals and standards, quality control, and continuing two-way communications. Restaurants, nonfood retailing, personal and business services, and a long list of other service businesses fall into [this] category." The Department of Commerce predicts that this type of franchise "will continue to offer opportunities for those individuals seeking their own businesses" (1987, 3).

In contrast to the business format type, the second category of franchises, product and tradename franchises, has been shrinking since the early 1970s. Franchises in this category "concentrate on one company's product line and to some extent identify their business with that company. Typical of this segment are automobile and truck dealers, gasoline service stations, and soft drink bottlers." A large portion of the decline in this type of franchise can be attributed to a rapid decline in the number of gasoline service stations. There was a net loss of more than 106,000 gasoline service stations between 1972 and 1986. (U.S. Dept. of Commerce 1987, 3).[7]

The possibility that increases in self-employment through franchises are related to business strategies relying on decentralized and divested operations seems to be supported by the Department of Commerce's analysis of recent trends. Its 1987 report concluded that increases in franchises providing business services "can be attributed to the large numbers of both small and large companies going outside of their own organizations to fulfill many service functions previously performed internally. This is demonstrated, for example, by the rapid rise of franchising services in accounting, collection services, mail processing, advertising services, message taking, package wrapping and shipping, business consulting, security, business recordkeeping, tax preparation, personnel services, and others" (6). Indeed, the number of franchises in the business aids and services category grew from approximately 40,700 in 1980 to an estimated 67,300 in 1990, an increase of almost 40 percent (*Statistical Abstracts of the United States*, 1992, 770).

In addition to franchising, subcontracting also allows industries in the service and manufacturing sectors to decentralize their operations. Russell (1984) points to taxi, construction, trucking, warehousing, logging, real estate, and sales operations as examples of industries in the United States using increasing numbers of independent contractors. He points out that although it is difficult to calculate the precise number of self-employed individuals who operate as independent contractors, Internal Revenue Service officials estimated in 1979 that their pending actions applicable to this group would affect approximately two million workers. Russell concludes that "[t]he evidence suggests that the present popularity of independent contracting is contributing to a reversal of the historic decline of self-employment in the U.S." (263). Globally, subcontracting has increased in a range of manufacturing industries (including garments, electronics, machine tools, autos, and plastics) for both labor-intensive production processes and services (Baud 1987; Beneria and Roldan 1987; Holder 1981; Mitter 1986; Pineda-Ofreneo 1983; Scott 1983; Sharpston 1975).

As "organizational devices" used by employers to mobilize new sources of capital, minimize investment risks, and reduce labor costs, franchising and subcontracting are part of the same broad trend of capital restructuring. For example, the interrelation between the two is clearly illustrated in the case of Advanced Technical Services, Inc., an electronics firm that subcontracts assembly work for larger companies. In 1982, ATS's founder announced his intention to expand his company by selling franchises that would use his procedures and customer leads in exchange for a licensing fee and royalties. His primary motivation was a need for more capital than his firm could generate by itself to expand. Looking to McDonald's and Burger King as examples, he found that cooking fast food and attaching semiconductors to printed circuit boards are similar businesses in that "both can be duplicated in several locations, a basic ingredient of franchising" (Potter 1982, 4D). Already a part of a vast network of subcontractors, ATS further decentralized electronics assembly through franchising.

A closer examination of the increasing use of franchises and subcontracting provides a clue as to how homework fits in with the broader trend toward decentralization of economic activity. For example, home-based franchises undoubtedly account for part of the overall increase in service-related franchises. Low start-up costs and overhead, the ability to take on a business that is already established, and increased flexibility are cited as the principal reasons why setting up a franchise in one's home is an increasingly attractive option in the context of today's competitive and unstable business world. While these potential benefits can have equal appeal to men and women, home-based franchises have been promoted as a way for working mothers to increase their flexibility to meet demands of both home and work. This is seen in the fact that businesses providing home repair, home decorating, and childcare training have targeted mothers as potential franchise owners (Marsh 1990; Alexander 1991).

Similarly, subcontracting arrangements on both a national and international scale often provide the organizational base of homework operations. In the international arena, subcontracting has, to some extent, replaced direct relocation of production by multinational corporations to the developing world. During the 1960s and 70s, integration of developing countries took place primarily through the establishment of wholly or partly owned subsidiaries in those countries. Today, industrial activity is becoming increasingly characterized by vertical disintegration. Multinational corporations subcontract to local firms, who subcontract to middlemen, who further subcontract to petty commodity producers or homeworkers. Thus, an elaborate chain of subcontracting is established. In this context, homework "represents decentralization carried to its logical extreme: shrinking the production unit down to a single individual in his or her home" (Mattera 1983, 391).

Recent analyses of economic restructuring in core countries

demonstrate how homework emerges as the end point in a chain of subcontracting in the developed world as well. As changes in the international division of labor have allowed a substantial transfer of production to the developing world in industries such as textiles, clothing, and electrical goods, subcontracting, often in the form of homework, is increasingly used by firms in developed countries in an attempt to match the low labor costs of their developing world competitors. For example, Lipsig-Mumme demonstrates that clothing manufacturers in developing countries have taken an increasing portion of the world market. This shift is reflected in the fact that as clothing exports from the developed market economies dropped from 80 percent to 63 percent of the world market between 1968 and 1977, the share coming from developing countries rose from 20 percent to 37 percent (1987, 45). While large enterprises in core countries can often match their competitors by creating subsidiaries in low-wage areas and phasing out operations in the developed nations, enterprises too small to shift production typically resort to subcontracting, often in the form of homework. In the European Economic Community, for example, between 1972 and 1977, 240,000 registered jobs in the clothing industry were lost to developing world production, subcontracting, and homework (Lipsig-Mumme 1987, 45). The spread of garment industry homework in advanced economies as a strategy to cheapen labor costs in the face of competition from developing countries is also documented by Coyle (1982) for London, van Luijken (1984) for the Netherlands, and the International Ladies' Garment Workers Union (1981) for the United States. Similarly, the use of homeworkers to counteract competitive pressures from abroad is common among U.S. electronics subcontractors (Carey and Malone 1980; Morales 1983).

Furthermore, decentralization of activities through subcontracting has emerged as a key economic strategy in the transformation of core countries from manufacturing-based to service-based economies. The continuing process of deindustrialization in countries such as the United States, West Germany, Canada, France, Australia, and Britain is marked by a shift from manufacturing to tertiary sector activity. In this context, vertical disintegration has allowed large firms to hire subcontractors to perform a variety of services formerly done in-house. Mingione explains why large firms have chosen to contract out for a range of services:

> The combination of the growing size of productive units
> leading to an expanding tertiarization in employment
> structure and the productivity gap . . . between manufac-

turing and service jobs caused vertically integrated organizations to become less and less profitable, and at the
same time increased the relative advantages of systems
which had developed different forms of "organized vertical disintegration" (Sayer, 1989), such as Japan or the
Third Italy. In this sense, a current important factor in
deindustrialization, and also one of the leading aspects of
contemporary trends towards vertical disintegration, is
the contracting out of operations involving the intensive
use of service labour. (1991, 201–202)

The reduction in labor costs associated with subcontracting
often follows from employers' ability to bust existing unions or
avoid expanding operations with unionized workers. For example,
Berger (1980a) argues that decentralization of production began
in Italy in the early 1970s in response to increased labor costs and
growing rigidity in the use of unionized labor in large factories.
Thus, large firms began to subcontract to smaller firms to avoid
workers who couldn't be laid off. Small firms, in turn, began to
hire homeworkers to reduce costs. According to Berger, the proportion of firms employing over 100 workers that subcontracted
out work rose from 80 percent to 98 percent between 1971 and
1975, while the number of firms employing fewer than ten workers
grew rapidly (Berger 1980a, 85).

The link between subcontracting that often results in the use
of homeworkers and deunionization is discussed by Lipsig-
Mumme (1987) for the Canadian garment industry, Mattera (1983)
for the information-processing industry in the United States, and
Katz and Kemnitzer (1983) for the electronics industry in Silicon
Valley, California. Not only is homework used in many cases as a
way to weaken existing labor organization, but it is sometimes
introduced in exanding industries to prevent unionization. For
example, as employment in the tertiary sector grows, so does the
potential threat of unionization. In the United States and Canada,
increases in telecommuting are occurring most frequently in the
banking, insurance, and communications industries, which are
potential targets for union activity. According to Lipsig-Mumme,
"homeworking in these high-technology service industries represents an attempt by the newest objects of unionization to decentralize the labour force before unionization crystallizes its collective power" (1983, 553).

In addition to the savings in wage costs that make subcontracting in developed countries competitive with production in less

developed areas, the flexibility it gives employers enhances its attractiveness in industries that are subject to fluctuating demand and nonstandard production runs. Mitter (1986) demonstrates that for the portion of the United Kingdom clothing industry subject to rapid fashion changes, subcontracting, often via home-workers, gives retailers access to suppliers who can modify orders on demand. "Flexibility of supply—the capacity to fulfill orders at short notice and the capacity to change an order with a minimum of time-lag—gives the domestic suppliers a competitive edge over their overseas counterparts" (1986, 46). The ability to ensure flexibility by decentralizion through subcontracting has, according to Mitter, resulted in a visible shift in production from the developing world to Western European countries in the 1980s. A similar link between subcontracting and the maintenance of flexibility in the high-fashion industry is also apparent in the United States, particularly in large cities such as New York and Los Angeles (ILGWU 1981). In certain segments of the electronics industry, the need for flexibility has also spawned the development of subcontracting chains. In the highly competitive production of printed circuits, the need for flexibility and minimization of costs derives from sharp cyclical fluctuations in markets and the fact that every individual order for printed circuits is a special case requiring detailed instructions subject to constant redesign (Scott 1983, 344).

The flexibility subcontracting can provide is also seen in its potential to allow companies to take full advantage of the fact that different stages of production have different levels of minimum efficient scales. On one side, large, capital-intensive firms may be best suited to produce a range of intermediary goods and services for a number of smaller firms. On the other side, small firms and single, self-employed people may be best at performing highly specialized tasks (Brusco and Sabel 1981, 103). Subcontracting also cuts the risk of long-term investment by allowing firms beginning to produce a new product to buy only the equipment necessary for that product and subcontract for the production of standard parts. It provides an easy way to deal with temporary labor shortages in main operations and to mobilize sources of labor not normally available for employment.

Economic Restructuring and Casualized Work: Using Home-Based, Part-Time and Temporary Employees

In addition to the proliferation of work arrangements based on the use of a "self-employed" labor force, capital has sought to increase flexibility and lower labor costs through the "casualiza-tion" of many of the jobs it provides. Recent increases in the use of part-time, temporary, and home-based employees are indica-tive. New strategies of capital accumulation and economic restruc-turing have hinged on the replacement of secure, full-time work with more irregular work arrangements. A journalist's report in the Paris newspaper Le Monde summarizes the thrust of this shift:

> The current economic situation and increasing un-employment are reshaping the classical model of employ-ment, which once was based on a full day's work and on lifetime employment with a single company, from train-ing to retirement. The concept of total employment has been replaced by one of floating, uncertain work. In the past few years new and atypical forms of employment have flourished: temporary jobs, substitutions, piecework, subcontracting, shared workplaces, short workdays, tai-lored hours. (Herteaux 1985, 38)

A 1986 New York Times article pointed to a trend in the American economy toward the weakening of ties between em-ployer and employee through the spreading use of "contingent" workers, such as those hired for part-time or temporary jobs (Serrin 1986, A1). The proportion of U.S. workers employed part-time increased from 15.4 percent in May 1954 to 22.1 percent in May 1977 (Applebaum 1987, 283). Since the late 1970s, however, while the number of part-time workers has continued to rise (from approximately 14.8 million in 1976 to approximately 20.7 million in January 1989) the proportion of American workers employed part-time has remained relatively constant (U.S. Dept. of Labor, Employment and Earnings, monthly reports). In other core coun-tries, a trend toward an increase in the proportion of part-time workers was evident by the early '70s, reaching 12 percent in Canada by 1973, 17 percent in Sweden by 1974, and 11 percent in New Zealand by 1972 (Lipsig-Mumme 1983, 560).

Greater use of temporary workers has proven to be an eco-nomic boon to employers and Bureau of Labor Statistics data show that their numbers have grown from more than 300,000 in 1978 to more than 700,000 in 1986. Employment growth in the temporary services industry has averaged 11 percent a year since 1973, compared with a 2.1 percent growth rate for all nonagricul-tural jobs (Applebaum 1987, 274). The temporary help industry, which "operates by putting workers on its payrolls and renting them out at a substantial profit to companies needing extra labor for varying lengths of time," allows employers the flexibility to expand and contract their workforces at will (Mattera 1985, 21). Temporary workers are now servicing a broad range of industries, moving beyond the clerical field that was once their mainstay. Applebaum identifies four main areas supplied by the temporary help industry—office clerical/office automation, medical, industrial, professional—with the use of temporary workers growing fastest in the medical field. By 1982, 46.2 percent of employment and 56.6 percent of total receipts of the temporary service industry were generated in nonoffice help areas (Applebaum 1987, 276).

Finally, the use of home-based employees (as distinct from home-based subcontractors who may be technically self-employed) is part and parcel of the trend toward creating increasingly casualized types of employment. Many home-based workers retaining "employee" status are telecommuters. Estimates in the 1980s indicated that there were approximately 250 U.S. companies, including New York Telephone, American Express, Walgreen's, and McDonald's, with a total of about 10,000 employees working at home using computer technologies (Applebaum 1987, 298). In addition, in her analysis of 1980 U.S. Census data, Silver (1989) reports a wide distribution of industries employing home-based workers, including more traditional areas such as agriculture, forestry and fisheries, private household services, and personal services as well as some of the leading growth industries such as real estate, retail trade, business and repair services, and nonmedical professional services (Silver 1989, 117).

Features of Homework: Advantages for Employers

Whether homeworkers are direct employees of a firm or "self-employed" contractors, their use accrues similar advantages to employers. While I have already mentioned some of the overall benefits of subcontracting, it is useful to focus on the precise ways those benefits are manifested in homework operations. Studies in the United States and abroad contrast homeworkers' wage and benefit levels to their counterparts' levels in the factory and office. For example, Carey and Malone (1980) discovered that by sending work home with factory workers, Silicon Valley electronics firms could eliminate about 10 percent of their labor costs for payroll deductions. They found that "a $9-an-hour job can be done for $6 or $7 an hour at home by a company worker" (1A). Furthermore, for illegal aliens, refugees on assistance, or welfare recipients, piece rate pay for doing assembly work at home drops below minimum wage. Beneria and Roldan (1987) similarly found that Mexico City homeworkers who performed tasks such as assembly for a variety of industries, plastic polishing, and garment-making earned, on average, less than one-third of the weekly minimum. While the 140 women they interviewed reported average earnings of $444 Mexican pesos (or $19.30 U.S. dollars) for a 48-hour work week, the federal minimum was set at $1470 pesos (or $63.90 U.S. dollars) (Beneria and Roldan 1987, 62). The fact that homeworkers' wage rates are typically determined in an arbitrary fashion by employers, with no consideration of federally imposed standards or the income needs of workers is clearly illustrated by the wage policy of one central New York electronics firm. In the words of the company owner and president, "we knew what our profit margin had to be and what the competitive price for the product should be, so from that we calculated how much we could pay our homeworkers."[8]

The savings in wage costs that accrue to employers hiring homeworkers can be further augmented by concomitant increases in productivity. As homeworkers become more adept at the operations they perform, the pressure to continually increase the pace and intensity of their work in an effort to increase earnings under the piece rate system tends to result in productivity gains for the employer. As Coyle (1982) explains in her discussion of homeworkers in the London garment industry, "[p]iecework is not a system of reward for increased productivity—it is a way of pushing wages down. Payment decreases proportionately as output rises and women receive only a portion of their increased productivity" (p. 19). In the case of telecommuting, productivity gains go hand in hand with the increased control that follows from employers' ability to closely monitor working times on the computer, as well as the potential for the employee to more efficiently use work time given her ability to work when she feels most productive rather than according to fixed work hours. One study of telecommuters estimates that productivity increases 20 to 40 percent when people are allowed to work at home (Schwartz 1987, 91).

Another boon to employers is the fact that a significant amount of unpaid labor time is typically applied to the completion of the homeworker's job. Left unremunerated in most cases is the time workers spend being trained to do specific tasks, picking up materials and delivering finished products, packing and unpacking materials, setting up and cleaning up the work area, and in some instances, inspecting their work to ensure it meets quality control standards. Furthermore, payment is made only for finished products that meet all the necessary specifications. If materials are damaged or quality control standards unmet, the worker receives nothing for her work time. The situation of the central New York homeworkers I studied is indicative. Most homeworkers who assemble transformers are trained on their own time by distributors. They are required to pick up raw materials, sort and count cores and wires according to size and color, and then deliver their finished products. If transformers are not wound properly, no payment is received for them.[9]

Finally, the wage bill for hiring homeworkers is further reduced by the fact that this type of employment usually does not include benefits such as paid vacations, sick leave, and insurance (health, social security, disability, and workman's compensation), except in the cases of directly employed homeworkers. With all homework operations, however, employers save money by avoiding responsibility for assuring that health and safety standards are met in the workplace. For example, in the electronics industry, without the enforcement of Occupational Safety and Health Administration regulations, homeworkers are often exposed to toxic chemicals. Acid burns, nausea, and headaches are common occupational hazards (Morales 1983). In the garment industry, health threats such as chronic exposure to cotton dust in poorly ventilated rooms, which is linked to byssinosis or brown lung disease, are potentially worse for homeworkers than factory workers. In industries that use homeworkers for packing and packaging products, storing and working with large quantities of paper products in cramped living quarters poses a fire hazard. For telecommuters, new demands that employers ensure adequate work breaks and periodic changes in work tasks for VDT operators subject to health problems such as stress, eye strain, radiation exposure, and muscular disorders, are almost certain to exclude homeworkers (*Technology Review* 1988, 16).

In addition to savings on wages and protective measures for workers, many overhead costs associated with in-house operations are avoided with homework. It is the worker, not the employer who pays for heat, lighting, cleaning, and maintenance of the workplace. Tools and equipment, which range from the inexpensive wire cutters and clamps used to make transformers in central New York to the pedal-operated machines the size of a can opener used to wind electronic coils in Mexico City (Beneria and

Roldan 1987, 59) to sewing or knitting machines costing a few hundred dollars (Green and Weiner 1981, 9), are usually purchased and maintained by homeworkers. In the case of clerical telecommuting, some have been required to purchase their own microcomputers or rent them from the employer, which probably represents the highest investment in work equipment by any group of homeworkers (Applebaum 1987, 299). For example, it is estimated that the average cost of working at home for an employee of Blue Cross-Blue Shield of South Carolina is $2,640, which covers machine, telephone, electricity, and maintenance costs (Lipsig-Mumme 1983, 550).

Converting in-house employment to homework results in a significant reduction of many of the risks and uncertainties most employers face. Absenteeism and tardiness are virtually eliminated, and the fact that companies pay only for correctly completed products cuts down their losses from wasted materials. More importantly, hiring homeworkers allows employers to respond to fluctuations in the market without leaving invested capital idle and without worrying about the need to comply with labor contracts that impose restrictions on the ability to hire and fire at will. Thus, this type of employment offers flexibility with regard to both capital and labor costs.

Finally, for some employers, homework provides opportunities to "superexploit" workers. Examples abound of jobbers who often refuse to pay illegal immigrants for work done (Webb 1982). Homework distributors in the Silicon Valley electronics industry are notorious for charging homeworkers a fee for the "privilege" of obtaining their jobs. For example, an exposé in the *San Jose Mercury News* revealed that a broker for black market work charged Indochinese refugees $150 to $250 for jobs as home assemblers (Carey and Malone 1980, 1A). In some cases, materials distributed to homeworkers are protected by severe and arbitrarily enforced rules, which result in large profits for employers. In their study of Mexico City, Beneria and Roldan report an instance in which homeworkers' weekly wages were not paid if their product was damaged. In another case, five times the value of the merchandise was deducted from wages for damage (62).

Restructuring in the Electronics Industry: The Spread of Homework

As discussed above, homework is a particular type of decentralized production arrangement whose expansion in recent decades is tied to processes of global capital restructuring. In certain branches of the electronics industry, it has played an important role for firms seeking to raise their competitive edge by lowering labor costs for producing electronic components. For many firms based in developed countries, homework has emerged as the answer to competition from low-wage production in developing countries. As such, it serves as a vehicle for "bringing the Third World home."[10]

According to the government's Standard Industrial Classification (SIC) system, four SIC groups commonly included in the electronics industry are office and computing machines (SIC 357), communications equipment (SIC 366), electronic components and accessories (SIC 367), and scientific instruments, measuring devices, control instruments and optical instruments (SIC 381–83) (Eisenscher 1984, 2). Within the electronics industry, homeworkers are sometimes employed for the assembly of electronic components. Since these components are eventually used in a wide range of electronic products, homework can be seen as an integral part of the manufacture of electronic devices that span all four SIC categories.[11]

Electronic components include semiconductors, passive components (resistors, capacitors, printed circuit boards, transformers, coils, switches, connectors), and nonsolid state active components (for example, electron tubes). It is in the production of passive components such as coils, transformers, and printed circuit boards that homework has been most prevalent in recent decades. Homeworkers have been used since the mid-1960s as changing patterns of competition in the industry have encouraged firms to seek ways to lower labor and overhead costs for labor-intensive production.

The mid-1960s through the early '70s is generally seen as a period of significant restructuring in the electronics industry (Moxon 1974; CSE Microelectronics Group 1980; Snow 1983; O'Connor 1984). The large-scale shift of labor-intensive production from developed to developing countries is identified as the most salient feature of this restructuring. For U.S. firms, in the absence of any credible foreign competition, the principal motivation for the transfer of assembly operations for electronic components such as semiconductors was increasing competition from domestic firms (Moxon 1974; O'Connor 1984). In addition, Moxon points out that price reductions were important during this period as semiconductors began to compete with other electronics technologies. For example, semiconductors began to compete with alternative computer memory devices and gradually replaced electronic tubes for many applications, including sophisticated military devices and consumer electronics products. Thus, he concluded in 1974 that the movement of semiconductor manufacture offshore could be seen not only as a defensive move against domestic competition, but also as an aggressive move intended to open up new markets (Moxon 1974, 25). For other types of electronic components, such as printed circuit boards, offshore assembly also became prominent as a strategy to establish "low cost assembly" operations (*Electronic News* 1976, 63).

While offshore production, either through direct investment, sourcing, or subcontracting, has been the predominant strategy to lower labor costs for electronic component production over the last 25 years, firms have used other methods to achieve the same goal. Depending on the specific characteristics of the production process, automation and/or changes in the organization of production can reduce or cheapen the labor component in electronics assembly. Restructuring plant layout to minimize movement of goods, improving quality control to reduce the number of testers and technicians required, and minimizing indirect labor (material planners, inventory clerks, production schedulers, and purchasers) are ways to reorganize production to cut costs (The High Tech Research Group 1986, 22) Employing homeworkers is another. In fact, in the semiconductor industry, homework was used alongside of offshore production in a truly internationalized production process. By the 1980s, it was common for semiconductor firms to have their chips manufactured in the United States, tested and assembled in low-wage countries abroad, and then brought home again for incorporation into other products (Morales 1983). It is at this last stage, when semiconductors are assembled or "stuffed" onto printed circuit boards for eventual use in a range of electronic devices, that homeworkers have been employed.

In order to zero in on the precise conditions under which homework becomes a viable strategy to cut labor costs for some firms, I will examine its use in the United States for specific electronic components, namely, transformers, coils, and printed circuit boards. I will examine the features of the production process that make homework possible and consider why it was chosen instead of offshore production and automation in the particular cases studied. My examples are taken from two geographical areas—central New York and Silicon Valley, California. I have chosen to focus on these areas because substantive research on homework is available for them. In addition, given the geographical concentration of electronics production in the United States, firms in New York and California are likely to represent overall practices in the domestic electronics industry. The majority of electronics manufacturing workers in the United States are found in seven states (California, New York, Illinois, New Jersey, Pennsylvania, Massachusetts, and Indiana), with California and Massachusetts together accounting for one quarter of all electronics employment (Snow 1983).

TRANSFORMERS AND COILS

A coil is one of three basic components from which all other electronic devices derive, including transistors and integrated circuits. The other two are resistors and capacitors. Coils (inductors) store energy temporarily. They vary in overall size, wire gauge, the number of times the wire is turned or "coiled," and the size of the coils. A transformer is composed of two coils combined into one with a bead (or core) acting as a connecting medium. Transformers also vary by wire guage and the number of times the wire is wound around the core. Transformers are attached to printed circuit boards and other devices. The variation in size and characteristics of coils and transformers depends on the particular electronic products for which they are made.

In central New York, a center for production of electronics components used in the cable television industry, coils and transformers have been assembled by homeworkers. The components are used in products such as the trap (or notch filter), a cylindrical device used to secure premium channels provided by the cable television system, and the directional tap, a generic device used by all television systems to siphon off a portion of the signal from the main telephone line to bring it into the home.

In the course of my investigation of electronics homework in central New York, I learned that at least six area firms have used homeworkers at one time or another since the late 1960s. I was able to obtain specific information about the operations of only three of those firms.[12] I will discuss each in turn. The first is MALCO,[13] a subsidiary of a large multinational corporation, with international markets for its electronics products. The company started using homeworkers in 1969, when the wife of one of its foremen began to distribute work in her community. When the firm began to "experiment" with homeworkers, it was looking for a foreign site for the assembly of transformers. After a short trial period, however, the homework distributor was able to underbid manufacturers in Haiti and Mexico for the job. According to the distributor's husband, a company foreman, MALCO hired home-workers because it was "too expensive to hire people in the factory for transformers." Domestic homeworkers were preferred over offshore production because when the latter was used, there tended to be problems with quality control, shipping lags that interrupted the flow of production, and occasional water damage to products transported by ship.

The firm continued to have its transformers assembled by homeworkers until 1981–82, when the New York State Depart-ment of Labor applied its homework law and forced distributors to halt operations. At that time, homeworkers were providing an average of 600,000 transformers a month for the company, work-ing through three different distributors. After the Labor Depart-ment's actions, the bulk of homework activities ceased as the company transferred production of transformers and circuit boards (formerly done in its central New York factory) to India and Haiti. One distributor saw the transfer overseas of the in-house circuit board line as a direct result of the company's inability to hire homeworkers to assemble the transformers des-tined for the boards.

After the Labor Department's failure to sustain its application of state homework laws to the electronics industry, homeworkers were hired again by the firm, but in much reduced numbers. One distributor, who had 45 people working for her when she was forced to cease operations in 1982, had work for about a dozen "on and off" at the time of our interview in 1984. Another interviewed in the same year, who employed approximately 50 homeworkers before his operations were stopped, admitted to having "a few" homeworkers remaining under his employ. In addition, he set up his own small factory/workshop and became a legitimate subcontractor for the firm. The third of the company's distributors, who had between 150 and 200 people working for her at any one time, had stopped doing work for the firm shortly before the state intervened to halt homework operations.

In the case of this firm, homework was part of an international production process. Homeworkers assembled transformers, which were attached to printed circuit boards in the New York plant. The assembled circuit boards were then sent to India to be put into directional taps. When homework operations were halted in 1981–82, the firm transferred transformer production and printed circuit board assembly overseas. Once the controversy over its homework operations subsided, with the Labor Department unable to uphold its application of industrial homework laws to electronics, some homeworkers were reemployed. By that time, however, the bulk of the work formerly done by homeworkers had been established offshore and was not returned. The company's continued need for some low-wage domestic labor was met by the new "workshop" set up by one of the homework distributors and a small number of homeworkers employed intermittently.

The second firm I studied, ENCO, was founded in the mid-1970s by a group of former employees from the first firm discussed above. It produced traps and directional taps for the cable television industry. By the early 1980s the new company employed 650 in-house workers and at least 40 homeworkers.[14] Its products were marketed internationally.

Here too, homeworkers were used to assemble transformers for use in circuit boards destined for directional taps. According to the vice-president and co-owner of the firm, it was not economical to have transformers made in the factory because the production process is so labor-intensive. He explained that materials were a very small portion of the product's cost and to remain competitive the wage bill had to be reduced. He also pointed out that the company had space limitations and could not hire the number of workers it needed to produce transformers in-house without investing in additional physical plant.

According to the company's co-owner, the need to cut the cost of building transformers resulted from price pressure from competitors on the overall product (the directional tap). The firm's three major competitors in the production of directional taps (one of which was MALCO) had substantial production operations in low-wage countries such as Taiwan and India. Like MALCO, this company preferred homeworkers to offshore production because of the delays in shipping and supply lines common to the latter.

ENCO was also affected by the state's enforcement of its homework laws. Forced to stop giving out homework in 1982, production of transformers, circuit boards, and the directional taps themselves was immediately moved to Sri Lanka and India. Production of other electronic devices continued at the New York plant. During our interview in December 1983, the company's co-owner explained that even though the Labor Deparment's actions against some electronics homework distributors had been overturned, the directional tap line, including assembly of transformers, would not be brought back to the United States. He added, however, that the company might be interested in hiring homeworkers in the future for operations such as stripping and salvaging equipment with technical defects.

The third firm, GILCO, was a relatively small enterprise that started supplying electronic components to larger firms in the area, including both companies discussed above, in 1975. It gradually expanded its market to include about 50 customers throughout the United States, Mexico, and Canada. At the time of my interview with the owner in 1984, the company was trying to secure contracts to supply electronic components to firms in France, West Germany, and the United Kingdom.

This firm began as a homework operation when its founder, who was a sales manager for a company that manufactured electronic test equipment, saw an opportunity to fill another firm's unmet demand for airwound coils. He and his wife began to produce the coils themselves and soon started hiring friends and neighbors to help. Within a few months, he had 150 people winding coils at home on a part-time basis and became the sole supplier of airwound coils for his original customer.

At the start of this homework enterprise, there was no machine available to successfully automate the process of winding the particular coils needed. While his business continued to grow through homework, the company founder explored possibilities for automation and eventually found a West German manufacturer able to modify an existing machine to make the coils he needed. Within a year of establishing his operations, he began to mechanize and eventually replaced all of the homeworkers. At the time of our interview in 1984, he had 11 machines and six in-house employees doing the job 150 part-time homeworkers formerly did. In the previous year, his company did $1 million in business on this product. In addition to using homeworkers for the production of airwound coils, 30 homeworkers were hired in 1980–81 to build transformers. With the intervention of the Labor Department in 1981, these operations were discontinued.

As the experiences of these three firms reveal, homeworkers have been used in the electronics industry as an alternative to offshore production and as a way to start a business without an initial investment in plant or equipment. In the cases discussed above, automation was not an alternative because of technological limitations. While the last firm was eventually successful in automating the production of airwound coils, assembly of most transformers still has not been mechanized. As one company manager explained, problems in automating for this component stem from constant variation in the size and characteristics (gauge of wire, number of times wire has to be wound around the core, size of the core) of transformers used in the cable television industry. With Labor Department action against electronics industry homework distributors in 1981–82, most homework operations were transferred overseas, though two of the three firms continued to employ some homeworkers.

PRINTED CIRCUIT BOARDS

The printed circuit board is the heart of most high-technology electronic equipment. It is a "flat piece of laminated insulator, plated with a metalic pattern, into which chips, resistors, and other components are inserted" (*Global Electronics Information Newsletter* 1984). In simple terms, it is a board with electronic circuitry etched onto it. Many industries use printed circuit boards, with the largest market coming from general electronics and aerospace firms. "Consumers of printed circuit boards mount electronic components onto the boards and these subassemblies are then inserted into various devices, such as caluclating machines, television sets, rocketry, and so on" (Scott 1983, 344).

The printed circuits industry is a highly specialized one, with boards made to buyer specifications. Accordingly, it is an industry characterized by a high degree of specialization and decentralization of production. A portion of the market in the United States is supplied by relatively large firms, many of which are vertically integrated as "captive plants" producing for particular customers. As of 1984, the top 26 producers accounted for 41 percent of the market. The two largest in this group, IBM and AT&T, supplied 7.7 and 6.4 percent of the market respectively, producing primarily for consumption in-house. Many of these enterprises are sheltered from external competition. On the other hand, more than half of the national market is met by independent suppliers (*Global Electronics Information Newsletter* 1984). In the independent sector competition is intense. In addition to pressure to cut costs, firms face uncertainty due to sharp cyclical fluctuations in markets and the fact that sales linkages are constantly recreated and renegotiated since each individual order for circuit boards tends to be a special case requiring new design instructions (Scott 1983, 344).

The production of printed circuit boards can be broken down into two broad sets of operations—the manufacture of the boards themselves (also referred to as fabrication) and the insertion of electronic components onto the boards (also referred to as stuffing or assembly). The manufacture of the boards consists of "the physical cutting of the laminate material into boards and the drilling of complex patterns of holes into these boards" and "the chemical etching of circuitry onto the boards, which are then covered with a coating of protective material" (Scott 1983, 344). The labor required for these processes is mostly unskilled or semiskilled. Subcontracting is commonly used by firms for operations at various stages of printed circuit board manufacture. For example, subcontractors are often hired for specialized operations such as drilling, multilayer laminating, solder fusing, and plating (Scott 1983, 359).

Inserting electronic components onto the boards is a time-consuming, labor-intensive process. Printed circuit board assembly is even less concentrated than manufacture. Here, again, subcontracting is a common practice. While many firms use legitimate subcontractors to do their assembly, others turn to "garage sweatshops" and industrial homeworkers. It is estimated that in Silicon Valley, California, there may be a few thousand workers illegally stuffing circuit boards in their homes. Offering low wages and no benefits, garage sweatshops and industrial homework have become "Silicon Valley's answer to foreign competition" (Carey and Malone 1980, 1A). As Katz and Kemnitzer (1983) explain, homework is analogous to offshore production because, in relation to in-house work, it is cheaper, more flexible, and eliminates the obligation to provide employees with benefits such as health insurance, sick leave, and paid breaks. It also removes the threat of unionization.

While there have been a number of studies exposing illegal homework operations in Silicon Valley (Carey and Malone 1980; Markoff 1980; Katz and Kemnitzer 1983; Morales 1983), there is little direct evidence of the use of homeworkers for printed circuit board assembly in other parts of the country. Nevertheless, Carey and Malone (1980) point out that electronics firms from the eastern United States, particularly Pennsylvania, have shown an interest in Silicon Valley's labor force of homeworkers. In addition, some of the homeworkers I interviewed in central New York had done circuit board assembly at home in the past, though it did not appear to be a widespread practice.

Variation in Patterns of Economic Restructuring

The electronics industry provides a useful illustration of the role homework has played in the restructuring of industries over the past few decades. While homework has been used by electronics firms as an alternative to offshore production for particular processes, it remains an integral part of a fully internationalized production system. Nevertheless, while it is important to understand the circumstances that have led to the use of homeworkers in this industry, it is equally important to acknowledge that homework cannot be explained merely by its suitability to the production of electronics components. Instead, the increasing use of homeworkers in a variety of industries over the last few decades is related to changes in economic conditions on the level of the world-economy as a whole. As firms have attempted to adjust to economic recession, heightened competition, and pressure to cut costs, homework has emerged as one strategy to meet new demands in a changing world market.

While I have argued that, for the most part, recent restructuring patterns have led to a weakening of labor vis-à-vis capital and a deterioration in working conditions, it is important to acknowledge the variation in outcomes of industrial restructuring for workers and local economies. Here too, the electronics industry serves as a useful illustration. In what follows I draw heavily on Benton's (1990) analysis of economic restructuring in order to compare her findings on the electronics industry in Spain with my findings on electronics firms in central New York.

In her discussion of productive decentralization, which includes an investigation of homework, Benton argues that recent trends have had different and contradictory outcomes for workers. She calls for an approach to studying these trends that allows us to capture the variation in experiences within and across countries:

> If sweatshops and economic backwardness would result from industrial restructuring in one place, while technological innovation and the revival of craft might emerge in another, one challenge was clearly to understand the factors responsible for shaping different patterns of industrial change. Underlying this approach is the conviction that no superior logic dictates how the profile of industry must evolve. The process will always be contingent on local political, social, and cultural forces that deserve to be placed at the center of economic analysis. (1990, 7)

Benton's aim is to identify the conditions that lead industrial reorganization in one direction or the other. She points out that for Italy, which has seen productive decentralization result in a vibrant, autonomous, small-scale industrial sector, an unusual mix of conditions prevailed.[15] These included a strong tradition of worker cooperatives, a high concentration of different industries in central Italy that allowed small firms to form associations to collectivize tasks such as bookkeeping, a high degree of political cooperation among business, local government, and workers in Communist-led municipalities, and a critical mass of skilled workers. In addition, the initial period of decentralization of production in Italy began in the early 1970s when global demand was still expanding.

In contrast, Benton points out that productive decentralization and the expansion of the informal sector has led to different outcomes in other parts of the world. In Latin America, the informal sector increased rapidly in many countries after the late 1970s in the context of falling real wages, weakening labor organization, and market contraction. Benton argues that

> the very success of the bureaucratic-authoritarian regimes in reducing real wages meant that industrial employers faced reduced incentives either to introduce innovations in established factories or to search for novel contributions from auxiliary producers. Industrial workers, meanwhile, having received ample benefits and protection from the state in the past, did not view informal labor as a desirable or acceptable replacement for coveted stable jobs. Nor were producers encouraged either by local or national governments to form cooperatives or other worker associations to improve their position. In short, the peculiar constellation of expanding demand, cooperativism, local government autonomy, institutional support for informal-sector ventures, and a strong position for skilled labor was absent as a backdrop to industrial restructuring. (1990, 22)

Benton found a similar contrast in outcomes when comparing the shoe and electronics industries in Spain. Decentralization in the shoe industry led to an increase in informal enterprises that remained dependent on established firms and relied on a system of "sweatshop labor," including homework. This process of informalization began in the late 1970s in response to a decline in the export market and a resurgence of the labor movement. A wave of plant closures was followed by the spread of small, informal shoe factories, which began to rely on homeworkers for labor-intensive tasks such as sewing uppers and finishing work. Benton points out that since these tasks had been done in the factory primarily by women, "employers have been able to rely to some extent on natural turnover—traditionally higher among women than men—to reduce the number of workers employed in these phases within the factories" (85). In addition, firms began to subcontract male-dominated tasks such as leather cutting, which resulted in the growth of informal cutting and sewing workshops.

Benton argues that informalization in shoemaking took the form it did because the industry had already passed through a period of rapid expansion and was characterized by a preponderance of small, family-run firms that had to adjust to a period of slower growth. In addition, the tasks that could be decentralized were low-skill, labor-intensive, and tended to take place at the beginning of the production process. This eliminated the possibility for worker-entrepreneurs to break away from established firms. Finally, in the context of a wave of plant closings, workers' bargaining power had been substantially weakened, making them vulnerable to employers' demands to intensify work and increase hours. Accordingly, restructuring in the shoe industry has resulted in "a two-tiered industrial structure, with an informal sector characterized mainly by poor labor conditions and the simple reproduction of tasks formerly carried out by formal firms" (Benton 1990, 98). The proliferation of waged homework is one of the most significant outcomes of restructuring in the shoe industry.

In contrast, the process of decentralization in electronics that occurred in Spain in the 1970s and 80s created a dynamic, small-scale sector providing well-paying, skilled jobs for workers. Benton credits this outcome to the fact that many of the productive tasks that were decentralized are capital-intensive and require skilled labor. She points out that many of the small electronics firms in the "auxiliary sector" were started by skilled workers "with strong convictions about making it on one's own" and a willingness "to experiment with new forms of associations that enable them to escape some of the difficulties of internal management and technical capacity encountered because of their relative newness and small size" (Benton 1990, 72). At the same time, productive decentralization of some labor-intensive, low-skill tasks occurred (assembling transformers and placing subcomponents on circuit boards) leading to the use of "unregulated or semi-regulated" labor, including homeworkers. Thus, the process of industrial restructuring produced both stable and more precarious forms of work.

The situation Benton found in Spain parallels what I found in the central New York electronics industry to some extent.[16] Large, integrated firms such as MALCO existed alongside of smaller firms that served as subcontractors. Two of the firms I studied were started by former employees of larger companies who saw an opportunity to fill a gap in the marketplace. Their history reveals a process of productive decentralization that led to stable work for in-house employees as well as more precarious work for a variable labor force of industrial homeworkers. One of the firms, ENCO, was started in 1975 by a group of former MALCO employees. Their aim was to compete with their former employer and other multinational companies in the production of directional taps. At the time large firms like MALCO were having components for their directional taps (transformers, for example) either made offshore in countries such as Taiwan, or assembled by homeworkers in the United States. ENCO started as a homework operation, but then grew to include more than 500 in-house employees and some homeworkers. After intervention by the State Labor Department in 1982, it shifted the assembly operations homeworkers did to India.

Another level of decentralization occurred in the mid-1970s as a business associate of ENCO's president formed a new company to supply ENCO's growing need for another product—airwound coils. This company, GILCO, also started by using homeworkers and continued to do so until its production process was successfully automated. The cases of these three companies illustrate a process of productive decentralization that resulted in the coexistence of large-scale, integrated firms and smaller subcontractors, each providing stable work for factory employees alongside of homeworkers.

A central question that underlies Benton's work is whether or not the informal sector, which includes casualized forms of work such as waged homework, can be transformed "from a degraded industrial substratum to a forum for innovation and development" (45). Her analysis of different circumstances and outcomes in various countries leads her to hypothesize that the answer depends, first of all, on the social relations of production in the workplace. For example, the outcomes of productive decentralization depend on whether or not industrial outworkers can overcome "a strictly subordinate relationship to producers at the top of the production ladder" and "abandon the organizational tenets of factory production—autocratic control over workers, de-skilling, and the atomization of tasks—and replace these with forms of production which enable them to capitalize on the peculiar strengths of their small size, skill composition, and the relative absence of state regulation" (Benton 1990, 22–23).

Secondly, Benton recognizes the importance of the social relations surrounding production, "including patterns of authority within the family and the character of political alliances which may constrain workers' actions" (23). In the case of waged homework, the social relations of production in the workplace combine with the gender division of labor in the family to render this particular type of informal production regressive rather than progressive for most—as a "refuge" for women whose place in the gender division of labor limits their "value" on the marketplace and their realm of choice within the home. This explains why, even in the midst of a generally "progressive" restructuring of industry (electronics in Spain and central New York), a substratum of industrial homeworkers is left out of the upward climb. This occurs not because homework is a residual category of work—not because homeworkers fill in to perform marginal tasks—but because the social relations that underlie this form of production provide a ready supply of a specific type of labor, whose availability conditions the development of the production process. Waged homework gives credence to Benton's claim that "social and political conditions we often think of merely as colorful background to larger, systemic shifts come to the fore and assert their power to redirect industrial development and reshape the world economy" (1990, 23). Waged homework continues to play an important role in conditioning economic development and the forms of work that emerge across the globe. The historical dimensions of that role reveal it as a structural feature of modern capitalism, the subject to which we turn in the next chapter.

4

Waged Homework: A Structural Feature of the Capitalist World-Economy

In conventional textbooks of economic history, the displacement of the "domestic system" by the "factory system" is commonly seen as the inevitable result of industrialization (Bythell 1978, 12). Similarly, labor process theorists in the Marxian tradition, most notably Braverman (1974), have focused on centralization of production as the optimal form in capitalist development. Consistent with these views, state policy regarding industrial homework has been influenced by the assumption that this form of production would eventually disappear. In the United States, for example, New Deal homework laws in states such as New York and Rhode Island were clear in their intent to regulate homework with the aim of facilitating its eventual (and inevitable) elimination.

The increase in waged homework (both industrial and service)[1] over the last two decades raises important questions about these assumptions. To what degree has decentralized production been sustained during the last century? Is homework, as a specific form of decentralized production, rooted in a past stage of capitalist development or is it compatible with modern enterprise? Is the recent spread of homework simply conjunctural or is this form of production a structural feature of capitalism? In order to answer these questions, it is necessary to trace the historical roots of homework and assess its compatibility with modern capitalism in theoretical and practical terms.

As a starting point, we must reassess conventional views that see centralization of production as a predominant and inevitable tendency. For example, analyses offered by economic historians

such as Landes (1969) and Ashton (1948), in stressing the impact
of technological change, imply that as capitalist development
proceeds increased mechanization will lead to the substitution of
capital for labor, the concentration of production in ever larger
units, and the inevitable decline of small-unit and labor-intensive
production. Similarly, labor process theorists such as Braverman
(1974) and Marglin (1971) see centralization as an inevitable
tendency, but not because of technological imperatives. Instead,
they emphasize that capitalists tend to centralize operations in
order to gain better control of the labor force. The assumption that
there is a continuous, one-way progression from mechanization
to capital intensity to concentration and large-scale production
has been challenged by those who have sought to explain the
persistence of decentralized, small-scale production throughout
the world-economy.[2] The perspective on economic development
and recent patterns of industrial restructuring that has emerged
out of scholarly debates on productive decentralization and the
informal sector provides an important framework for analyzing
forms of production such as waged homework that deviate from
the factory model. At the same time, analysis of the conditions
under which industrial homework emerged in the nineteenth
century allows us to clarify, in theoretical terms, the compatibility
of decentralized production with modern capitalism. By tracing
industrial homework's historical origin, we can see the early
coexistence of centralized and decentralized production and
identify the precise conditions that allow both to be used concur-
rently. We can also clarify the distinctions between different types
of production historically carried out in the home. This allows us
to specify the point at which domestic labor becomes integrated
with, and a part of, capitalist production and to pinpoint the
difference between various forms of domestic labor, such as the
putting-out system and industrial homework.

The Emergence of Industrial Homework
as a "System of Industry"

As I have argued elsewhere (Dangler 1986), Carl Bucher provides
a useful framework for analysis of the emergence of industrial
homework as a form of production with a specific set of relations
that distinguishes it from other forms of domestic production,
such as the putting-out system.[3] He contends that the process of
industrial development involved a series of stages characterized

by five different "systems of industry," four of which involve some form of home-based production. The first system of industry is housework (or domestic work) which involves industrial production for household use. Next, under the wage work system workers produced directly for consumers who provided them with raw materials. According to Bucher, wage workers constituted an independent professional class of industrial laborers who, in contrast to their predecessors whose industrial skill "was exercised in close association with property in land and tillage," became independent of property in land (162). Those who labored under this system were either itinerant workers who worked at their customers' homes (dressmakers and seamstresses, for example) or "home workers" who had their own place of business and usually received piece rate wages for their work (the linen weaver, miller, or baker working in the nineteenth century countryside).

Bucher saw handicraft production as the third system of industry. While the handicraft worker, like the wage worker, was involved in custom production and paid on a piece rate basis, he differed from the latter because he owned his own raw materials and means of production. As a result he could accumulate business capital and transform his status from wage earner to capitalist.

Under the fourth system of industry, the commission system, both wage workers and handicraft workers were transformed from custom producers working directly for those who purchased their products to employees of commercial entrepreneurs. In contrast to workers under the wage work and handicraft systems, commission workers had lost all direct contact with the market. In fact, under this system merchant capital organized and controlled the market. Moving a step beyond this level of control, the fifth system of industry—the factory system—gave capitalists (now in the form of industrial capital) control over the entire production process as well as the market.

Bucher's description of the commission system corresponds to what is more generally known as the putting-out system. Production under this system took place in the homes of people scattered around the countryside or in outbuildings or cottages where workers would gather to work. According to Albrecht (1982), the putting-out system for British textiles, which dates back to the fifteenth century, was gradually transformed so that "cottage industry" came to replace home-based work as the major form of organization. During the early years of putting-out, workers typically owned their own tools (spinning wheels and looms, for example) and worked at home. Eventually, merchants owned and equipped cottages where workers would gather to perform tasks previously done in the home. This type of cottage industry was also a major form of organization in the putting-out system for British woolen manufacture and was found in nail making, glove sewing, cutlery manufacture, and basket-weaving (Albrecht 1982). Among the industries in which the putting-out system prevailed in the United States (New England) were the boot and shoe industry (Blewett, 1983), textiles and related products (spinning of flax and wool, weaving), glove-making, straw-braiding, and palm-leaf hat-making (Clark 1979; Stansell 1983; Dublin 1985). In New England, home-based and cottage industry forms of putting-out often coexisted.

While cottage industry is a particular form of the putting-out system, it is often perceived as the transitional stage in an inevitable shift from home-based to factory production. The transition from home-based putting-out to cottage industry to the factory was not always linear, however. Putting-out did not always become transformed into more centralized production. In many nineteenth century industries, a new form of decentralized production—industrial homework—emerged as an alternative to factory production.

Bucher's model provides us with the historical space within which to insert industrial homework as another "system of industry," integral to modern capitalism and characterized by its own form and relations of production. While his formulation is basically one of sequential stages, we can reject the implied rigidity of stage theory in order to consider the possibility that different production systems could coexist, not simply because of overlap during transition periods, but because of their simultaneous suitability for modern enterprise. Bucher's model allows us to pinpoint the historical emergence of industrial homework as a form of production different from, though emerging out of, previous forms of domestic labor. As a "system of industry," it emerges after the stage described by Bucher as commission work and exists alongside of factory production. Thus, the commission work system was replaced by a dual system of factory work and industrial homework. While the location of work differs for each of the latter, they are the same with regard to social relations of production, degree of proletarianization of the workforce, and workers' loss of contact with the market.

To clarify the similarities between industrial homework and factory work it is useful to show how the former differs from previous types of domestic labor. Before the nineteenth century, domestic laborers who worked as custom wage workers or independent artisans were likely to own their own tools and materials, own the products of their labor, sell their products directly to local customers, and, if they were artisans, have the potential to accumulate capital. The transition to commission work saw the elimination of these conditions and greater dependence on employers.[4] Then, the transition from commission work to industrial homework was marked by a shift from the control of domestic labor by commercial capital to its control by industrial capital and the removal of any remnants of worker independence, such as access to the means of subsistence. In short, the industrial homeworkers who emerged during the nineteenth century were fully proletarianized, unlike their predecessors who engaged in industrial production from their homes.

The process of proletarianization of domestic workers is described by E.P. Thompson in his discussion of the British textile industry. Through the course of the eighteenth and nineteenth centuries, the "customer-weaver," who "lived in independent status in a village or small town, much like the master-tailor making up orders for customers," was replaced by the coexistence of three other types of weaver: the self-employed artisan who worked "by the piece for a choice of masters," the journeyman weaver who worked in the shop of a master clothier or in his own home, and the "farmer or smallholder weaver, working only part-time in the loom" (Thompson 1963, 270). According to Thompson, these three types were gradually replaced by the proletarian outworker:[5]

> We may simplify the experiences of the years 1780–1830 if we say that they saw the merging of all three groups into a group, whose status was greatly debased—that of the proletarian outworker, who worked in his own home, sometimes owned and sometimes rented his loom, and who wove up the yarn to the specifications of the factor or agent of a mill or of some middle-man. He lost the status and security which [the self-employed weaver and the journeyman weaver] might expect, and side-earnings of [the farmer or smallholder weaver]: he was exposed to conditions which were, in the sense of the London artisan, wholly "dishonourable." (271)

Historians such as Blewett (1983) and Clark (1979) provide a glimpse of similar processes of proletarianization among domestic workers in the United States during the eighteenth and nineteenth centuries. Moreover, they highlight a key feature of the transformation of domestic industry during this period, namely, its feminization. Whereas workers under the putting-out or commission system were just as likely to be male as female, women (and also children) became the main source of labor for industrial homework.

In her discussion of the New England shoe industry, Blewett describes the process through which shoemaking was transformed from a "family labor system" of putting-out controlled by male artisans to a system based on a detailed division of labor between female outworkers and male artisans, with the "shoe boss" controlling the labor of both. According to Blewett, the putting-out system in the shoe industry was transformed in the following way. Before the 1750s it was characterized by domestic production with male artisans working in houses or attached sheds. By the 1780s male artisans had moved out of the house and into "self-contained work area[s]" or outbuildings called "ten footers." After 1780 production was expanded by merchant capitalists who owned the materials used by shoemakers and marketed the products of their labor. Experiencing a labor shortage in the face of expanded production as well as decreasing control over profits, male artisans turned to female family members to sew uppers:

> Those shoemakers who owned no leather and who accepted work from capitalists had only their labor from which to profit. They divided up the work among the men in their shops and augmented their wage income from labor by recruiting additional family members for work: their women. The male head of the shoemaking family disciplined and controlled women's work in the home. The merchant capitalist, who had no control over the assignment of work in the artisan shop or family, welcomed the new potential for production. As entrepreneurs, they paid no wages directly to women workers and did not need to supervise their work. By adapting to the new work, women added their traditional household labor to their family's income in ways which continued to permit them to combine family and work roles. (Blewett 1983, 223)

This system of family control of female domestic labor had declined by 1830 since the "shoe boss," not artisan family members, began hiring female homeworkers. In this case, the locus of control over women's labor shifted from the family (that is, male artisans) to industrial capital. By the nineteenth century the homeworker was a proletarianized "domestic worker" and the power of male artisans to control the work process had declined markedly:

> This disassociation of women's work from the family labor system affected the ability of the shoemaker to coordinate the work process. The shoe boss assumed responsibility not only for hiring female workers, often from non-shoemaking families, but also directed and coordinated the work process from his central shop. The shoemaker had to wait, sometimes for hours, for the shoe boss to provide him with bound uppers. The shift in the coordination of the work of binding and making to the central shop represented a decline in the power of artisans to exert control over the work process. (Blewett 1983, 225)

The proletarianization and feminization of domestic industry are also revealed in Clark's (1979) discussion of the development of market exchange in the Connecticut Valley between 1800 and 1860. He explains how the household manufacturing system collapsed in the face of the influx of cheap British clothing and textiles, the growth of American manufacturers, disruption of the rural exchange system based on credit and trade in goods, and the gradual increase in landless and land-poor people who were forced to sell their labor or engage in trade (Clark 1979, 175–76). As a result of these changes, market relationships came to undermine the system of household production for family or local consumption. Here, too, control of domestic production shifted from the family to commercial and eventually industrial capital. During the first half of the nineteenth century the increase in factory work in Connecticut and neighboring states was accompanied by "new sources of outwork, at first in small textile mills along the Mill River in Northampton and Williamsburg, and subsequently in the button trade of Williamsburg and Easthampton, and finally in the palm-leaf hat industry, which was centered largely in Amherst." Outwork was an important source of income for married and unmarried women. It gave them "a chance to accommodate their work to the needs of other household tasks, in the way that had been possible under the household system" (Clark, 1979, 179)

These historical examples show that in contrast to the pre-nineteenth century domestic laborer, the homeworker who emerged during the Industrial Revolution in Britain and the United States was likely to have more in common with her current factory counterparts than with earlier domestic laborers. By then she had become part of what Marx identified as "an outside department of the factory":

> This modern so-called domestic industry has nothing, except the name, in common with the old-fashioned domestic industry, the existence of which pre-supposes independent urban handicrafts, independent peasant farming, and above all, a dwelling-house for the labourer and his family. That old-fashioned industry has now been converted into an outside department of the factory, the manufactory, or the warehouse. Besides the factory operatives, the manufacturing workmen and the handicraftsmen, whom it concentrates in large masses at one spot, and directly commands, capital also sets in motion, by means of invisible threads, another army; that of the workers in the domestic industries, who dwell in the large towns and are also scattered over the face of the country. (461)

Marx adds further clarification to the role of industrial homeworkers in modern capitalism in his discussion of the industrial reserve army. He argues that as the proportion of variable capital tends to fall in relation to total capital, the capitalist accumulation process produces "a relatively redundant population of labourers, i.e., a population of greater extent than suffices for the average needs of the self-expansion of capital" (630). This surplus population is not only a product of accumulation but "becomes, conversely, the lever of capitalistic accumulation, nay, a condition of existence of the capitalist mode of production. It forms a disposable industrial reserve army, that belongs to capital quite as absolutely as if the latter had bred it at its own cost. Independently of the limits of the actual increase of population, it creates, for the changing needs of the self-expansion of capital, a mass of human material always ready for exploitation" (Marx 1967, 632). For Marx, workers in "domestic industry" constitute a component of the surplus population he labels the "stagnant" portion.[6]

> The third category of the relative surplus-population, the stagnant, forms a part of the active labour army, but with extremely irregular employment. Hence it furnishes to

capital an inexhaustible reservoir of disposable labour-power. Its conditions of life sink below the average normal level of the working-class; this makes it at once the broad basis of special branches of capitalist exploitation. It is characterised by maximum of working-time, and minimum of wages. We have learnt to know its chief form under the rubric of "domestic industry." (643)

Historical accounts of industrial homework reveal the important role it played in the development of capitalist production in Europe and the United States. Still, it remains to be demonstrated in theoretical and empirical terms that industrial homework was more than simply a transitional phenomenon whose existence in the twentieth century is related to conjunctural factors such as economic crisis or large-scale immigration. Reevaluation of labor process theory provides a useful starting point for analysis of contemporary waged homework.

Marxian Labor Process Theory: A Historically Specific Analysis

In his discussion of changes in the labor process during the industrial revolution, Marglin (1971) implies that the centralized factory model represents the most effective means for controlling labor, and, therefore, the inevitable choice of capitalists. But his discussion of the factory is a historically specific one. His objective is to uncover the impetus behind centralization of production in the nineteenth century, and evidence he presents to support his claims elucidates reasons the factory afforded a better way for capitalists to organize most of their activities at that particular time.

Marglin provides evidence of widespread concern among capitalists about their inability to discipline and coordinate dispersed workers in the eighteenth and early nineteeth centuries. In his view, the lack of discipline or "laziness" eighteenth century observers attributed to workers reflected the latter's ability to determine exactly how much work they needed to do in order to obtain wages sufficient to secure their livelihood. Aside from the fact that many of those working under the putting-out system maintained some independence through subsistence farming, rising wages allowed them to limit the time they devoted to wage work. "Thus, the very success of pre-factory capitalism contained within it the seeds of its own transformation. As Britain's internal commerce and its export trade expanded, wages rose and workers insisted in taking out a portion of their gains in the form of greater leisure. However sensible this response may have been from their point of view, it was no way for an enterprising capitalist to get ahead. Nor did the capitalist meekly accept the workings of the invisible hand" (Marglin 1971, 46). For Marglin, discipline and supervision were inadequate under the putting-out system only from the point of view of the capitalist, not of the worker. The alleged need to increase both reflected a class issue rather than an issue of technological efficiency since "a lack of discipline and supervision could be disastrous for profits without being inefficient" (44). Thus, "the capitalist's salvation lay in taking immediate control of the proportions of work and leisure. Capitalists' interests required that the worker's choice become one of whether or not to work at all—the only choice he was to have within the factory system" (47).

The strength of Marglin's argument rests on its historical specificity. He has demonstrated that in order for capitalists to expand their control over production in the nineteenth century, workers had to become fully proletarianized. The gradual displacement of the putting-out system occurred hand in hand with the separation of workers from the means of subsistence, the steady distancing of domestic producers from the markets for their products, and, finally, the concentration of workers in factories. It is with the latter that the process of proletarianization received its full expression.

But the evidence Marglin presents may in fact lend support to some of the points made previously concerning the viability of homework in the late nineteenth and twentieth centuries. I argued that the industrial homeworkers who emerged in the mid-nineteenth century had more in common with their factory counterparts than with earlier domestic laborers, and that the similarity between the two lay in the fact that by then both had become proletarianized. Since nineteenth century homeworkers had lost those privileges that previous domestic laborers enjoyed (ownership of tools and materials, access to markets, ownership of products, means of subsistence) they became encased in the same relations of production, vis-à-vis capitalists, as factory workers. In other words, once the social and economic relations that formed the basis of the putting-out system were dissolved, dispersed production could be reinstituted by capitalists under conditions that were compatible with their imperatives.

Marglin's analysis would seem to support this conclusion precisely because of its thoroughness in demonstrating the fact that the decision by capitalists to centralize production in the late eighteenth and early nineteenth centuries was a response to the specific conditions that confronted them at the time. Marglin takes pains to emphasize that the preproletarian status enjoyed by workers engaged in putting-out gave them substantial power to resist capitalist exploitation. Once that status was transformed and workers became substantially weakened vis-à-vis capitalists, however, what Marglin identifies as the prime motive for centralizing workers into factories loses its urgency. While organizing workers into factories may have been necessary to obtain control over the labor process at a particular historical moment, maintenance of that control has not necessarily required that all subsequent production be carried out in the factory. Furthermore, Rubery and Wilkinson (1981) show that the advent of labor unions presents a challenge to Braverman's and Marglin's assumptions that factory organization provides capital with complete and permanent control over the labor process. Given the potential power of unions to constrain capitalists in their efforts to increase profitability at the expense of workers, "outwork and cheaper forms of labour present attractive propositions both in reducing costs and providing a countervailing power to labor organization in factories" (119).

The Diverse Outcomes of Technological Change

While Braverman and Marglin saw the need to control workers as the factor that made centralization of production an imperative for capitalists, economic historians such as Landes (1969) and Ashton (1948) saw technological change as the driving force behind the inevitable decline of small-unit, labor-intensive production. Here too, developments in the twentieth century reveal the diverse outcomes of such change—outcomes that point to the compatibility of decentralized forms of production such as homework with modern enterprise. Rubery and Wilkinson (1981) point out that technological development does not proceed uniformly across all sectors of the economy and that some industries have not experienced the technological or market conditions to provide incentives for initiating fully mechanized, integrated production. They identify the construction and cutlery industries in Great

Britain as prime examples. Given their continual need to reorient activities to specialized, rapidly changing markets, these industries are prevented from standardizing their operations and function optimally through a decentralized structure that can utilize specialized (often labor-intensive) production techniques. Similarly, Piore and Sabel (1984) provide a detailed analysis of the conditions under which decentralized production has been optimal in particular regions and industries in recent decades. They show that small-scale custom production in specialty steel, precision machine tools, specialty chemicals, textiles, and other industries has been highly successful in parts of Italy, West Germany, Austria, and elsewhere.

Another illustration of the point that technological change has led to diverse, and even contradictory, outcomes is seen in the fact that technological advances (and the consequent spread of mechanization) in some segments of industry have been associated with increases in labor-intensive processes in others. For example, the contradictory effects of mechanization are revealed in the case of the sewing machine. Schmiechen (1984) argues that the introduction of the sewing machine in nineteenth century Britain caused a speedup in production that facilitated the spread of homework. Despite predictions to the contrary, mechanization did not alter the basic pattern of organization that characterized the "sweating system" in garment-making:

> Early predictions that the sewing machine would encourage the centralization of production in the factory turned out to be unfounded: most machine-made clothes were not made in a factory. Other machines were developed for high-speed stitching, band-stitching, machine-filling, collar-padding, buttonholing, cutting, lacemaking, and embroidery, but with few exceptions these, too, were machines for the home and small workshop. . . . As late as 1915 there was probably no industry as untouched by factory production or in which the methods of production had been standardized so little as the manufacturing of clothing. (Schmiechen 1984, 26)

The link between the sewing machine and the proliferation of homework was also seen by Stansell (1983) in her examination of the New York City garment industry. She contends that the sewing machine actually solved one of the major problems the homework system presented to employers—the production of nonstandardized work ("garments sewn too differently from each other to be sold for a unit price"): "In the 1850s, employers hard pressed by growing competition took steps to solve the problem of standardization by introducing the sewing machine, which standardized the stitch, and by putting out detail work instead of whole garments. Home workers sewed pieces of the garment—cuffs, buttonholes, sleeves—which were then assembled in an inside shop" (89).

In more recent times, technological progress in the U.S. semiconductor industry has created both capital- and labor-intensive production. As Keller (1983) indicates, increased mechanization in the fabrication stage of semiconductor production (that is the stage at which silicon wafers are prepared as integrated electronic circuits) has been accompanied by increased labor-intensive production at other stages. Thus, increased integration at one stage can reopen the opportunity for fragmented production at another—a situation that has made homework an attractive and viable option for some electronics firms. In sum, variation in production techniques and organization suggests that we cannot view large-scale, integrated, fully mechanized operations as the paragon that small-scale, decentralized, labor-intensive firms must strive to become. Instead, we must recognize that different types of production units can coexist with structures that are equally suited to an advanced capitalist economy.

Waged Homework: Structural or Conjunctural?

I have tried to show that neither technological change nor the need for labor control led to the inevitable decline of small-scale, labor-intensive, decentralized production. However, even if we have established that decentralized forms of production such as homework are plausible in the modern economy, we need to clarify the precise role they have played. In general, those who have documented the coexistence of homework and factory production into the twentieth century have stopped short of recognizing its long-term, structural role in the world-economy. For example, one of the most significant studies of nineteenth and early twentieth century "domestic outwork" is Duncan Bythell's *The Sweated Trades*.[7] He argues that outwork in domestic premises was used alongside of factory work during this period, though the extent to which it was the sole form of production in key industries declined steadily during the nineteenth century. While Bythell recognizes the importance of domestic outwork for nine-teenth century industries such as textiles, clothes, boots and shoes, and nail-making, he concludes that it becomes statistically insignificant around the turn of the century. Relying on official estimates of industrial homework available in Britain after passage of the Factory Acts, he depicts twentieth century homework as "abnormal."[8] Moreover, he contends that the attention given to homework and "sweating" by turn-of-the-century social reformers arose precisely because the situation of domestic outworkers contrasted starkly with the steadily improving conditions experienced by the general workforce. As I have argued elsewhere, Bythell believes that domestic outwork "became a social issue only after it had become rare and highly localized (e.g., in London). In his view, it became intolerable when it became abnormal" (Dangler 1986, 263).

Bythell's designation of turn-of-the-century homework as "abnormal" is based on its quantitative decline as reported in official government records. Yet, there is considerable reason to doubt the accuracy of such records. In the United States and Britain, government statistics have typically captured only those homework operations employers are willing to disclose or illegal operations uncovered by special government investigations. In Britain, a decline in the number of registered homeworkers accompanied public concern about its potential abuses in the first two decades of the twentieth century (Hakim and Dennis 1982).[9] As the number of known homeworkers dwindled, public concern was assuaged. Davin (1981) believes that interest in homework faded with the First World War because of the assumption that it was a survival of an older form of industry and would inevitably decline with modern progress. In fact, concern about exploitative homework seemed to generally disappear in Britain until the 1970s, when a series of government reports revealed its "reemergence."[10] The relative absence of homework in official counts and public consciousness for a good part of the twentieth century (roughly from World War I to the 1970s) does not mean it did not exist at significant levels, however. For example, recent research has uncovered the fact that it flourished between the two world wars in the hat trade in Luton, Lace-making in Nottingham, and the garment industry in London (Edwards and Flounders 1977).

In the United States, while homework ceased to be a focal point of public debate during the interwar years, efforts to refine and expand state and federal homework laws continued through the New Deal period, indicating that it continued to be recognized as a problem that needed addressing. Nevertheless, the focus of government regulatory efforts was fairly limited. The main target was "traditional" homework industries, leaving homework in other areas outside the realm of government enumeration and investigation.

While the inaccuracy of government statistics on homework will be discussed in detail in chapter 6, at this point we can assert that the assumed decline of homework after the turn of the century in Britain and the United States has been greatly overstated. Keeping this in mind we must relinquish the assumption, which I think is implicit in Bythell's analysis, that homework became effectively controlled once it was regulated in the United States, Britain, and other European countries in the early part of this century. To the contrary, recent studies have documented the perisitence of homework throughout the twentieth century across the world eonomy.[11] Most of these studies focus on illegal homework operations—those not captured in official government figures.

In recent years the literature on homework has grown, probably because of its rediscovery during the economic crisis conditions of the 1970s and '80s. While historians and other social scientists are trying to piece together the history of this largely hidden form of work, its association with crisis conditions overshadows a more comprehensive picture of its use in the twentieth century. While evidence does indicate that the use of homework has increased markedly in periods of crisis, as occurred in the United States during the Depression of the 1930s and worldwide during the economic crisis of the 1970s and '80s (Benson, 1989; Blackwelder, 1989, ILGWU, 1981), a closer look reveals that a sustained pattern of use underlies these intense episodes of expansion. This sustained pattern of use reveals homework's structural nature. It is structural in that it persists because of the logic of capital and the persistence of the social relations that support it.

Conditions that Make Waged Homework a Viable Production Option

While centralization of production has been the dominant tendency in capitalist development, homework and other forms of decentralized production have been used to meet recurring needs not met through centralized work arrangements. In order for homework to be a practical option for meeting these needs, certain conditions must be present. First of all, the production process must be easily fragmented and physically dispersed. The extent to which this condition exists has varied considerably across time and by industry. In industries where fragmentation has remained a constant feature despite changes in technology, such as garments, jewelry, and shoes, homework has been a relatively permanent form of production for more than a century. It is indeed a structural feature of these industries, for without it they would have to undertake significant restructuring of their production processes.

Throughout the economy in general, however, the use of homework has been more sporadic. It has been introduced, expelled, and reintroduced as changes in technology, the availability of capital and labor, the nature of markets, and the intensity of competition have influenced capitalists' choice of production methods.[12] Thus, despite its impermanence within most industries, it has been a permanent feature in the economy at large because of recurring conditions across the world-economy that allow homework to retain its position as a viable form of production, intermittently used and then set aside until conditions are once again ripe for its recall.

The suitability of homework for labor-intensive processes has made it a potentially viable option during the start-up phase of a wide range of new businesses. Once new industries gain a firm position in the market, however, they are likely to become more capital-intensive and eventually eliminate the need for homework. For example, some electronics firms have used homeworkers in the initial stage of product development, when cost minimization is important and investment in plant and equipment too risky. As mentioned in the previous chapter, this was the case with one of the firms I studied in central New York, which started as a homework operation when lack of resources prevented an initial investment in physical plant.

Reluctance to invest in the capital goods needed to centralize operations can also be found among mature firms. In some cases, discontinuity in demand combines with intense competition to discourage investment in capital-intensive production. According to Scott (1983), the highly competitive printed circuits segment of the electronics industry is characterized by sharp cyclical fluctuations in markets and constant changes in product design. The structure of the industry thus lends itself to multilayered subcontracting, with homework used by many small contractors (*Global*

Electronics Information Newsletter, 1984). Similarly, in the high fashion segment of the garment industry, intense competition, frequent style changes, and seasonal changes have made subcontracting and homework a more flexible arrangement than centralized factory production. Coyle estimates that one-half of the output for London's fashion trade is produced by homeworkers (Coyle 1982, 18). A similar situation exists in U.S. cities such as New York and Los Angeles (Haggberg 1980; ILGWU 1981; New York State Dept. of Labor 1982a).

Homework and other forms of subcontracting are also used by capital-intensive firms for routine work, ancillary services, or hand processes associated with mechanization. Examples include packaging operations for pressed metalware, hospital supply kits and plumbing supplies; detailed finishing work in the lace industry; hand-sewing in the shoe industry; assembly of basic components used in sophisticated electronic devices; painting and decal work on consumer products and novelty items; and photo-retouching (Beach 1989; Dangler 1989; Edwards and Flounders 1977; New York State Dept. of Labor 1981; Rubery and Wilkinson 1981). Rubery and Wilkinson found that in a wide range of industries hand processes associated with mechanization are often given to homeworkers because demand for such labor fluctuates and switching the regular labor force to hand production often disrupts an integrated production cycle. "Outwork can therefore be used as a means of integrating stages of a mechanized production cycle, freeing the direct labour force for continuous work on the main production process" (Rubery and Wilkinson 1981, 121).

Another condition which fosters the reintroduction of homework is cyclical labor shortage. In the current period, shortages of skilled workers in technical and professional fields have caused firms to seek more attractive work options to offer prospective employees. Institution of work-at-home programs for journalists, engineers, accountants and other salaried workers can be seen in this light. At the other end of the spectrum, shortages of workers willing to take minimum wage jobs, or high turnover of in-house employees in "undesirable" jobs can prompt companies to seek sources of labor not normally available. Rural women confined to the home because of childcare responsibilities or physical isolation have been a primary source of labor for "detail work" employers claim factory workers are unwilling to do. Subassembly of electronic components in central New York and hand sewing of shoes in Maine are two examples (Beach 1989; Dangler 1989).

Finally, homework is often introduced by employers as a means of gaining more control over their workforce. Mattera (1980) argues that the wave of decentralization of production, including homework, that began in Italy in the 1970s was a direct political response to the success of worker struggles in the late 1960s. Similarly, in the United States, unions such as the Service Employees International Union and the International Ladies' Garment Workers Union see homework as a union-busting tactic in their industries. In expanding high-technology service industries in the United States and Britain, homework is often seen by management as a way to decentralize the labor force before union inroads are made (Lipsig-Mumme 1983).

I have tried to show that homework is a structural feature of modern capitalism since it persists because of the logic of capital. My argument hinges on identification of recurring conditions that make its use possible. Whether they are sufficient conditions is another matter. First of all, even under otherwise favorable circumstances, there may be disadvantages to using homeworkers, such as those arising from logistical problems (transport, coordination of operations, reliability of supply and so on). Furthermore, the legal status of homework, and, if illegal, the likelihood of successfully evading the law, and political conditions, which could affect enforcement of labor laws and support for workers' rights and labor unions, affect employers' decisions about which production options to pursue. Equally important, however, are the social conditions that affect the likelihood of homework's use. The feminization of waged homework (that is, the persistent use of the same type of labor across time, geographical space, and industries), is a crucial dimension of its structural nature. Recognizing that dimension forces us to combine an anlysis based on economic factors with an understanding of the social relations that give rise to its use. Not only capitalists' prerogatives, but also worker agency, plays a role in the development of the production process. With this in mind, we must uncover the social and ideological conditions under which workers accept, and often press for, home-based work options. If we add this perspective to our analysis, we can grasp the complexity of social and economic relations that underlie homework's use. We can also combine our search for appropriate theoretical and empirical generalizations with an understanding of the tremendous variation in forms of production across the world-economy.

The Social Dynamics that Sustain Waged Homework

A conceptual framework for an analysis of the social and economic factors that converge to support waged homework has emerged out of scholarly debates about the "informal sector" of the economy. The informal sector analysis is relevant to our discussion for two reasons. First, it helps clarify the economic role and significance of waged homework in the modern economy. Homework can be understood as one of a number of "informal productive structures"[13] that exist within and not outside of modern capitalism. Second, recent contributions to the informal sector debates, most notably those of Benton (1990) and Mingione (1991), highlight the significance of social and cultural factors in shaping economic development and patterns of work across the world-economy. The perspective they offer allows us to differentiate various forms of informal work in order to understand their specific origins and different outcomes for workers. This is important for an analysis of waged homework because it allows us to uncover its uniqueness vis-à-vis other types of informal production. Earlier discussions of informal work obscured important distinctions because they failed to specify how the gender division of labor and social power helps shape patterns of work.

In its early formulations the informal sector concept embodied a dualist approach to understanding the coexistence of "traditional" and "modern" productive activities in peripheral countries. In the literature of the late '60s and early '70s the informal sector was seen as encompassing a range of activities associated with the urban poor, who were thought to play a precarious role in the modern economy. According to Bromley (1978), the analysis put forth in the International Labour Office's World Employment Programme report on Kenya in 1972 typified the common distinctions drawn between the formal and informal sectors. While formal activities were seen to be characterized by corporate ownership, large-scale operation, difficult entry, capital-intensive production, frequent reliance on overseas resources, formally acquired skills and protected markets, informal activities were defined by opposing characteristics. Family ownership, small scale operation, ease of entry, labor-intensive production, reliance on indigenous resources, informally acquired skills, and unregulated and competitive markets defined informal activities.

The first break with a dualistic analysis of the informal sector was provided by Keith Hart who, in his studies of Ghana, portrayed the informal sector as a "complex, organized, and highly dynamic component of the urban economy" (Portes and Walton 1981, 81). This analysis has been extended by those who have tried to show the interconnectedness of "formal" and "informal" activities within one economy. For example, Portes and Walton (1981) conclude that the informal sector is not "traditional" in either its means of production or types of activities (as portrayed in earlier writings) and exists in "close articulation" with firms in the capitalist economy. They see the informal sector as "formed predominantly by small-scale activities conducted outside the state and the state-regulated private sectors. Contrary to stereotypes, such activities do not generally correspond to traditional subsistence production, but embody continuously changing requirements and opportunities in the 'modern' economy" (Portes and Walton 1981, 81). The examples of informal activities they cite include enterprises in transportation, construction, manufacturing of clothes and footwear, and urban commerce. In their view, one of the defining features of informal activities is the absence of state regulation. With the predominant use of unpaid family labor and/or the payment of wages below the official minimum with no social security protection, the informal sector functions to provide goods and services at a lower cost than could be realized under formal production arrangements and is, therefore, "a structural feature of the process of peripheral accumulation" (83, n40).

Bromley and Gerry's (1979) discussion of the variety of production arrangements found across the world economy allows for an extension of the informal sector analysis beyond peripheral countries. Their concept of "casual work" incorporates a range of informal work arrangements that exist alongside of more formal work in the modern economy. Casual work includes "any way of making a living which lacks a moderate degree of security of income and employment" (Bromley and Gerry 1979 5). It contrasts with stable wage work, where the risks of losing work are relatively low and job loss is usually compensated for through social provisions such as unemployment insurance, sickness benefits, pensions, redundancy pay, and so on (7).

The first type of casual labor Bromley and Gerry define is "short-term wage-work," which is paid and contracted by the day, week, month, or season for fixed terms or tasks. The second, "disguised wage-work" takes place when a firm or group of firms regularly and directly appropriates part of the product of a person's work without that person legally being an employee of the firm or group of firms" (6). Third, "dependent work" takes place when an enterprise is "dependent on one or more large enterprises for credit, the rental of premises or equipment, or monopolistic or oligopolistic supply of raw materials or merchandise, or a monopsonistic or oligopsonistic outlet for its production" (6). Finally, with "true self-employment" a person owns his own means of production, works independently, and has a relatively free choice of suppliers and outlets.

Through this classification scheme, Bromley and Gerry hope to show the integration of various types of production relations within the capitalist economy. For example, they explain that many of those typically described as "self-employed" are in fact "disguised wage-workers" or "dependent workers":

> The conventional division of the labour market into "wage-employment" and "self-employment" obscures the variety of forms of working relationship, and particularly the extent to which individual workers and small enterprises may be harnessed to the needs of large enterprises without a legal employment relationship. Our classification into stable wage-work and casual work, and the division of casual work into four main categories, is intended to form the basis for a focus on relationships between large and small firms, between firms and workers, and between the State and the labour process. (7)

The analyses of the informal sector and casual work discussed above provide a basic outline of the conceptual discussions most relevant to an understanding of the role of waged homework in the modern economy. Portes and Walton (1981) include homework in the range of production "strategies" that are part of the informal sector, while Bromley and Gerry see homework as a type of "disguised wage-work" within their broader category of casual labor. They argue that even though homeworkers are not officially defined as employees in most countries (but as subcontractors instead), they are employees because of the precise nature of their relationship to those for whom their work is done.

> 'Disguised wage-employment"[14] will have virtually the same characteristic relations of production as the classical forms of wage-employment: hours of work may be more flexible and subject to the petty producer's own discre-

tion; petty producers may be scattered around throughout
the city and its surrounding area; remuneration may be
less stable than in situations of unambiguous wage employment. Nevertheless, the fundamental mechanisms of
exploitation (both through the labour process and the
market) will be the same as in the factory. Very often the
status of such disguised wage-workers will be unrecog-
nized by State institutions, the Labour courts or by private
"disguised employers"; these workers may appear on the
surface to be artisans, craftsmen or whatever, but are de
facto wage workers, even if de jure they are considered
not to be so. (247)

While the informal sector/casual work analysis outlined above
provides a useful framework for understanding the economic role
of homework, it falls short of helping us understand the social
relations that underlie it and the conditions that support its
adoption. For example, Beneria and Roldan (1987) point out that
although, according to definitions in the literature, homework can
be viewed as part of the informal sector, a number of conceptual
confusions remain that continue to cloud our understanding of
this type of production. They argue that the diversity of work
included in the informal sector obscures important class distinctions among the workers involved. Not only homeworkers but
jobbers who use homeworkers, artisans, petty commodity producers,[15] and workshops that hire labor and operate illegally are
considered to be part of the informal sector.

The conceptual confusion has several dimensions. One
aspect is that when these different agents of production
are included within the general concept of informal sector, no distinction is made between their different class
categories. Yet, it is important to distinguish between the
owner of a workshop and his or her wage workers, and
between these and family labor, and each of the categories
of domestic pieceworkers. The distinction is essential for
understanding the process of labor appropriation and the
dynamics created by conflicting class interests. (Beneria
and Roldan 1987, 70)

In addition, earlier informal sector analysis ignores important
gender issues which are essential to an understanding of waged
homework. Beneria and Roldan point out that the fact that wom-
en's choices are extremely limited is not well developed in the

informal sector literature. Women may "choose" to engage in homework as opposed to work in the formal sector, but their "choice" is severely constrained by their need to combine different roles as well as by objective limitations on their work options. They argue that homeworkers' lack of choice is related to "direct limitations," such as their husbands' opposition or the need to care for children, and/or "indirect limitations," such as a lack of employment options resulting from class and gender discrimination (72).

Recent analyses of economic restructuring and the proliferation of decentralized and informal work arrangements allow us to address the shortcomings in previous discussions of the informal sector. For example, by emphasizing the importance of "worker agency" and the "social economy" in determining the forms of production adopted in different locales, Benton (1990) and Mingione (1991) pave the way for an analysis of how social relations mediated by gender and class shape particular work experiences. Mingione is critical of the tendency to interpret informalization from points of view "almost exclusively concerned with its macro-economic origins and impact." Instead, he argues that more attention must be paid to "social organizations, life-styles and survival strategies, which should be viewed as original co-determining factors in the heterogeneity of working activities, rather than as mere consequences of it" (76).

It seems to me that Mingione's perspective provides the conceptual framework for an analysis of homework that puts gender relations on center stage. Homework emerges as a production option not simply because it is imposed by capital or arises out of external economic forces, but because it develops as a result of the interaction between economic factors and social relations at the family and household level. An attempt to understand the origins of homework and its outcomes for workers from a "social economy" perspective forces us to recognize that the gender division of labor and sex-based power differentials are among the social factors that shape patterns of work. With this in mind, an analysis of waged homework as a form of production must be sensitive to the likely variation in the experiences of homeworkers in different locales (variation related to social, cultural, and economic differences among them), but it must also recognize the common link that joins them across the world-economy. That common link—their position in the gender division of labor— reveals another important dimension of waged homework's structural nature. The recurrence of conditions that make homework a practical production option for capital and the persistent use of the same type of labor for homework, testify to its permanence as a structural feature of the capitalist economy.

Gender as Agency in the Shaping of Household and Labor Market Relations

The most common reasons given to explain why waged home-workers are generally women and not men are that

- women have primary responsibility for maintaining the home and caring for children, the elderly, the sick, and the handicapped. Working at home allows them to fulfill these obligations;
- women are very often not the primary wage earners in the household, and homework is a convenient way to supplement their family income;
- under pressure from their husbands or because of their own perceptions about their proper role, some women are reluctant to work outside of the home.

The problem with these explanations is that they take for granted that women bear such responsibilities and fail to explain how the gender division of labor, both within the household and in the external labor market, emerged historically. My task in this chapter is to move beyond simple descriptions of household and labor market relations and elucidate the historical processes that have shaped those relationships over time. In order to do that it is necessary to consider the interplay of ideological and objective factors. How has gender ideology shaped labor market conditions and, in turn, how do labor market conditions reinforce gender ideology? When applied to the study of waged homework, this question leads to an analysis of homework's role in the family economy as well as its important effect on the course of capitalist development in the nineteenth and twentieth centuries. Accordingly, homework gives us a particularly strong vantage point from which to understand how gender relations have conditioned modern capitalism.

The cornerstone of my analysis is a critique of labor market segmentation theory. While the latter has provided an important conceptual and empirical description of women's role in the economy, it is limited in its ability to analyze the development of new forms of "casualized" work and identify the historical processes involved in the segmentation of labor markets. Understanding the latter is crucial to an analysis of economic development that recognizes the active role of gender in shaping the occupational structure and production processes.

Ideology and the Gender Division of Labor

The ideological separation of home and work that took place in the early nineteenth century influenced the manner in which women were incorporated into the paid workforce. The desire to preserve the home as a sanctuary in response to the mounting pressures of industrialization and urbanization required a constriction of women's roles which placed motherhood and homemaking at the center of their lives.[1] This ideology of "separate spheres" has had a significant impact on the way women's economic role has been portrayed. According to Allen (1983) "in the kind of sociological theory which developed to explain the nature and consequences of industrialization, the separation of home and work became a taken-for-granted assumption on which the sociology of work and the sociology of the family have proceeded" (650). Those who have accepted this separation identify the home as the site of reproduction and consumption and assume that it is only in the external sphere of the paid economy that productive activity takes place. Historically, this perceived separation of home and work took objective form in the opposite roles assigned to men and women in the social division of labor. It was believed that men, who assume the role of "breadwinner," must obtain paid work in the external economy to provide resources for the household's consumption. Women, on the other hand, were to assume the roles of wife and mother and confine their activities to the realm of household reproduction and maintenance.

This ideological construction of male and female gender roles has as its corollary the conceptual separation of paid from unpaid work. Paid work is considered to be the real productive activity of capitalist society, and in its "pure" form it is done by men on a full-time, regular basis in the external economy. Unpaid work (hardly considered as "work") is done by women within the household. The artificiality of the distinction between paid and unpaid work and its tendency to obscure women's economic contributions is revealed by the range of "hidden" economic activities women have engaged in since the nineteenth century. For example, in the United States, in addition to industrial and service homework, childminding, taking in boarders and laundry, household crafts, and local sale of women's accessories and household items (Avon and Tupperware, for example) are among the largely "invisible" sources of income women have relied on. These income-generating activities have been largely overshadowed by the plethora of unpaid tasks women perform on a regular basis. Official records tend to underestimate them, and, thus, as Allen points out, it is problematic to "uncritically accept officially defined female economic activity rates as though they describe what women actually do" (Allen 1983, 651).

Despite the objective reality of women's economic lives, gender ideology supported the marginalization of their paid work. In this context, "wage work would be judged by whether it enhanced or, minimally, did not detract from home roles" (Kessler-Harris 1982, 51). By masking the association of women and waged work and apparently preserving the image of women as primarily wives and mothers, homework became one way of incorporating women into the workforce while preserving prescribed gender roles within the household. As Stansell points out in her discussion of nineteenth century industrial homework, "[t]he outside system masked women's involvement in wage labor; they appeared to be peripheral to industrial production and their identity as workers seemed secondary to their roles as wives and mothers" (Stansell 1983, 95). Recent debates about homework reveal that this nineteenth century ideology remains intact for some segments of American society. For example, Boris (1987) argues that in the 1980s controversy over the proposed repeal of federal homework restrictions under the Fair Labor Standards Act (for example, in the case of the Vermont knitters), homework was seen by some as a way to reconcile traditional notions about women's family roles with economic need:

> even the most diehard supporters of motherhood as woman's noblest profession, like Senator Jeremiah Denton (R-

Ala.), recognized the economic necessity for two-earner families and thus viewed homework as a necessary compromise between economic reality and cultural preferences. Acknowledging the entrance of married women with small children into the official labor force, the Heritage Foundation supported letting Americans work out of their homes. Moreover, the Center on National Labor Policy claimed that such homework offers a huge "nonmonetary advantage" to society. Because of its flexible hours, homework gives women more time than a factory or office job to do nonpaid work, such as volunteer work, nurturing activities, and other traditional women's tasks. (1987, 108–09)

Paradoxically, homework defies the very ideological separation of home and work it is purported to uphold. For homeworkers the complete integration of home and work becomes apparent as paid work is interspersed, physically and temporally, with domestic chores and childminding.[2] Furthermore, as the process of production becomes interconnected with the process of reproduction, the artificiality of the separation between paid and unpaid work is revealed.

Gender and the Formation of Labor Markets

While the gender division of labor within the household has made waged homework a socially acceptable form of paid work for women, its practicality has been enhanced by women's overall position on the labor market. The widespread acceptance of the ideology of separate spheres has placed severe constraints on women in the paid labor force, where they have been viewed, for the most part, as "supplementary" wage earners at best. Allen (1983) points out that the idea that women are or should be dependent on a male breadwinner has served to define the terms on which their labor is sold in the external economy.[3] This has been so despite the fact that not all women live in male-headed households.

The sexual division of labour is not a division between male "breadwinners" and female "housewives" or domestic labourers. The importance of this distorted conceptualization of the division of labour is the ideological force which it carries. The sexual division of labour is between women as unpaid workers within the household and the relative freedom of men in this respect and the differential bases on which women and men are integrated as paid workers into the system of production. (Allen 1983, 659)

Kessler-Harris (1975) lends support to Allen's analysis in her assertion that women's perceptions of their roles, combined with the changing economic needs of the capitalist economy, have conditioned their labor force participation. She concludes that by the late 1920s, most male and female workers in the United States were segregated from each other "largely by prevailing norms about proper roles, but increasingly by protective legislation and by an educational structure that reflected those norms and channeled women into jobs deemed appropriate" (Kessler-Harris 1975, 232).

That women have been largely confined to the lowest-paying, lowest-status jobs in the economy has been amply documented by labor historians, economists, and sociologists alike. This concentration of women in the lower levels of the occupational structure has been explained by some in terms of the systematic segmentation of labor markets. According to labor market segmentation theorists (Doeringer and Piore 1971; Gordon et al. 1975), the workforce is divided into distinct segments that compete differentially on the labor market. Thus, in contrast to a single pool of labor that enters the market with everyone having equal chances to compete for jobs in terms of education and skill requirements, the workforce is split along class, race, and gender lines so that different groups are matched to specific branches of the occupational structure. In its simplest form, labor market segmentation theory (also called dual labor market theory) posits the existence of a two-tiered labor market, which corresponds to the kind of dual industrial structure identified by dual economy theorists such as Averitt (1968). Thus, the proposed division in the economy between large-scale, mechanized, fully integrated producers enjoying relatively stable markets and small-scale, labor-intensive firms subject to intense competition is complemented by a corresponding dualism in working conditions, wages, and mobility patterns among the working class. While it is believed that the stable production and sales patterns of large-scale firms lead to the development of specific job structures and internal relations reflecting that stability, firms in the competitive sector develop significantly different employment patterns consonant with their unstable production and demand. Herein lies the distinction between what dual labor market theorists term primary and secondary sector employment.

The general attributes of secondary sector employment include low wages, little or no security or advancement, no elaborate work structures, and an absence of well-defined workers' rights. This sector is composed of a variety of production and nonproduction jobs, including unskilled work in nonunion factories, several categories of low-wage services, lower-level clerical, lower-level retail and wholesale trade, and migrant agricultural work. In general, women, racial minorities, and immigrants tend to be concentrated in secondary sector employment.

In contrast, primary sector jobs are characterized by relatively stable employment, job security, high wages, well-defined occupations with paths for advancement, and linkages between successive jobs a worker may hold. This sector is further divided into subordinate primary and independent primary tiers. The former includes unionized lower-level clerical, sales, and administrative work in major retailing, utilities and manufacturing firms, while the latter includes professional, managerial, and technical jobs.[4]

In its description of women's employment patterns, labor market segmentation theory reveals the concrete effects of the ideological separation of men's and women's work. As a result, it provides an important starting point for an analysis of the relationship between gender and labor market formation. To refine that analysis, however, we must overcome its limitations.

To begin with, recent patterns of industrial restructuring have led to the development of forms of work that fall outside of the primary and secondary sector categories defined by dual labor market theorists. Mingione (1991) argues that in the context of increased international competition, previous patterns of labor market segmentation have led industry to search for new ways to organize production. He explains the relationship between industrial restructuring and the segmentation of labor markets as follows:

> Segmentation produces an increasing rigidity in the industries which mainly operate with labour in the primary market. Increasing international competition forces these industries to find ways of creating a cheaper and more flexible labour force. This cannot be done by straightforward dismantling of the segmenting mechanism as this

would have devastating social consequences and might be met by strong political opposition, and not only from the workers' political and trade union organizations. Therefore, the paths followed in order to achieve more flexibility have involved vertical disintegration, relocation of labour processes, and the re-emergence of various old and new forms of subcontracting. Such conditions further heighten the heterogeneity of work. Both the primary and the secondary segments survive and, often, the new workers cannot be classified as belonging to either. The social and geographical impact of de-industrialization, relocation and new ways of organizing industry leads to a striking and expanding range of working activities. (1991, 77)

Mingione also points out that while labor market segmentation theory offers a description of the occupational structure in the manufacturing sector, it does not adequately explain patterns in the service sector, which has a more heterogenous employment structure (1991, 78).

Labor market segmentation theory is further limited by the fact that while it may provide a useful description of divisions in the workforce, it fails to explain how these divisions emerged historically. As a result, dual labor market theorists assume precisely what needs to be explained: how specific groups come to occupy particular roles in the social division of labor. This question is central to an understanding of the relationship between gender and capitalist development. Dual labor market theorists seem to accept the gender division of labor as given, thereby precluding an analysis of gender relations as a determining force in the structuring of the economy. For example, Kenrick argues that dual labor market theory is discriminatory in its implications since it maintains a primary interest in "adequate family finance (in which it is assumed that a male breadwinner earns the principal wage)" (171). She points out that Doeringer and Piore (1971), who sought to reconcile the needs of business with the political demands for full employment in the 1960s, were concerned with improving the chances of minority males trapped in secondary sector jobs, but not of females. In her view, "at the level of policies directed at changing individual worker characteristics [Doeringer and Piore] focus on the ways in which subcultural experiences appear to render (male) blacks unsuitable for primary employment (and suggest training policies by which this might be changed); but they discuss the way in which women's family responsibilities fit them for the secondary sector. They even suggest ways in which this might be incorporated into training programmes for casual labor" (171).

Another problem with dual labor market theory is its failure to consider the role of conflict between labor and capital, and conflict among different groups of workers, in fostering segmentation. Dual labor market theorists see the historical emergence of different forms of work in capitalist society as related to technological, market, and control factors. The emphasis is on how technology created specific options for industrial development, how the character of markets limited the suitability of certain industrial structures, and how the desire to control the workforce resulted in capitalist initiatives to segment labor markets. What is missing is the role of labor-capital conflict in influencing industrial development as well as an analysis of how cultural and ideological factors that serve to divide the workforce along gender, race, and ethnic lines have influenced patterns of labor force participation among various groups. An important problem in this context is to explain how the existence of certain groups, such as women, condition the development of the occupational structure—how different occupations become defined in terms of the specific characteristics of the workers potentially available to fill them.

The gender division of labor in the household and the ideological perceptions about men's and women's roles that follow from it, have fostered an artificial distinction between men's and women's work so that regardless of the nature of the activities performed, work that is done by women is imputed with certain characteristics that distinguish it from work that is done by men. As a result, in the external sphere of paid work, women have been perceived as different from the "typical" male worker. As such, the occupations they have historically occupied have been tailored to fit their supposed characteristics and assumed needs. They have generally been relatively low paid (since women supposedly need only a "supplementary" wage), they have often been part-time (since their primary responsibility is to the household), and they have remained largely unorganized (since it is believed that the lack of a lifetime commitment to work on the part of women makes unionization pointless). Moreover, when women have entered occupations that are traditionally male, job definitions and descriptions have been altered to accommodate their perceived needs.[5] These patterns reveal the inextricable link between women's social roles in the household and the structuring of the economic system (Allen 1983; Kenrick 1981; Kessler-Harris 1975; West 1982). A closer look at waged homework helps clarify that link by illustrating the transformation of certain industries to match production processes to the perceived characteristics of a female labor force.

It is clear that the availability of a labor force of homeworkers affected the development of the production process in some industries. For example, Blewett shows how the recruitment of women homeworkers in the late eighteenth and early nineteenth century shoe industry significantly altered the organization of production:

> The introduction of the sexual division of labor into an artisan craft represented a major change in the mode of production. Work was redefined and relocated, new words were coined and new procedures devised for supervision. The work assigned to women took on social meanings appropriate to their gender. Female family members adapted their traditional needle skills to hand sew the leather uppers of shoes in their kitchens without disrupting their domestic duties or their child care tasks. Needle work on leather uppers, a relatively clean part of the job, was accompanied by a new tool designed exclusively for women's work: the shoe clamp. The woman shoeworker would not have to straddle a shoemaker's bench, but would use a long, flexible wooden clamp which rested on the floor and which she held between her knees, holding the pieces of shoe upper together and freeing her hands to ply her needle. Her work was given a new name: shoe binding, which became a major category of women's work in the early nineteenth century. (224)

Similarly, Stansell's analysis of homework in New York City reveals how gender divisions in the household were "replicated" in industry: "A sexual division of labor developed between branches of New York manufactures, based primarily on outwork; trades like clothing that relied on put-out work became women's trades, while those that did not mostly remained closed to women. The consequence was a segmentation of industry that limited women in the city to a few trades." These were the manufacture of paper boxes, hoopskirts, shirts and collars, millinery, artificial flowers, and ladies' cloaks (80).

In recent times, the availability of homeworkers has similarly affected the development of production processes. One of the most interesting aspects of the history of electronics industry homework in central New York is the fact that the viability of homework as a stable form of production was "discovered" by firms as women bound by family responsibilities and limited job options actively sought this type of employment. Beginning in the late 1960s, electronics firms in the region transformed their production process in response to the availability of a "new" labor force (in the case of MALCO) or developed their production process around homework from the start (in the cases of ENCO and GILCO).(See chapter 3 for a discussion of these firms.)

Homeworkers' Conflict Between Economic Need and Gender Ideology

To the extent that the ideology that separates home and work in capitalist society is accepted, the link between women and work becomes ambiguous. Separated from the sphere of work ideologically yet forced to become part of it as a result of objective need, women have often come to adopt ambivalent attitudes about the paid work they do. Here, too, the experiences of homeworkers are telling. One explanation for homeworkers' willingness to accept low wages is their propensity to see their work as "casual" and "supplementary." Hakim and Dennis (1982) explain this ambivalence in terms of a distinction between a behavioral commitment to paid employment and a subjective identification with work roles. In their view,

> a strong behavioral commitment to paid employment does not necessarily lead to strong identification with the work role (in the sense of adopting the self-label of a "working woman") and . . . among married women, both commitment to and identification with paid employment [are] affected by the attitudes of others—such as the husband's attitudes and those of friends and family. This perspective suggests that homeworkers may adopt a behavioral commitment to work without adopting any identification with their work role, producing apparently conflicting and ambivalent attitudes to work which could affect their attitudes to pay. (4)

Allen observed the same type of ambivalence about work in her study of 90 homeworkers in the West Yorkshire region of Great

Britain. A majority of the workers she interviewed expressed the belief that their homework was not a "proper job." This was most clearly evident in their opinions on the possibilities of organizing homeworkers into trade unions. On the basis of her observations, Allen concluded that "the ambivalent attitudes of the women who do this kind of work reflect the ambiguities and contradictions of a system of economic and social relations outside and inside their homes which together denies them any rights as workers. It is not therefore surprising that many saw themselves and their work as falling outside the concern of unions and at the mercy of those with power, the suppliers and their husbands" (1982, 407). While most of the electronics industry homeworkers I interviewed in central New York saw their jobs as comparable to paid work outside the home, a few expressed the kind of status devaluation found by Allen and by Hakim and Dennis. In one woman's view, "Homework is not like a real job because it's voluntary—to earn money at home" (Interview 16).

For Allen (1982), the denial of women's rights as workers relates to "the conditional nature of the link between women and paid work." She explains that while work is both a right and a duty for men, its significance for women varies with ideological and material circumstances. This is borne out by the fact that "unemployment is only recognized as critical when men are without paid, full-time regular work, whereas it can be and is argued that at least a partial solution to unemployment is the return of women into the home" (Allen 1982, 383). She concludes, therefore, that "the conditional nature of the link between women and paid work is a denial of a basic economic right. This denial is not related in any simple way to the economic demand for women's labour. It does, however, affect the terms under which this labour is supplied and used and the degree of recognition given to it" (1982, 384).

In addition to focusing on the subjective perceptions of workers in our effort to understand the status of homework in the occupational structure, it is important to appreciate the impact of the state in marginalizing it and shaping the conditions under which it is done. For example, in the United States, the unevenness of homework regulation across states and industries, together with inadequate enforcement provisions, have allowed homework to flourish "underground" with wages and working conditions below legally mandated levels. In addition, inconsistency in the legal status accorded homeworkers vis-à-vis employers has allowed many firms to treat them as independent contractors who are not entitled to benefits, job security, or a minimum hourly wage. One obstacle to developing consistent national policies regarding these issues is that taxation and labor statutes often have conflicting definitions of the employer-employee relationship. This has affected electronics industry homeworkers in New York State and garment industry homeworkers in California (Fernandez-Kelly and Garcia 1989).

The controversies over homeworkers' legal status in the United States revolve around a range of issues, including workers' rights, economic need, working conditions (how much control and supervision is present), and whether or not training is provided by a particular company. While these legal issues and their implications will be discussed in detail in chapter 6, for present purposes it is important to recognize the extent to which gender ideology is often superimposed on discussions of legal technicalities. For example, in my interviews with attorneys involved in the 1980s court cases regarding electronics industry homeworkers in central New York, the perception that prohibitions on industrial homework were unreasonable because this type of work was somehow "naturally acceptable" for women was apparent. During our interview, an attorney who represented homework distributors in their battle with the State Labor Department mixed analysis of the legal issues of his case (workers' rights, due process, liberty of contract) with statements that seemed to justify the exploitation of the workers he represented: "Because we live in a capitalistic society there's always going to be segments of the workforce that are exploited no matter where they work. Women have been exploited for years. [I don't think] legislatures dominated by men should create paternalistic laws that prevent women from doing something in their homes that they want to do" (Interview 46). The Labor Department's lawyer expressed his belief that the Industrial Board of Appeals' decision in favor of the homework distributors (which overruled the DOL's application of the state's anti-homework statute and allowed homework operations to continue) was not based on the legal issues. In his view, the case focused on "what little ladies are doing in their homes" (Interview 44).

In Great Britain, too, the poor conditions associated with homework (low wages, health and safety risks, and so on) are made possible by the state's refusal to recognize this form of work as legitimate employment. Because homework is defined as self-employment, homeworkers are excluded from the benefits and protection extended to other British workers. Since they cannot claim coverage under the country's National Insurance program, they are ineligible for unemployment, sickness, and maternity insurance. Similarly, they are not covered for industrial injuries under the Health and Safety Work Act. It is obvious that the exclusion of homeworkers from the set of institutions established to protect British workers is either a gross oversight or an intentionally discriminatory policy on the part of the British government. The fact that it is possible for homeworkers to contest their self-employment status and become classified as employees under common law (a possibility realized in a precedent-setting case heard before the Industrial Tribunal in 1976) indicates that there are no legal barriers to securing homeworkers' rights—only customary restrictions against doing so. The fact that most homeworkers are unaware of their right to fight for a change in legal status, plus the expense and trouble involved in doing so, means that the ability to change the situation facing this segment of the workforce is in the hands of the state.

The failure to recognize homeworkers as employees stems in part from the general perception of this form of work as "casual" in nature, (that is, as involving women with only a temporary or casual commitment to paid work). Those who view homework as "casual" often adopt the position that homeworkers would not ordinarily be engaged in paid employment if not for the fact that homework provides them with a unique and particularly convenient opportunity to earn extra money. This conception of casualized work takes a specific form within the Wages Council system in Britain.

Wages Councils are set up to establish minimum rates of pay and conditions in industries traditionally unprotected by trade unions. If homework takes place in Wages Council industries, homeworkers are entitled to the same protections extended to factory workers in those industries. Although the Wages Councils set industrywide minimum rates, they have the ability to assign differential (lower), rates for persons deemed not to be "ordinary workers" (Jordan 1977). The concept of "ordinary worker" is difficult to operationalize, and its application is left to the descretion of Wages Council inspectors—who supposedly acquire the expertise to define what is and is not "ordinary" work. The fact that homeworkers are often assigned a status below that of "ordinary worker" reflects the devaluation of their work in the eyes of the authorities. The common explanation as to why homeworkers are often considered not to be "ordinary workers" is that they work in suboptimal conditions in the home (with frequent interruptions) and that it is impossible for them to achieve factory level standards of efficiency and output. Contrary to this assertion, Hakim and Dennis (1982) point out that existing research does not support the conclusion that homeworkers are inefficient, poorly organized, or unskilled. By looking at the ratio between hourly earnings and minimum rates of pay for homeworkers and factory workers in the same Wages Council industries, they found that earnings distributions for homeworkers paralleled that for inworkers. This supports the conclusion that there is little difference between the two groups in terms of skill and productivity.

Another practice by Wages Council authorities that reflects their depiction of homework as "casual" labor has to do with how minimum pay rates for homeworkers are established. It has been brought to the attention of Wages Council inspectors that homeworkers bear overhead costs such as heating and lighting when doing their work, and that these expenses should be taken into account when minimum pay rates are set. The Wages Council inspectorate assumes, however, that the homeworker would normally be at home during the day, even if not doing homework, so heating and lighting expenses are not taken into account when wage rates are set unless a separate room is used exclusively for homework. The problem here is that homeworkers are compared with persons who would be home anyway, rather than with inworkers who are away from home during working hours. Thus, the perception of homework labor as something that is subordinate to factory labor, even if engaged in similar types of production, is reinforced (Hakim and Dennis 1982).

Is Homework Simply for "Pin Money"?

As Allen (1982) has pointed out, historically the link between women and paid work has been conditional, varying with both ideological and material circumstances. As such, the conditional nature of this link has affected "the terms under which [women's] labour is supplied and used and the degree of recognition given to it" (Allen 1982, 384). Homework provides a prime example of the subordinate status accorded women's work and the implications that status holds for the lives of workers. Widely seen as an extension of women's household activities (especially in the needlework industries), homework has, for the most part, been viewed not as an occupation, but as a sideline activity taken on by women to earn extra money. More recently, new types of homework, such as knitting by rural women in New England, have been characterized as providing middle-class wives with supplemental income to help raise their families' discretionary spending. Both of these views have fostered a widespread indifference to the plight of the nation's homeworkers and the significance of homework jobs to the occupational structure. As a result, policy measures aimed at allowing the uncontrolled spread of homework (such as the elimination of existing homework regulation) are supported by both ideological and economic arguments based on a view of such work as a secondary and supplementary activity.: In order to dispel this misconception, it is important to understand the significance of the income earned by many homeworkers to household budgets and local economies.

The importance of homework earnings to household budgets has been documented in case studies of homeworkers in the United States and abroad. While the degree of importance varies considerably, depending in large part on whether another wage earner is present in the household, the use of homework earnings for essential expenditures has been widely shown. Studies of ethnic minorities employed as homeworkers in developed countries tend to reveal the primacy of homework jobs. For example, Lebanese, Yugoslavian, Greek, and Vietnamese migrants in Australia, who are faced with substantially higher unemployment rates than nonmigrants, engage in homework to provide essential income for their families (Australia Asia Worker Links 1982). Similarly, immigrant families in Silicon Valley, California, depend on the wages of female homeworkers as a primary means of support (Katz and Kemnitzer 1983; Morales 1983).

In developing countries such as India and Sri Lanka, the importance of homework earnings varies from being a supplemental but necessary income to being the sole support for women and their families. In a study of women coir workers in Sri Lanka, Risseeuw (1987) found that in one village, 30 percent of households derived their income from female homeworkers alone while 51 percent obtained earnings from both sexes and 19 percent from males alone (Risseeuw 1987, 184). Bhatty (1987) also found diversity in the proportion of household income contributed by homeworkers in the beedi industry in India, with an average of 45.5 percent provided by the women across income groups. Among the poorest households, homeworkers contributed as much as 85 to 95 percent of household income (Bhatty 1987, 40–41). Similarly, Rao and Hussain (1987) found that among garment homeworkers in Delhi, wages earned through homework are often the sole income for households supported by women who receive little or no help from their husbands.

In Britain and the United States, homeworkers' contribution to household income also varies, though studies reveal the importance of homework earnings to family budgets. For Britain, both Hakim (1980) and Allen (1983) conclude that while many homeworkers work to supplement their husbands' wages, the income they provide is essential. In Hakim's study of 50 homeworkers in four British cities, only a small minority (those with highly paid husbands) reported that their homework earnings were insignificant.[6] For the rest, homework provided an important addition to the family budget, typically used for emergencies, holidays, major purchases such as furniture and cars, or to reduce financial pressures when the cost of supporting young children put a strain on the household budget. Homework earnings were also reported to provide a cushion against fluctuations in husbands' earnings, especially loss of overtime. In Hakim's view, "for most, homework was the solution adopted to meet the need to work for financial reasons at a time when young children made it difficult or impossible to work outside the home" (1109). Based on her study of 90 homeworkers and 12 ex-homeworkers, Allen (1983) reveals that many have no male partners and provide the sole income for their households. For those with male earners present, the contribution to family income ranged from 2 to 76 percent. Nevertheless, aside from three women who reported using their income for "extras," the money earned by these homeworkers was used for essential budgetary items such as food, electricity, rent or mortgage, clothes, and shoes.

For the United States, as early as 1945 Sayin reported that among workers in the knitted outerwear and women's apparel industries, homework was more than just pin money. In his sample of 125 workers, 36 percent reported homework as providing their family's only means of support, while 61 percent used it as a necessary supplement to the income earned by other family members. Only 3 percent did homework to obtain "extra" money" (Sayin 1945, 32). In recent times, while the depiction of some groups of homeworkers implies the accessory nature of their work (the accounts of New England home knitters), it is evident that women accepting homework jobs in a variety of industries do so out of economic necessity (U.S. House of Representatives 1987; Walsh, 1987).

Among electronics industry homeworkers in central New

York, the importance of homework earnings to family budgets is clearly illustrated by the relatively low incomes of most families in this group. Of the 39 homeworkers I interviewed, only six reported family incomes above $20,000 a year. The rest ranged between $10,000 and $20,000.[7] While the majority reported homework as one of two essential incomes for their families, many emphasized that the periodic unemployment of their husbands due to layoffs in blue-collar jobs often made their income from homework their only support. Only four reported that their income from homework was "extra" money used for discretionary consumption. The situation of central New York homeworkers demonstrates the extent to which such work can be an essential component of family income—one needed to keep many working-class families above the poverty level. One woman summarized the economic situation facing homeworkers in her area in the following way: "Most people I know are not living the good life. They're just managing, just getting by. They don't even have enough money to take their kids to the movies. They have no savings, nothing to fall back on in an emergency. We're all just living from week to week" (Interview 24). To illustrate the desperation of many of the homeworkers she employed, one distributor explained that she had people driving from as far as an hour and a half away every two weeks to pick up materials for work.

Many central New York homeworkers related stories of how difficult it was for those who lost the opportunity to do homework to maintain decent living standards after they lost their jobs as a result of the rigorous enforcement of anti-homework law by the State Labor Department in 1981. They explained that while some were able to get minimum-wage jobs to replace homework, others were forced to apply for welfare or simply "make do," "get by," and "settle for much less." "I'm really not sure what they [unemployed homeworkers] are doing now," explained one woman who spoke of a friend who had such a difficult time adjusting after losing her income from homework that "she may have lost a baby over it." The importance of the income from this work to the maintenance of adequate living standards for central New York homeworkers clearly demonstrates the extent to which current depictions of "cottage industry" as a new source of "pin money" for well-off women seeking constructive uses for their time is mistaken. As one homeworker put it, "It's not a fun job. People who do it do it because they need the money."

Who Are Today's Homeworkers?

As demonstrated in chapter 3, current research has dispelled the myth that homework is a unique problem of the needlework industries and other traditional occupations such as cigar-making and assembly of artificial flowers. Another related myth that must be challenged is the primary association of this form of production with immigrant labor. While studies in developed countries continue to document that the link between homework and poor immigrants remains strong (Katz and Kemnitzer 1983; Mitter 1984; Morales 1983; New Jersey Dept. of Labor 1982; Webb 1982) an equally significant literature has revealed the widespread use of urban and rural nonethnic, nonimmigrant, working- and middle-class women in contemporary homework operations.[8]

According to studies in the United States and Britain, married women with dependent children constitute the predominant group from which homeworkers come (Allen 1982; Berch 1985; Edwards and Flounders 1976; Hakim 1980; Trades Union Congress not dated).[9] While many such women are, in fact, poor urban immigrants, most are just as likely to be nonimmigrants from rural or urban areas and to come from working- to middle-class families as from the ranks of the poor. For example, in her analysis of the increase in homework since the mid-1970s, Allen (1982) concludes that most homeworkers in Britain are not members of ethnic minorities. Similarly, the Trades Union Congress (not dated), cutting across class and ethnic lines, describes most British homeworkers as mothers with childcare problems. For the United States, recent accounts of working- and middle-class women engaged in a variety of homework occupations (Belsie 1986), of "homebound wives" who provide labor for electronic outwork (Berch 1985), and of rural seamstresses and knitters in middle America (*Blair and Ketchums Country Journal* 1980; Hosenball 1981; Norwood 1986) have confirmed that a wide spectrum of women are fueling the expansion of homework. My study of electonics industry homeworkers in central New York is also instructive in this regard. As discussed in chapter 2, since 1969 rural, nonethnic, nonimmigrant, working- and middle-class women have been the source of homework labor for electronics firms in this area.

Why Women "Choose" Homework

Homework emerges as a practical alternative for women workers in the face of a set of constraining factors which limit their freedom on the job market. Limited job opportunities (due to high unemployment and sex segregation in the labor market) combined with the need to manage the double burden of paid work and family responsibilities have fostered the spread of homework as an attractive work option. The practicality of homework for many women is aptly illustrated by the situation of central New York homeworkers. Their "choice" to do homework can only be understood in the context of two related factors: the subordinate position they occupy in the local labor market (their lack of other employment options and/or relegation to low-wage jobs) and the subordinate position they occupy in the household economy (the fact that they bear primary responsibility for household maintenance and childcare). When asked why they decided to do homework instead of outside work, all of the female respondents indicated that they needed to remain at home with their children, were unable to "afford" an outside job, or both. The meaning of this response, in terms of the actual conditions facing homeworkers in central New York and elsewhere, becomes clear when reviewing the results of current case studies.

The fact that women continue to bear primary responsibility for household maintenance and childcare, and the difficulty that poses for those who need to work for wages is widely documented. As Hakim (1980) discovered in her study of British homeworkers, the lack of adequate childcare often combines with the inability to find flexible work arrangements to make homework the only option for some workers.[10] In this study, most of the women interviewed said they would have preferred outside work if they didn't have children and regarded their choice of homework as a sacrifice made on behalf of their families. Many also reported that their husbands did not want them to work outside the home, and that homework allowed them the flexibility to adjust work times to family commitments such as school holidays and to coordinate their work and free time with their husbands' work shifts.

The choice of homework as a means to better coordinate paid work with family responsibilities is also documented in studies by Allen (1983), Baud (1984), Beach (1989), Beneria and Roldan (1987), Morales (1983), and Roldan (1985). Thus, the social constraints placed on women as a result of their "double burden" combined with structural factors such as the lack of affordable childcare and the failure of employers to respond to women's need to reorganize work to meet family needs (by allowing more flexible work schedules and more liberal maternity and paternity leave, for example) have forced women to scramble to adequately meet all of their responsibilities.

Ironically, despite common perceptions, the effectiveness of combining homework with household chores and childcare is questionable. For many homeworkers, doing paid work at home allows little time for meeting family responsibilities. In its recruitment of telecommuters, Pacific Bell discouraged homework as a childcare option. According to Walsh (1987), a spokesperson for the company has described telecommuting and childminding as "two separate full-time jobs." Furthermore, a 1986 study of home-based clerical workers at a Wisconsin insurance company found that homeworkers were unable to successfully combine their paid work with childcare (Walsh 1987, 208). Some central New York homeworkers also expressed the incompatibility of their work with family responsibilities. One homeworker's comments are indicative: "It takes a lot of hours and time when you're doing homework. You can neglect your kids. If you work outside and your kids are in school, when you come home you can be with them. When you get behind in your homework, this takes away from your kids. At times you get angry at them when they interfere with your work. My husband complained if I was behind and had to do the wires at night, and couldn't spend time with him" (Interview 27).

The position women occupy in the labor market and the limitations this places on their employment options is another key factor explaining why women often see homework as a practical work option. For central New York homeworkers, the fact that minimum wage jobs were the only outside jobs available, (which is amply demonstrated by their employment histories),[11] the cost of travelling to work from their remote residences, and the cost of childcare meant that working outside the home "didn't pay." Most of the women I interviewed believed that even at wages below the minimum, homework yielded more spendable income than minimum-wage jobs outside the home. "When you work at home you don't need to make minimum wage because you don't have expenses for travel, clothes, and babysitters" (Interview 19).[12]

Similar views were expressed by homeworkers in studies done by Clark (1981) and Webb (1982). Recounting the view of a woman she interviewed in the knitted outerwear industry, Clark reveals a common sentiment among homeworkers.

What is all this talk, [the homeworker] wonders, of insurance benefits, the paid holidays, and paid vacation, the unemployment compensation and other fringe benefits they say she's missing out on as a home worker. Jeff [her husband], who is also self-employed, doesn't get any of those fringe benefits. And her friends who work at the box factory or at the ski resort are lucky to be getting minimum wage. (Clark 1981)

The recent attention paid to the prevalence of homework in rural America brings to light the particular constraints faced by people in such areas that make homework attractive. For example, many central New York homeworkers had small farms, large garden plots, or a few farm animals that provided a major source of support and needed considerable care—care that could be provided in between hours spent on homework. Others heated their homes in winter with wood stoves that need constant tending. For most, however, their physical isolation and the cost of transportation to the towns and cities where work might be available led them to seek homework jobs. The common problems faced by women workers in general (finding babysitters, being available for family emergencies such as a child's illness) are compounded for residents of rural areas (Norwood 1986).

Aside from the economic considerations that made homework a more practical alternative than outside minimum-wage jobs, some women I interviewed expressed their preference for homework in terms of its potential to provide them with a more satisfying and dignified work experience than they could hope to get in outside jobs available to them. They spoke of the unpleasantness of working on assembly lines—of tedium, boredom, overwork, and sexual harassment. As one woman put it, "people get more abuse in the shop than they do at home." In the words of another, although electronics homework is just as tedious and boring as assembly line work, "at least at home you can break up the boredom by doing other things in between." When weighing the disadvantages of working at home (such as the isolation) against the disadvantages of working in minimum-wage factory or service jobs, most women revealed their qualified preference for homework. "This kind of work at home is too monotonous to do as a full-time job," explained a woman who gave up her homework job to work in hospice care for $5 an hour, "but if I had to go back 'on the line' I might choose homework as an alternative." Once again, in the context of other available job opportunities, homework provided these women with comparable pay, plus the added benefits of convenience, flexibility, and a sense of greater control over their work experiences.

According to Morales (1983), for minority women in the Silicon Valley electronics industry, taking a homework job can be a way of avoiding sexual exploitation in the workplace and gaining status as entrepreneurs. She concludes that "[f]or a significant number of women, homework . . . makes it possible to earn an income without having to submit to the gender stereotyping prevalent in the factory. While men gain satisfaction through promotions and job stability, minority women gain that satisfaction by acting as entrepreneurs outside of the plant. Status devaluation is less apparent if a woman doesn't have to consciously acknowledge gender and race stratification on the job" (Morales 1983, 177).

In sum, the attractiveness of homework to women seeking more creative solutions to the problem of their "double burden" cannot be overemphasized. In the case of central New York workers, as for many others, homework must be viewed simply as the best of a bad lot. While exploitative conditions remain an inevitable feature of most types of homework (from rural electronics work to urban garment-making, to suburban telecommuting), the apparent support for homework voiced by many women workers can only be understood with an eye toward the broader context of economic, social, and political powerlessness from which women make the "choice" to become homeworkers. In the absence of structural changes that would allow women to participate in more full and meaningful work experiences (changes such as alterations in the gender division of labor in the household, an end to discrimination against women in the labor market, flexible work time for all workers, and high quality, low-cost child care), the resurgence of homework in the modern economy promises to contribute to the continued subordination of women in economic, political and social aspects of life. As it stands now, most women homeworkers lack a vision of better and realistic alternatives around which to organize their lives, and, as a nation, we have failed to provide the structural basis for such a vision. If this void persists, homeworkers will continue to press for the right to choose homework from among a group of equally dismal employment alternatives.

Social Class Divisions Among Homeworkers

While waged homework reveals the significance of the gender division of labor in shaping the occupational structure and the choices open to women for paid work, it is important to acknowledge that social class mediates the effect of gender relations on women's lives. This issue underlies my discussion in chapter 1 of different types of home-based work in the United States. I argue that waged homeworkers occupy a fundamentally different set of social relations than professionals and the self-employed who work from their homes. While women in all of these categories face a common set of constraints that distinguish them, as a group, from men, their social class differences also separate them from each other in significant ways. The work experiences and economic outcomes associated with women's waged homework vary considerably from those associated with women's home-based self-employment and professional employment. The differential impact of the gender division of labor in each case helps explain their divergent experiences.

In the case of women's waged homework, the gender division of labor conditions the process of workers' "choice" and employers' search for production options in a direct and unequivocal way. For poor and working-class women, the search for employment is constrained by the demands of household work and childcare and the limited labor market options that have followed from a gender ideology that portrays their paid work as supplementary and conditional. Thus, homework can be the "ideal" choice from both workers' and employers' points of view. In the case of home-based self-employment and professional employment, the effect of the gender division of labor is more obscure. First of all, workers in these categories are just as likely to be male as female. For professional and self-employed men, there is little evidence to suggest that family responsibilities are a primary motivator in their choice of home-based work. For example, in a study that compared male and female homeworkers to their counterparts working outside of the home, Silver found that men who work at home "whatever their occupations, spend no more time on housework or childcare than men working elsewhere" (Silver 1993, 301). The desire to avoid long commutes and traffic congestion in urban areas and the search for greater autonomy are more likely to be the motivating factors.[13] Thus, the gender division of labor is not at work in fostering the growth of this group in general.

Still, studies have shown that women in these groups are more likely to choose home-based work for family reasons than their male counterparts (Silver 1993). Nevertheless, women choosing to work at home from a position of strength on the labor market, even if family considerations are at the heart of their choice, are not subject to the same labor market and household constraints that the gender division of labor imposes on most waged homeworkers. For example, professionals who choose to work from home because they can arrange their work schedules to better accommodate family needs (time flexibility for medical emergencies, being there when their children get home from school, and so on) are in a different situation than women in low-wage occupations who must work at home because they can't afford after school childcare or get jobs that allow time flexibility. In the former case, the gender division of labor is certainly significant. However, while such women may choose this option because they believe it enhances the quality of their family life by allowing them more time with their children, objectively they are likely to have a wider set of options for combining work and family demands. For example, as Hertz (1986) has shown, well-paid professional women are often able to transfer the responsibilities imposed on them by the traditional gender division of labor onto other women whom they hire as housekeepers and childminders. In contrast, waged homeworkers are less likely to have this option, and "choose" home-based work because they are likely to have no better alternative. The gender division of labor is firmly in place in both cases, but its direct impact on women of different social classes varies.

6

State Regulation of Homework: Historical and Contemporary Perspectives

In previous chapters we saw how capital and labor have been key actors in the history of homework, each providing part of the impetus behind its expansion in the modern economy. What remains to be shown is that the state has also influenced homework's course of development. In particular, state policy has helped shape the organization of homework over the past century—its distribution across industries, geographical space, and the labor market. It is important to examine the state's role as the "third actor" in the homework drama by considering how the form and content of homework legislation in the United States (its unevenness across states, its focus on specific industries, and its inadequate enforcement provisions, for example) influenced the pattern of homework's use as a production option. Furthermore, the contradictory policies and perspectives of state agencies have led to confusion and inconsistent actions with regard to homework.

For the most part the state has been given fairly narrow treatment in studies of homework. For example, discussion has focused on the role government regulation has played in the expansion or contraction of homework during key periods such as the turn of the century, the New Deal, and the 1980s (Derber 1959; ILGWU 1981; Miller 1941; Sayin 1945; Van Kleeck 1910). A related set of questions is typically posed: What legislative efforts were needed to curtail exploitative homework operations in the past? Have particular homework laws been effective in reducing or eliminating homework? What kind of laws might be needed in the future to prevent the expansion of exploitative homework? The end point of such analyses centers on how homework legislation might be reformed to solve the homework problem. Reform proposals range from those of the political right (eliminate homework laws to bring it out from "underground," thereby affording homeworkers the opportunity to report labor law violations) to those of organized labor (ban homework outright by expanding anti-homework laws). An important step beyond this narrow conception of the state's influence on the expansion and contraction of homework is provided by Fernandez-Kelly and Garcia (1989), who, in their study of garment industry homework in Miami and Los Angeles, found that local and federal government agencies have played an important role in the expansion of the informal economy. Their analysis takes us an important step toward understanding that the focus on legislative reform as a solution to the homework problem misunderstands the complex role of the state as actor in the homework debate. In this, as with other issues, the state is directly enmeshed in the contradictions of capitalism (Giddens 1981). The source of the homework problem lies within the contradictions inherent to the capital-labor relation and the gender division of labor in society. The capitalist state, far from being a locus for resolving those contradictions, often perpetuates them.

In order to specify how state policy and actions have affected the pattern of homework's use in the United States, it is necessary to explore the contradictory interests of the state and how it has responded to conflicting pressures from key participants in the struggle over homework—namely capital, labor, and social reformers. The variable form and content of homework legislation across the nation reflect the contradictory character of state policy-making and have helped to create conditions under which homework could flourish.

The State as Mediator in the Homework Debate: A Contradictory Role

Historical accounts of legislative efforts to regulate homework in the United States typically portray the state as a mediator in the conflict over homework policy—juggling the interests of capital, organized labor, social reformers, consumers, and homeworkers themselves (Miller 1941; Sayin 1945). Others underscore the contradictory aspects of the state's role in the political struggle over homework. Rather than serving as an impartial mediator, the state is seen as acting in accordance with a view toward dominant class and gender interests (Daniels 1989; Boris 1985). In general, the state has been given insufficient analytical treatment in the homework literature. In order to understand why state policy regarding homework took the form it did, we must examine closely the contradictory interests of the state and how various "pressure groups" supported or opposed those interests.

The importance of the state as an actor in capital-labor conflicts has been acknowledged in recent contributions to the debate surrounding neo-Marxist theories of the state. Rejecting early formulations, which saw the state as acting primarily in the interests of capital and possessing a "relative autonomy" (as in the work of Miliband 1977 and Poulantzas 1973), later works separated state power from class power, recognizing that the state has and is able to pursue its own interests (Skocpol 1979). In addition, the role of the state in capital-labor conflicts is understood in terms of the former's ability to organize and manipulate political power. Accordingly, Giddens sees the state as "a set of collectivities concerned with the institutionalized organization of political power," while Skocpol emphasizes that state structures, which vary nationally and historically, "determine the ways in which class interests and conflicts get organized into (or out of) politics in a given time and place" (Giddens 1981, 220; Skocpol 1980, 200). These formulations reject the Poulantzian view of the state as simply an "arena" of class conflict or a "concentration of class relations" and see it as possessing more autonomous power. For example, Giddens seeks to explain "the sources of state power and the scope of the sanctions which the state is capable of wielding" (217).

Mann (1988) sees the autonomous power of the state as derived from its three main attributes: the necessity of its existence (based on the need for enforceable rules to hold together a diverse society), its multiplicity of functions, and its territorial centrality. These attributes give the state an independence from civil society that brings with it some degree of autonomous power. In Mann's view, the state differs socio-spatially and organizationally from the major power groups of civil society (that is, economic power groupings, ideological power movements, and military power). He points out that while power groups are "quite capable of keeping watch on states they have propped up" they are unable to do the state's jobs themselves because of their socio-spatial and organizational structure:

Even if a particular state is set up or intensified merely to institutionalize the relations between given social groups, this is done by concentrating resources and infrastructures in the hands of an institution that has different socio-spatial and organizational contours to those groups. Flexibility and speed of response entail concentration of decision-making and a tendency towards permanence of personnel. The decentred, non-territorial interest groups that set up the state in the first place are thus less able to control it. Territorial centralization provides the state with a potentially independent basis of power mobilization being necessary to social development and uniquely in the possession of the state itself. (18)

Thus, the necessity, multiplicity of functions, and territorial centrality of the state underlie its autonomous power. In Mann's view, this autonomous power gives the state an independence from civil society, "which is no less absolute in principle than the power of any other major group." Accordingly, the state "is not merely a locus of class struggle, an instrument of class rule, the factor of social cohesion, the expression of core values, the centre of social allocation processes, the institutionalization of military force (as in the various reductionist theories)—it is a different socio-spatial organization. As a consequence, we can treat states as actors, in the person of state elites, with a will to power" (Mann 1988, 18–19).[1]

The premises advanced by Mann and others in theoretical discourse about the capitalist state provide the groundwork for an understanding of the state's crucial role in organizing class interests and conflicts with regard to homework. Examination of legislation and government policies in the United States reveals the contradictory interests of the state and how various power groups supported or conflicted with those interests. The end result was an uneven system of homework regulation that fell short of the full demands of all affected interest groups but allowed for the perpetuation of an exploitative system of homework.

Historically, the capitalist state has had at least three general concerns: maintaining the conditions needed for production and economic growth, securing the stability of social relations, and ensuring its own political legitimacy. For example, in the interest of maintaining economic growth, the state has taken action on behalf of capital and labor. Government subsidies and loans, protective tariffs, and regulatory activities advanced to stabilize the economy are seen as directly benefiting capital. Legislation to maintain wage standards, improve working conditions, and stabilize industrial relations by protecting collective bargaining rights are seen as concessions to labor. Taken together, such actions promote stability, thereby creating conditions needed for expansion of production and economic growth. In addition to its concern with production, the state must act to ensure the stability of social relations, which is essential for attaining required levels of consumption. State policies aimed at improving living standards, economic security, and quality of life are relevant here, with social welfare, education, and antipoverty legislation directed toward these ends. Finally, state action is influenced by the need to ensure political legitimacy. Faced with the need to regulate interclass social relations, the state must "integrate all elements of the population into a coherent system, win mass loyalty, and legitimate itself and society" (O'Connor 1973, 69).

Accordingly, the state's role as mediator among various classes and interest groups is a contradictory one. It seeks to balance two related sets of concerns: the need to secure production against the need to advance consumption and the need to ensure labor's subordination to capital against the need to secure the reproduction of wage labor. The process of policy formation regarding homework illustrates the playing out of this contradictory role. In an effort to confront the conflicting need to support production (and thus respond to the interests of capital and organized labor) and consumption (and hence respond to the interests of social reformers) the state created an uneven and somewhat arbitrary system for regulating homework—a system that, in turn, had a significant impact on the organization of homework as a form of production.

In the public debates that surrounded legislative activity regarding homework, key "pressure groups" articulated their positions and policy suggestions. Through organized lobbying and public presentation of their concerns, employers, labor unions, and social reformers came to influence the course of legislative action on this issue.

> Beyond the kitchens of homeworking women, negotiations over homework policy reflected the different interests brought to bear on the state over the issue of women's work at home. In opposition to homework, social reformers sought to reinforce the division between the public and private spheres by banning homework entirely: they

believed women—mothers—should not work at all. Joining them, labor unions opposed homework on the grounds that homeworkers posed unfair competition to unionized, male factory workers. On the other side of the debate, manufacturers who sought to exploit working mothers for their cheap labor defended the rights of women to work and argued that the state lacked the authority to interfere in the "privacy" of the home. (Daniels 1989, 14)

Beginning with the turn-of-the-century period of state-level efforts to regulate homework and continuing through the New Deal efforts to expand homework regulation, considerable public pressure came to bear on the state through the efforts of social reformers, a heterogeneous group that included social feminists concerned with the welfare of women and children, consumer organizations, and public health and housing reformers.[2] In the early 1900s, focusing on the health hazards associated with products made in tenements and sweatshops, organizations like the Consumers' League of New York published the reports of investigators who "were appalled to find homeworkers with infectious diseases sorting coffee beans, cracking nuts with their teeth, and using coats sent home for finishing as bed covering at night" (Daniels 1989, 23). During the New Deal period, the activities of the National Child Labor Committee, the Women's Trade Union League, and the federal Labor Department's Women's Bureau helped arouse public awareness about the abuses of homework and influenced the course of legislative activity. According to Boris (1985), the "New Deal Network of Women," led by Eleanor Roosevelt, Secretary of Labor Frances Perkins, and Democratic National Committee Women's Division Chief Mary Dewson, influenced policy development regarding women and homework. For example, when an executive order was drawn up in 1934 to exempt certain groups of people from the homework provisions of the National Recovery Administration (NRA) codes (the elderly, those with disabilities, and those caring for the disabled), the women in the Labor Department made sure mothers were not given an exemption, as had been proposed by some officials in the Roosevelt Administration. Their opposition to the exemption was motivated by the belief that mothers should not work and that homework "most undermined motherhood because its low piece rates meant long hours, jeopardizing their health and family life" and that working women, presumably single, belonged in the factory in order to benefit from minimum wages and better working conditions (Boris 1985, 751).

Thus, for more than four decades, pressure from social reformers was a constant in the arena of conflict over homework. In
fact, the identification of homework as a social problem that
warranted legislative action can be attributed in large part to the
activities of reformers. Overall, they had a dual impact on the
development of homework legislation in the United States. First,
they provided a constant source of pressure on the state to develop
and expand homework legislation. Second, they influenced the
content of homework laws by striving to ensure that statutes
prohibited homework for women with children.

As mentioned earlier, a major aspect of the unevenness of
homework regulation in the United States is its focus on specific
industries. It is in this regard that the interplay of the other main
actors in the homework debate—capital and organized labor—had
significant impact. To begin with, the state has been faced with a
divergent set of demands from capital on this issue. While employers have generally resisted efforts to regulate homework,
either through attempts to influence lawmakers, challenge homework statutes in the courts, or simply evade existing regulations,
segments of capital have, at times, supported its regulation or
abolition. For example, during the years of the New Deal, employers from large, capital-intensive, mechanized and unionized firms
often supported the abolition of homework on the grounds of
unfair competition (Silver 1989, 105). Employer opposition to
homework, and hence support of homework regulation, has also
been prevalent among small firms in highly competitive industries
where homework has been a mainstay for decades. In the more
recent controversy over the lifting of the seven Fair Labor Standards Act (FLSA) Prohibitory Orders, manufacturers in the knitted
outerwear industry and the Federation of Apparel Manufacturers,
which represents 5500 firms, voiced their opposition to the deregulation of homework on the grounds of unfair competition (Hosenball 1981; Rauch 1981; Webb 1982). It is likely, however, that
the relatively high incidence of unionization among firms in these
groups has had some bearing on their position with regard to
homework. The relatively high level of worker organization in the
needle trades and union success in winning state and federal
homework prohibitions in their industries has shaped the content
of homework laws and separated the anti-homework from the
prohomework employers.[3]

The union struggle against homework dates back to the 1880s
and can be credited with achieving the first legislative attempts to
regulate it. The public campaign waged by the Cigar Makers

International Union resulted in the first piece of legislation prohibiting homework. Passed in 1884 but struck down by the courts
shortly after, this first attempt at state regulation of homework
marked the beginning of a long union battle. Faced with continual
failure on the legislative front, unions such as the Cigar Makers
turned to direct economic action (strike demands) and the institution of the union label as ways of combating the use of homework in the early decades of the century (Daniels 1989; Miller
1941). It was not until the New Deal period that union influence
converged to affect the passage of firm state and federal homework
laws. Reflecting union strength in certain industries, homework
bans were enacted in the most highly organized trades.

In addition to responding to the needs of social reformers,
capital, and organized labor, state policy-makers were often influenced by their ideological convictions regarding women and work
when deliberating on the homework issue. Daniels (1989) points
out that legislators in New York State were reluctant to regulate
homework in the early decades of the twentieth century because
they "viewed the cure of the homework problem as worse than
the disease." In Daniels' view,

> legislators were less concerned with upholding ideal stan-
> dards about the separation of home and work than they
> were in making sure women stayed at home. And by
> exempting homeworkers from all forms of regulation, they
> could also avoid the public recognition that the traditional
> patriarchal family was not functioning as it ideally
> should. In the end, this failure to act evinced the deeper
> commitment of legislators to the mystification of the sex-
> ual division of labor—one that guaranteed that home-
> workers would continue to labor under the most exploit-
> ative working conditions. (1989, 27)

In her analysis of the unintended effects of public policy on
the structures of gender dominance and subordination, Boris
argues that New Deal homework legislation "reinforce[d]—and
perhaps extend[ed]—the sex-gender division of social life" despite the fact that it curtailed the exploitation of women and
children (1985, 748). She points out that defending "sacred motherhood" was at the heart of the discourse of proponents and
opponents of homework. Social reformers and labor unions
sought an end to homework because it degraded motherhood by
forcing women to neglect their home and children. Using the flip
side of the same ideology, the business community supported

homework on the grounds that it helped preserve women's essential functions regarding home and family. Absent from the homework debate, and from New Deal policy, was a recognition of the real problem of women's employment in the home—the double burden of paid and unpaid work and the absence of childcare services. "Because organized labor and the Women's Bureau focused on conditions in the paid labor force, because they considered the work of married women and mothers as temporary responses to economic hard times, neither seriously analyzed the question of child care as part of the problem of women's employment. Central to their policy remained the ideal of the family wage and the concept of full-time motherhood" (Boris 1985, 756). Thus, homework regulation was couched in a New Deal policy that accepted the separation of economic life into men's and women's spheres. As a result, it neglected the root of the homework problem and helped sustain the conditions for its continuance.

In sum, the state was faced with conflicting pressures from the key participants in the homework debate. On the one side, the majority of employers fought to exempt homework from government regulation. On the other side, certain segments of capital, social reformers, and organized labor pressed for homework regulation, though with different, and sometimes competing, agendas. Superimposed on the debate was an ideological commitment on the part of many lawmakers to the gender division of labor in the home. As such, policy-making regarding homework reflected an attempt to manage the contradictory aspects of women's dual role and at the same time respond to the interests of groups that represented important consumption and/or production concerns of the state.

The Unevenness of Homework Legislation in the United States

The system of homework regulation developed in the United States during the first half of the twentieth century illustrates the contradictory outcomes of state intervention in labor-capital conflict. The state's need to balance conflicting demands resulted in uneven and largely ineffective homework regulation. In what follows, I outline the main features of state and federal homework legislation and show how the inconsistant application of government regulation to homework manifests itself in disparate state homework statutes, federal and state regulation targeted at specific industries, and inadequate enforcement provisions at both the state and federal levels. This will lay the groundwork for a discussion of the specific ways government policy has affected the organization of homework in the United States.

The first efforts to regulate homework took place on the state level at the turn of the century. Pressure to regulate homework was brought to bear on many states through the combined efforts of unions such as the United Garment Workers of America, which fought homework through strikes, publicity, and demands for state investigations of the homework problem, reform groups such as the Anti-Sweating League, formed by a group of young intellectuals in New York City, and the support for homework regulation voiced by factory inspectors in states such as New York. According to Miller, "by 1890 the cry against the sweating system had been taken up across the country by press and pulpit, and popular resentment against the system had reached a high pitch" (Miller 1941, 15). In response to public concern about industrial homework and the "sweating system," twelve states tried to regulate tenement manufacture and homework between 1891 and 1899. Aimed at protecting consumers from the health problems associated with purchasing goods produced under unsanitary conditions, state homework laws prohibited the manufacture of certain articles in dwelling places and required shops in nonliving quarters to meet certain sanitary and health provisions.[4] The states adopting such laws were New York, New Jersey, Massachusetts, Illinois, Maryland, Pennsylvania, Ohio, Indiana, Missouri, Connecticut, Wisconsin, and Michigan.

While the public outcry against the abuses of tenement manufacture diminished somewhat with the passage of these laws, continued concern about the abuses of industrial homework were reflected in efforts to refine and expand homework legislation. According to Miller (1941), government investigations carried out between 1907 and 1929 indicated that the anti-sweating laws enacted after 1890 were inadequate in combating the problems of industrial homework. For example, a 1909 congressional study of homework in the clothing industry in New York, Chicago, Philadelphia, Baltimore, and Rochester showed that despite anti-sweating laws, tenement manufacture and homework were still being done under unhealthy conditions for low wages and long hours, often with the use of child labor. Findings by the New York State Factory Investigating Commission illustrate how ineffective existing laws were in controlling homework abuses during this period. In its 1911 study, the Commission discovered tenement manufacture and homework were being used in the production of 62 articles in addition to the 41 prohibited under New York State law. Thus, homework was found to be much more extensive than previously imagined. As a result of these findings, the state strengthened its homework law in January 1913 by adding to the list of items barred from homework and tenement manufacture, extending licensing provisions for such manufacture, requiring that employers obtain permits before giving out material for tenement manufacture, and extending the Child Labor Law to cover such operations (Miller 1941, 23). Despite these new provisions, an investigation conducted ten years later found that practically nothing had changed. It was around this time that state authorities began calling for the total elimination of homework rather than simply its regulation.

Although other states followed New York and attempted to strengthen existing anti-sweating legislation during this period (Tenessee, California, Maryland, New Jersey, Wisconsin, and Pennsylvania, for example), most states had either very weak laws for the regulation of homework or no laws to deal with the problem at all. In 1936 only 16 of 48 states had some form of legislation to control homework and there was little uniformity among existing laws. In an attempt to remedy this problem, the International Association of Governmental Labor Officials endorsed a "model bill" to serve as a guide for states in the drafting of homework legislation. This model bill, Proposed State Law to Regulate and Tax Industrial Homework, called for the "complete prohibition of homework on certain items such as food and toys, for the licensing of all manufacturers and homeworkers on other items, for the creation of health and economic standards in operation, and for the keeping of extensive records. It also delegated power to the state labor commissioner to order cessation of homework in any industry if investigations revealed a threat to the health of homeworkers or to the economic position of factory workers. As a means of paying for the administrative costs of the law and at the same time reducing the economic advantage over factory production, a system of fees to be paid by the homework employer was also drawn up" (Derber 1959, 8). The model bill proved to be a valuable guide since, after its publication, some states replaced or revised old laws along the newly proposed lines, while others took measures to regulate homework for the first time. By 1940, two more states and the territory of Puerto Rico added some form of homework regulation.

The system of state-level homework regulation that was solidified during the New Deal period and remains basically intact to this day did not create a uniform regulatory apparatus to control homework. First, the system lacks consistency *across states*. Aside from the fact that many states lack homework statutes altogether, existing homework laws are quite disparate. For example, laws in states such as Illinois, New Jersey, and New York focus on prohibiting homework in certain industries, with those targeted varying from state to state. The Illinois Homework Act of 1937 prohibits homework for articles perceived to be dangerous to the worker or the public. Thus homework is prohibited for the processing of articles of food or drink, drugs or poisons, medical and surgical bandages, sanitary napkins, cotton batting, fireworks, explosives, toys, dolls, tobacco, and metal springs. Similarly, New Jersey's law prohibits homework for many of the same industries.[5] In nonprohibited industries homework can be done as long as the appropriate employer's permit and homeworker's certificate are obtained.

In contrast, New York State's homework law focuses on industries with a long history of worker exploitation and/or union pressure to eliminate homework. After 1935 homework was prohibited in boys' outerwear, men's and boys' neckwear, gloves, artificial flowers and feathers, and direct mail services unless employers had permits prior to the date of the applicable prohibitory order and homeworkers meet certain hardship criteria based on age, physical or mental handicap, or the need to care for an invalid at home.[6] In addition, a prohibitory order for all other industries was enacted in 1945. Unlike the specific industry orders it did not prohibit homework but restricted it to employers and homeworkers licensed between 1944 and 1945.

A second problem that has plagued the system of state-level homework regulation is the transfer of homework operations to states with no homework laws, or with weak ones. The first report on interstate shipment of homework, published in 1936 by the U.S. Department of Labor, showed that in New York alone 171 manufacturers were sending work to 1,452 homeworkers and to a large number of contractors in 16 other states and Puerto Rico. Seven of the states had no homework laws (Miller 1941, 33).

A third problem with state homework laws is the inconsistency of their application *within states*. In other words, existing homework statutes are not always interpreted and applied evenly. The case of New York is a useful illustration. Through examination of Labor Department records on legal homework permits and interviews with officials in the Division of Labor Standards, I identified four "problem areas" that have contributed to an overall inconsistency in the enforcement of New York's homework statute. First of all, it appears as if homework permits (to employers) and certificates (to workers) have been issued in direct violation of the law. For instance, while under the 1945 order restricting homework in all industries an employer cannot obtain a permit unless he was already licensed to employ homeworkers between 1944 and 1945, Labor Department data reveal a number of cases that violate this condition. Despite claims by officials that the Labor Department "has not issued permits in more than 30 years" some permits have been given out over the last three decades (Burg 1986, 14). Of 43 permits reissued in 1980, 27 were originally issued after 1945. According to one Labor Standards investigator, homework permits may have been issued in error over the years because people staffing the district offices of the Department of Labor, where permits are issued, may not always be aware of the homework regulations (Interview 40 1984). Furthermore, it is possible that some of these permits were issued at the direction of the Commissioner of Labor, who has some power to make exception to the homework law. This discretionary power has led to inconsistency in the application of New York State homework statutes—inconsistency that reflects variation in state officials' response to different pressure groups.

In a paragraph described by an attorney for the Department of Labor as "confusing," Section 351 of Article 13 of New York State Labor Law gives the industrial commissioner the authority to make exception to the homework law. The precise conditions under which exceptions can be made are not specified.[7] It appears, however, that in the early 1980's the policy of the commissioner was to grant "variances" in nonprohibited industries for those who need to work at home because of age, disability, or the need to care for an invalid regardless of whether employers met the "pre-1945" requirement (U.S. House of Representatives 1987, 187).

In the view of one attorney who represented electronics industry homeworkers whose operations were curtailed by enforcement of Article 13 in 1981, willingness to make exception to the homework law has varied with different commissioners. In his view, homework permits "were issued freely" before 1976, when

Lillian Roberts took the office. He pointed out that 30 permits were issued between 1945 and 1976 despite the "prior to 1945" rule, which corresponds closely to the data presented above (Interview 46 1984). A homework distributor whose operations were also curtailed by the enforcement of Article 13 made a similar observation, alleging Commissioner Roberts has enforced Article 13 more rigorously than her predecessors because of her ties to organized labor as a former union organizer (Interview 47, 1984). In this case, the discretionary power of the commissioner has been challenged by one pressure group (capital), which sees the state as acting against its interests and in favor of a competing group (organized labor).

Inconsistencies in policy that stem from the commissioner's discretionary power are compounded by the fact that her decisions can be overruled by the state's Industrial Board of Appeals (IBA). In the controversy over electronics industry homework in the 1980s, the IBA consistently overruled the Department of Labor and the commissioner in their attempt to subject electronics industry homework to Article 13. Criticisms from Labor Department officials about the inconsistency of the IBA in its rulings abound. According to one labor standards investigator, the IBA has tended to rule in favor of the Labor Department on most homework cases, with the exception of those involving electronics. In her view, certain members of the IBA "personally support the position that there is nothing wrong with homework" despite their mandate "to make an objective decision about the legal aspects of the case" (Interview 40 1984).

Another "problem area" in the application of New York State's homework law has to do with varying levels of commitment to regulate homework among different divisions of the Department of Labor. In particular, cuts in funding for enforcement since the late 1970s have made it difficult for the Labor Standards Division to adequately confront the problem of illegal homework. In the words of one investigator, "there's a lack of commitment to preventing homework on the level of the Governor's office and in the Division of the Budget" (Interview 40 1984). It is interesting to note that in their study of garment industry homework in California, Fernandez-Kelly and Garcia (1989) also found variation over time in enforcement of state homework statutes. They concluded that in the 1980s, under the conservative administration of Governor George Deukmenjian, "sanctions against employers in general were de-emphasized in the name of greater respect for the free play of labor supply and demand" (254).

Finally, inconsistencies in the application of the homework law in New York State were compounded by the fact that preconceptions about homework among state officials (as expressed by those I interviewed in Labor Standards in 1984) had not kept pace with current developments—particularly the use of homework for computer-based occupations. Article 13 exempts clerical work (typing, stenciling, transcribing, copying, bookkeeping, and stenographic work) from regulation under the homework statute. Offering their interpretation of the clerical work clause during an interview in 1984, officials in the Labor Standards Division expressed the view that computer-based homework is "more acceptable" than homework in traditional homework industries. Interviews with two Labor Standards officials revealed a "double standard" in assessing the exploitative potential of different types of home-based work and, thus, the legitimacy of regulating various homework occupations. One of the investigators felt the law's exclusion of clerical work (including computer-based work) from regulation is reasonable because with the advent of the computer "it is possible to ensure that minimum wage is paid by monitoring working hours." Another official similarly equated exploitation from homework with violation of minimum-wage laws, implying that if minimum wage could be ensured, homework would be acceptable. When asked if they thought telecommuting should be controlled under the homework law because it is potentially exploitative in other ways, one replied that it was not the job of the Labor Standards Division to prevent exploitative work unless the exploitation was directly related to the violation of laws such as those governing minimum wage, hours, and child labor. In this investigator's view, the kind of exploitation identified with telecommuting was not in violation of any labor laws (Interviews 40 and 41 1984).

Despite the opinions offered above, the commissioner's official policy on computer-based work at home makes a distinction between homework involving an extension of routine office functions and professional telecommuting. In his testimony before the House of Representatives Subcommittee on Labor Standards, Joseph Armer, director of New York State's Labor Standards Division, explained the commissioner's policy as follows: "where there is an extension of routine office functions, billing, or something of that nature . . . it is homework. . . . However, [for] the person who has an arrangement to do professional programming or something of that nature, it would not be homework, as indeed it would not be if it were a professional working at home but not using a computer" (U.S. House of Representatives 1987, 187). It seems possible that the apparent discrepancy between official policy and the interpretation of the homework law by labor standards investigators could result in the inconsistent application of Article 13 to new computer-based work at home.

Preconceptions about electronics industry homework also permeated the legal controversy during the 1980s over the interpretation of New York State's homework statute. My interviews with lawyers on all sides of the controversy (those representing homework distributors, the Labor Department, and the Industrial Board of Appeals) revealed a tendency to draw a distinction between the electronics industry homework they were dealing with and more traditional, "exploitative" types of homework. For example, while the Labor Department attorney seemed committed to seeing the "letter of the law" enforced, he revaled his ambivalence about the work electronics assemblers were doing in their homes. He told me during an interview that he did not believe there was "anything too awful about homework" in central New York. The lines of distinction drawn by his legal opponents were more pronounced. The chief attorney for the Industrial Board of Appeals stated his belief that it may not be "reasonable" to apply the homework law in all cases and that "new industries should be given review" before doing so. Similarly, an attorney representing homework distributors said he believed the homework law was "overly broad" and "not intended to cover the situations we're dealing with in central New York."[8] It is interesting to note that there are parallels between the situation I found in New York State and that found by Fernandez-Kelly and Garcia in California. They discuss the uneven application of California homework laws in the case of the electronics, textile, and garment industries. While California labor law bans all homework in the garment and textile industries, there is no specific prohibition for electronics. They conclude that field enforcement officials believe "there is justification for the asymmetrical application of the ban on homework in the positive public image surrounding the electronics industry." They point out that this perception is held despite the fact that "electronics firms are as likely to be cited and fined for violations of wage and hour regulations as garment manufacturers" and the use of chemicals in electronics assembly can make homework hazardous (Fernandez-Kelly and Garcia 1989, 252).

In sum, inconsistencies in the application of New York State's homework law derive from the following: errors in the granting of homework permits, ambiguity in the law itself, particularly with reference to the Industrial Commissioner's discretionary power and the veto power of the Industrial Board of Appeals, varying levels of commitment to control homework on the part of different divisions within state government, and a limited and historically specific view of homework on the part of key officials and judicial bodies involved in the interpretation and enforcement of the homework law.

FEDERAL HOMEWORK LEGISLATION

During the 1930s the development of federal homework legislation was seen as the only way to stop the interstate transfer of homework and to solve other problems inherent in the state-level system of regulation. An examination of federal efforts to control homework reveals the government's failure to provide an adequate and comprehensive program to meet those goals. The concentration of federal homework law on specific industries, which resulted from successful union pressure to regulate homework in unionized trades, has served to duplicate the kind of unevenness that plagues state-level regulation. In addition, shortcomings in enforcement of federal statutes (a problem for state-level regulation as well) have weakened their ability to prevent interstate transfer of homework operations and maintain uniform labor standards for homeworkers across industries throughout the country.

The first attempt to regulate homework on the federal level came with the passage of the National Industrial Recovery Act (NIRA) in 1933. Under the NIRA, many industries adopted "codes of fair competition" which included provisions for the regulation or elimination of homework. Although the NIRA was invalidated in 1935, the Women's Bureau of the U.S. Department of Labor concluded that during its two-year career it eliminated homework in 22 industries and regulated its use in many others.[9] Based on a study of industries not protected by NRA codes, which revealed widespread violation of wage and hours regulations among homeworkers, the Department of Labor concluded that where homework was not prohibited by codes old problems continued and intensified.[10] Aside from its direct impact on homework during the years of its implementation, however, the NIRA was also significant for its effect on future homework legislation. First of all, its perceived success—and the reported resurgence of homework abuses after its abolition—demonstrated the need for new and more comprehensive regulation.[11] Its unique approach to combating the problem also set an agenda for subsequent lawmaking. By setting up standards on the basis of industry, it provided a way for controlling the flow of homework between states. This set a precedent in attempting to prevent employers from transferring homework operations from regulated to unregulated areas. In addition, the NIRA differed from previous efforts to control homework by being one of the first to focus on the need to protect workers from exploitation and prevent the undercutting of factory labor. Most homework legislation up to this time focused on the need to protect consumers from goods produced under unsanitary conditions.[12]

After the invalidation of the NIRA adoption of the federal Fair Labor Standards Act in 1938 was the next effort to regulate homework on a national basis. Although the FLSA did not make specific reference to homework, it declared that all employees producing goods for interstate commerce were subject to the act's provisions "regardless of the nature of their place of employment" (Derber 1959, 9). Accordingly, homework manufacture had to meet federal standards for minimum wages, overtime pay and child labor as established by the FLSA, and homework contractors and their employees had to keep records of hours worked and wages earned. In addition to these general provisions, additional control over homework was implemented in subsequent amendments to the FLSA. By 1949 Congress had approved special regulations (called the federal prohibitory orders) to prohibit homework in seven specific industries (jewelry, gloves and mittens, knitted outerwear, buttons and buckles, women's apparel, handkerchiefs, and embroidery). The bans were enacted because of the difficulty the Department of Labor had enforcing the FLSA in these industries despite the recordkeeping system it put in place (U.S. House of Representatives 1987, 311). These prohibitory orders could be waived for persons unable to work in a factory for reasons of age, health, or the need to care for an invalid at home. However, homework was permitted under such circumstances only for persons already employed in the particular industry prior to a specified date "unless evidence of unusual hardship was shown or the worker came under the supervision of a state vocational rehabilitation agency or a sheltered workshop" (Derber 1959, 9).

The FLSA, like the system of state-level regulation put in place during the New Deal, failed to comprehensively regulate homework. While it may have had the potential to standardize homework regulations across states, its concentration, up until the 1980s, on seven specific industries and its shortcomings in enforcement weakened its impact. With regard to the former, the designation of specific industries as "prohibited" has focused enforcement and public attention on those industries, allowing the use of homework in nonprohibited industries to remain largely invisible. With regard to enforcement, the federal Department of Labor and state labor departments display similar inadequacies. A discussion of both will illustrate a key factor in the overall ineffectiveness of homework regulation in the United States.

State and Federal Enforcement Problems

In general, enforcement of homework laws has been based on response to complaints and/or selected inspections in targeted areas. On the federal level, inspection on complaint has been predominant. For example, after passage of the Fair Labor Standards Act, the sheer volume of reported violations with respect to industrial homework forced the federal government to limit itself to investigating reported violations rather than making regular inspections (Miller 1941, 47). Since the 1940s the federal homework statutes have been enforced primarily in response to complaints of workers being paid subminimum wages (Keller 1984a, A18).

Enforcement methods on the state level may change over time, as the case of New York illustrates. Between 1935 (when New York's homework law was adopted) and 1962, a special homework unit operated to police permitted homework (to ensure compliance with minimum wage, hours, and child labor regulations for employers operating legally under the state's homework permit system) and to enforce sanctions against the illegal distribution of homework. In 1962, after concluding that the homework law had been enforced with "apparent success," and thus the homework problem eliminated, the State Department of Labor abolished this special unit (New York State Dept. of Labor 1982a, 13). Between 1962 and 1976 New York's homework regulations were enforced on a cyclical basis (door-to-door inspections with special patrols in suspect areas) as well as by complaint. Since 1976 budget and staff reductions have limited enforcement to investigation on complaint only (New York State Dept. of Labor 1982a, 71).[13] Despite these general enforcement practices, it is possible that the branch offices of the State Labor Department vary in the primary enforcement mechanism they use. For example, despite the claim that investigations are initiated mainly on complaint statewide, the chief Labor Standards investigator for the Labor Standards Division based in Brooklyn reported that less than 5 percent of the investigations conducted by his department are initiated this way. At his division enforcement is based mainly on intercepting illegal homework in targeted areas of the city.[14]

On the federal level, shortcomings in recent enforcement of labor standards for homeworkers were identified in the context of public debate over the Reagan Administration's actions to lift the prohibition on homework in the seven industries targeted by the FLSA. According to the House of Representatives Subcommittee on Labor Standards, which held public hearings in 1986 to discuss the administration's proposal to lift the homework bans, there had been a "drastic reduction of compliance officer staff years devoted to FLSA enforcement" since 1980. A decrease in staff years from 1098 in 1980 to 895 in 1984 led to a 16 percent reduction in the number of FLSA investigations (U.S. House of Representatives 1987, 4). At the same time, the number of workers covered by the FLSA rose from 60 million in 1980 to more than 72.5 million.[15] Pointing out that this increase in responsibility has not coincided with an increase in enforcement capability, the subcommittee concluded that the Department of Labor "can no longer adequately enforce FLSA, particularly in homework settings that present many unique barriers to DOL compliance officers" (U.S. House of Representatives 1987, 315).

Despite Reagan Administration claims that enforcement activities for the Fair Labor Standards Act increased during its tenure even as staff reductions occurred, a close examination of Department of Labor reporting practices reveals otherwise. In its tally of investigations completed each year, the DOL counts all compliance actions, including so-called "conciliatory complaints," those routinely resolved with a single phone call to the employer. Thus, the House Subcommittee on Labor Standards concluded that "while the [Government Accounting Office] reported an increase in the number of FLSA 'investigations,' from 66,943 in 1985 to 72,641 in 1986, this is mitigated by the fact that many of these reported 'investigations' are conciliatory complaint resolutions." According to the GAO, the number of conciliations rose by 13 percent between 1983 and 1986, from 16,315 (26 percent) to 28,095 (39 percent). At the same time, the number of actual investigations fell from 46,729 (74 percent) in 1983 to 44,522 (61 percent) in 1986 (U.S. House of Representatives 1987, 316). Aside from the fact that it inflates enforcement statistics, heavy reliance on "telephone enforcement" is particularly ineffective with regard to homework, where on-site investigation is essential.

In addition to the recent reduction in enforcement activities, Department of Labor monitoring of homework is further mitigated by enforcement policies. For example, when investigating homeworkers, the DOL relies on company owners for lists of employees and addresses. Furthermore, the policy of making appointments with employers and workers in advance of an investigation can allow subjects to correct or hide violations (although, as we will see below, a significant number of violations tends to be found even when subjects know in advance of an inspection).

During the Reagan years, critics charged that the repeal of the seven prohibitory orders would further dilute enforcement efforts by forcing the Department of Labor to concentrate on investigating employers who apply for certification. In the words of Jack Sheinkman, secretary-treasurer of the Amalgamated Clothing and Textile Workers Union, "The program the Secretary [of Labor] has put together is not an enforcement program. Compliance officials are investigating employers who identify themselves by requesting certification. Other investigations are on a 'complaint only' basis and complaints are few and far between" (U.S. House of Representatives 1987, 155).

Regardless of the primary method used to uncover violations of homework laws or the resources devoted to enforcement, the overall effectiveness of enforcement on both the state and federal levels has inherent limitations. The physical isolation of homeworkers has made it difficult for authorities to identify illegal homework operations through inspections of targeted areas. Similarly, enforcement on complaint is likely to result in identifying a tiny proportion of potential violators of homework statutes. For example, homeworkers themselves are unlikely to report their employers' failure to meet minimum wage, hours, and overtime regulations for fear of jeopardizing their jobs. In addition, immigrants, who constitute a substantial portion of the homework labor force in industries such as garment-making have other reasons to fear disclosure of unfair labor practices.

The workers most susceptible to suffering as a result of non-compliance have a number of reasons not to identify themselves for government scrutiny. As newly arrived immigrants they may be unaware of services available, unable to communicate in English or, based on experience

of corruption in their native countries, distrustful of government agencies of any kind. There are the additional
possibilities . . . that the employees are: illegal immigrants; working while on public assistance or collecting
unemployment insurance benefits; not paying income and
social security taxes. (New York State Dept. of Labor
1982a, 14)

Even among legal homework operations, enforcement of minimum wage, hours, overtime, and child labor laws is problematic.
Writing on behalf of the International Ladies' Garment Workers
Union in 1941, Teper and Weinberg summarized enforcement
difficulties that are just as relevant today as they were more than
50 years ago:

Various agencies have frequenty referred to the impossi-
bility of securing evidence of child labor law violations in
cases of industrial homework because before the door is
opened to the inspector there is ample time to hide all
signs of work by children. To discover violations of overtime provisions is well nigh impossible without station-
ing an inspector in every home where industrial homework is carried on. In fact, resistance to the abolition of
homework is based in large part on the fact that its
disappearance would close off an avenue whereby the
regulation of hours of work may be defied with impunity.
(U.S. House of Representatives 1982, 113)

I have tried to identify the most salient flaws in state and
federal labor law enforcement mechanisms with regard to homework. Perhaps a more telling indictment of the regulatory apparatus is the fact that the small number of inspections that do take
place tend to yield significant violations. A close examination of
the data on compliance with regulations for homework operations
actually investigated by state and federal authorities illustrates
the pattern of widespread noncompliance with homework laws.
Virtually all government investigations uncover homework violations. In the words of one labor standards investigator in New
York State, "We don't go out and inspect and not find violations."[16]
Widespread evasion of homework statutes has been documented for early as well as current laws. As already mentioned,
the first round of state laws designed to regulate tenement manufacture and homework at the turn of the century were largely

unsuccessful. Government investigations carried out in the decades after their enactment found that unhealthy conditions, long hours, low wages, and child labor were still rampant in homework operations (Miller 1941). For example, in 1910 Mary Van Kleeck, Secretary of the New York Committee on Women's Work, reported the results of a random investigation of homeworkers licensed under New York State law. Among the 42 families visited, 59 children under 14 years of age were found working in violation of child labor laws (Van Kleeck 1910, 145).

The failure of the 1933 National Industrial Recovery Act codes to improve conditions for most homeworkers was also well documented. A 1935 report from the Women's Bureau of the Department of Labor identified 31 industries in which homework was prohibited by NRA codes but noncompliance was found. In addition, while the report claimed that homework was eliminated for 22 products protected by codes, 23 industries with no codes or no regulatory provisions for homework specified in their codes were identified as employing homeworkers (U.S. Dept. of Labor, 1935, 41, 47, 48). In a discussion of Texas homeworkers in the 1930s, Blackwelder confirms widespread violations of NRA regulations. "In San Antonio and Laredo NRA regulations that controlled the wages and conditions of homework were flagrantly violated and homework conditions in the late 1930s mirrored a situation that the National Recovery Administration had tried to eradicate" (Blackwelder, 1989, 77). Hand-sewing (mostly on infants' and children's wear) and pecan-shelling were the two main occupations of homeworkers in Texas. While hand sewing on infants' and children's wear at home was allowed but regulated under the NRA codes, pecan-shelling was an industry whose codes had no regulatory provisions for homework (U.S. Dept. of Labor 1935, 43–47).

More recently, studies and special investigations conducted at the state and federal levels reveal violations of homework statutes for both legal (certified) and illegal homework operations. For Illinois, labor law enforcement data collected between 1977 and 1981 reveal the extent to which standard enforcement procedures fail to uncover labor law violations for homework while special investigations tend to uncover significant violations. Though the number of homework violations uncovered yearly was relatively constant for 1977 through 1979 (with 33, 74, and 37 violations respectively), a large jump in the number of violations was reported for 1980 (395 violations). The large number for 1980 reflects the greater effectiveness of enforcement for that fiscal year. Between June and August of 1979 the Illinois Department of Labor undertook a special project to investigate legal homework operations, (those licensed under the state's homework law). Out of 162 licensed establishments investigated, 41 were found in violation of one or more labor laws, including 395 violations of the industrial homework law, 315 violations of the state's minimum-wage law, one violation of the child labor law, 40 violations of the Wage Payment and Collections Act, and 59 violations of the Illinois Six Day Week Law (Illinois Dept. of Labor 1980, 14). In 1981, when no special investigation of homework employers took place, homework violations dropped to 62.

In a special study of industrial homework published in 1982, the New Jersey Department of Labor found labor law violations among unlicensed firms as well as certified homework employers. Out of 332 total inspections, 193 firms were found in violation of one or more labor laws. Seventy-nine of these were distributing homework without a permit to a total of 217 uncertified homeworkers. The illegal homework operations also accounted for 126 wage-related violations, 32 child labor violations, and 144 record-keeping violations. A month after the special investigation ended, ten additional firms were found distributing homework without permits to a total of 162 uncertified homeworkers (New Jersey Dept. of Labor 1982, 30).[17] In New York State, a study of working conditions in the garment industry revealed that out of 101 manufacturing plants inspected in 1980 in response to a variety of complaints, which represented 1.4 percent of apparel manufacturing establishments on record in the state, violations of the homework statute were found in 33 (New York State Dept. of Labor 1982a, 14).

On the federal level, controversy over the Reagan Administration's rollback of homework regulations under the Fair Labor Standards Act focused attention not only on the Department of Labor's poor enforcement practices but also on the high incidence of labor law violations among firms actually inspected during the 1980s. After rescinding the FLSA ban on homework in the knitted outerwear industry in 1984, the administration developed a certification program that would allow employers in that industry to hire homeworkers as long as they maintained handbooks to record hours worked, wages paid, the number of pieces issued and returned, a description of the article and operation, and the date the work was issued and returned. The stated objective of the program was to ensure that homework operations took place in accordance with labor laws. As of April 1986, investigations of certified knitted outerwear employers under the new program revealed that approximately three-fourths of those investigated (27 out of 35) were found in violation of one or more of the FLSA recordkeeping requirements (U.S. House of Representatives 1987, 63).

Contradictory Policies Among State Agencies

The regulatory difficulties stemming from an uneven system of homework legislation in the United States are compounded by the contradictory perspectives and policies of state agencies that play a role in governing labor-capital relations, establishing taxation policies, and determining appropriate locations for business and industrial activities. Accordingly, whether or not home-based work is "legal" depends on different and often contradictory regulations governed by local, state, and federal agencies. On the local level, zoning laws often contain provisions pertaining to home occupations and may prohibit specific activities or establish conditions under which work in the home can be done. Since zoning laws tend to focus on protecting neighborhoods from disruptive activities such as noise and traffic, it is likely that much home-based work never comes to the attention of zoning enforcement officers. Nevertheless, an example of a zoning law that has affected otherwise unobtrusive kinds of home-based work is a Chicago ordinance that prohibits the use of electrical equipment in a home occupation. The author of a "work-at-home sourcebook" for prospective home-based workers points out that Chicago's law "means no calculators, no typewriters, no computers." She sees this zoning restriction as one of many "outdated zoning laws around the country" and informs the reader that the "city council in Chicago is working on a new ordinance that will be more accommodating to home work" (Arden 1992, 5).

The variability of zoning laws makes it difficult to generalize about their overall effects on homework. In the case of labor and taxation laws, however, we can identify more salient issues that are being debated and resolved (often in the courts) across the nation. Most importantly, disagreements about the definition of the employer-employee relationship illustrate how competing perspectives and agendas of state agencies have affected homework.

In their study of garment industry homework, Fernandez-

Kelly and Garcia (1989) point out that the definition of the
employer-employee relationship in California Department of Industrial Relations statutes differs from the definition used by the
Internal Revenue Service. At issue is the distinction between
"employee" and "independent contractor." While the Department of Industrial Relations has a "straightforward definition" of
employee ("anyone hired to perform any kind of service in exchange for a wage or a salary"), the IRS has a more complex
classification scheme. For the IRS, there are two types of employees—"common law" and "statutory" employees. The ability to
classify homeworkers as "statutory" employees brings IRS rules
into conflict with the labor code. Statutory workers do not fit the
precise definition of a "common law" employee. Instead, "[t]hey
are self-employed individuals providing services for payment
outside of an established place of work, but their condition as
employees (different from that of the self-employed or independent contractors) has been determined by statute, generally issued
by courts of justice examining class actions" (Fernandez-Kelly
and Garcia, 1989, 256). Following IRS rules, homework is legal
even though labor laws may classify it as illegal work. Accordingly, Fernandez-Kelly and Garcia conclude that the technical
distinctions between different types of "employees" made by the
IRS for tax purposes "opens a loophole allowing employers to
circumvent bans on homework" (256).

The contradictory statutes of taxation, business, and labor law
were also at the heart of the legal battles over application of New
York State labor codes to electronics industry homework in the
mid-1980s. Moreover, disputes regarding the meaning of the labor
code's definition of "employee" complicated the issue. To begin
with, the workers I interviewed were advised by homework distributors to obtain a certificate to do business (a DBA), which,
under the general business laws of the state, identifies them as an
"independent business entity" that can enter into contracts. According to a lawyer who represented homework distributors,
"homeworkers who wanted to be independent contractors would
want to file one of these" (Interview 46). Indeed, homeworkers
believed that obtaining a DBA assured their status as independent
contractors. At the same time, state labor law defined industrial
homework in terms of an employer-employee relationship. In its
actions against homework distributors, the Labor Department
argued that home-based electronics assemblers were employees;
thus their work violated the industrial homework law as well as
minimum-wage and hours regulations.

According to the chief attorney for the Industrial Board of Appeals, the Board's decision to overrule the Labor Department's application of its industrial homework law in one case (*Jesek Industries, Inc. v. Commissioner of Labor*) was justified by the argument that the distributor had "a long-standing operation," and had "established that his workers were independent contractors over a long period of time" because he required that they obtain business certificates, did not supervise them, and made sure that they used 1099 forms to pay income taxes. At the same time, in another case (*DK Electronics Assembly, Inc. v. Commissioner of Labor*), the homework distributor was found to be in violation of the industrial homework law because "she couldn't establish independent contractor status" for her workers since they applied for business certificates "after the case was brought to proceeding." According to the IBA lawyer, the IBA's view was that "it wasn't an established practice." The IBA lawyer also stated that in the latter case, the IBA "had established that there was control" by the distributor over workers (Interview 44).

The different rulings in these two cases puzzled me because I had interviewed both distributors and workers each employed. I could see no difference at all in the way the two operations were set up or in the work process, method and manner of payment, and degree of control and supervision (see chapter 2 for my descriptions of each). These cases reveal the subjectivity involved in interpreting legal statutes as well as the contradictory outcomes of different regulations. The state's general business law used different criteria to determine employee and independent contractor status, which, in turn, conflicted with industrial homework statutes as well as unemployment insurance law.[18]

The Effect of State Policy on the Organization of Homework

In addition to considering state response to the proliferation of homework, it is equally important to view the state as an actor in the shaping of homework as a production option. For example, state policy can create conditions conducive to the birth or revival of homework. It also can affect the structure of homework operations, especially its spatial organization and its characteristics vis-à-vis existing employment standards.

The development of protective legislation to regulate the relations between labor and capital in the United States has played a role in creating conditions for the expansion of home-work during key periods. Kessler-Harris (1982) draws a distinc-tion between two broad categories of protective legislation. "The first kind of labor legislation aimed to preserve the worker's independence by providing safe and clean working conditions, minimizing health hazards, putting a floor under wages, shorten-ing hours, and eventually by compensating workers for job-related accidents" (Kessler-Harris 1982, 180). In some instances, particu-larly at the onset of such legislation, employers turned to home-work as a way of avoiding new restrictions. For example, Miller (1941) points out that widespread violations of the industrial homework provisions of the Fair Labor Standards Act after its passage indicates that the act itself may have led to increased use of homework in some industries. Some employers saw homework as a loophole for evasion of the FLSA and "were capitalizing on the recognized difficulty of enforcing the wage and hour provi-sions as they effected homeworkers" (Miller 1941, 47). Similarly, passage of labor laws in New York State during the 1920s to regulate hours and conditions of female and child employment encouraged the decentralization of hand-sewing and resulted in the farming out of work to homeworkers in states with less restrictive regulations. The New York garment district sent such work to Texas, Connecticut, New Jersey, and Pennsylvania before and during the Depression (Blackwelder 1989, 79).

It is interesting to note that protective legislation had a similar effect on homework in Britain and France at the turn of the century. In 1908 the British government's Select Committee on Homework stated that

> the imposition by law of conditions and obligations upon owners and occupiers of factories and workshops tends to encourage employers to resort to Home Work in order to avoid compliance with the requirements of Parliament and the visits and supervision of the inspectors who are appointed to enforce them. The more numerous and strin-gent these regulations become the greater is the tempta-tion to evade them by employing persons who work under conditions to which they do not apply. (Quoted in Pen-nington and Westover 1989, 107)

In France, turn-of-the-century legislation that limited the working day for women and children in all enterprises except "family workshops" caused homework to flourish (Boxer 1986). In the 1930s, limitation of the working day to 40 hours and the introduction of paid holidays for factory workers is said to have spurred a revival of homework in France at that time (Paulin 1938).

A second type of protective legislation provided a more indirect, though no less significant, impetus to the use of homework. Restrictive or prohibitive laws, aimed at excluding some workers from certain jobs "applied almost exclusively to women." The jobs they covered "might be defined by the time and place where they were performed or by the nature of the task" (Kessler-Harris, 1982 181). By adopting such laws and effectively barring women from certain kinds of employment, the state played a primary role in marginalizing women workers and institutionalizing their secondary status in the labor market. "Protective labor legislation divided workers into those who could and could not perform certain roles. It therefore bears some of the responsibility for successfully institutionalizing women's labor force position" (Kessler-Harris 1982, 181). The position women have occupied on the labor market, marked by limited job opportunities, low pay, and conditions incompatible with household and childcare responsibilities has, in turn, created a supply of female labor willing to accept homework as an employment option. This has undoubtedly played a role in employer decisions to use homework.

In addition to creating conditions that can lead to a birth or revival of homework, state policy can contribute to homework's decline. The adoption of homework legislation, if adequately enforced, can lead to a reduction in this type of work since employers may be deprived of the main incentives for hiring homeworkers. In view of my previous argument that problems with enforcement have plagued homework legislation in the United States, it seems plausible to assert that this has not been the general tendency. Furthermore, while some homework operations may have been curtailed through legislation, it is more likely that the wider effect of homework laws has been to alter the structure of homework (in terms of spatial distribution and organization of production) as employers developed new strategies to escape regulatory controls.

With regard to spatial distribution, the unevenness of state-level regulation has fostered the concentration of homework in states without homework laws or with relatively weak ones (Blackwelder 1989; Derber 1959; Miller 1941). Moreover, employers sometimes transferred operations from urban to rural areas in response to legislation since they assumed rural families would be less likely to be aware of rights under the Fair Labor Standards Act (Derber 1959, 11). In recent years, the overseas transfer of homework operations from the United States has accompanied continued interstate transfer of such work to escape regulation. In the early 1980s, enforcement of New York's homework law against employers in the electronics industry caused the movement of operations to developing countries such as India, Sri Lanka, and Haiti.

The state's influence on the organization of production in homework operations can be seen in the development of the contractor or middleman to mediate between employers and workers. As Benson points out for the jewelry and lace industries in Rhode Island, government intervention played a role in shaping the organization of homework in the 1930s. "Rhode Island homeworkers had long dealt with factories directly, but as the government required employers to impose certain conditions on homeworkers and to police their compliance, manufacturers turned to contractors as intermediaries" (Benson 1989, 58). Although contracting via middlemen existed in some industries before the New Deal, employer response to homework legislation may have strengthened this organizational tendency.

The response of homeworkers to government legislation has similarly affected the organization of production in homework operations. Out of fear for their jobs, workers have upheld a "conspiracy of silence" to prevent enforcement of laws that might undermine employer incentives to continue hiring homeworkers. Accordingly, homeworkers have been willing to keep their work a secret and accept terms dictated solely by their employers (Pennington and Westover 1989). This has allowed most homework employers to keep their operations considerably below prevailing labor standards.

Finally, government legislation has institutionalized a split between legal and illegal homework operations—each with differing organizational traits. In industries where homework is prohibited by state or federal statutes, there has been a tendency for such work to be pushed "underground." This is especially true of the needlework industries for which homework prohibitory orders were issued under the federal Fair Labor Standards Act and some state homework laws. Continued demand for a cheap, flexible workforce for labor-intensive operations and unfavorable labor market conditions for poor, urban women fueled the maintenance of a relatively permanent base of illegal homework which has continued into the current period. The conditions associated with such work fall far below prevailing labor standards.

In contrast, where homework was regulated but not prohibited by legislation, there emerged a relatively small amount of homework carried out in accordance with labor standards. In such cases employers typically followed the permit procedures put in place by homework laws, thus registering their operations with the authorities. For example, comparing studies of homeworkers in Pennsylvania before and after New Deal legislation, Sayin (1945) concluded that the "pitiful conditions" identified with homework in the earlier study had disappeared by the 1940s. The postlegalization study discovered better wages, working conditions, and sanitary and health conditions among homeworkers than the earlier study revealed. Child labor had also been significantly reduced.[19]

Nevertheless, evidence indicates that the establishment of legal homework operations in conformance with labor standards was by no means a predominant trend. Studies such as Sayin's (1945), while describing improvements in "legal" homework cannot account for the proportion of homework operations that may have been pushed underground by homework laws. In addition, as discussed earlier, studies reveal significant violations of labor laws even among registered homework operations (Illinois Dept. of Labor 1980; New Jersey Dept. of Labor 1982; U.S. House of Representatives 1987). It is likely that homework laws created a small subset of homework in compliance with labor laws while remaining powerless to curtail the much greater incidence of illegal homework in violation of prevailing labor standards. Furthermore, due to the uneven character of homework legislation across industries and geographical space, the state must be seen as playing a determining role in shaping the character of the split between legal and illegal homework.

Finally, the state has affected the organization of homework through its influence on the public perception of such work. By defining the "homework problem" in a particular way, the state has set a context in which certain types of homework are generally perceived as outside the realm of legislative concern. This has become especially relevant in recent years in view of considerable public support for the rollback of New Deal homework legislation.

First of all, existing homework legislation implies that most homework takes place in the manufacturing sector. Recent research has shown, however, that homework is used in diverse industries (Dangler 1989; Silver 1989). The focus of legislation on manufacturing industries such as the needlework trades has reinforced the common perception that the "homework problem" is specific to a limited group of traditional homework industries and has furthered the notion that attempts to enforce existing laws in nontraditional areas is unreasonable. For example, New York State Department of Labor efforts to enforce its homework law outside of the garment industry during the 1980s were met with widespread accusations that the state's law was no longer justified and that the Labor Department was simply "going through the motions" without looking at present day situations or simply "dusting off an antiquated statute that was passed to end the so-called 'sweatshop' abuses of a bygone era" (Baden 1981; Burg 1986). In national debates over the Reagan Administration's rescission of the Fair Labor Standards Act Prohibitory Orders, proponents of homework played on the public perception that the poor working conditions associated with homework when the orders were issued were no longer prevalent in the 1980s, and certainly were not a factor in other homework industries (U.S. House of Representatives 1987, 291).

Aside from its role in defining the "homework problem" in limited terms, the state's consistent underrepresentation of this type of work has reinforced the view that exploitative homework is an anachronism in the modern economy and, thus, that there is no need for legislative control. Since the 1930s, government efforts to keep an accurate account of homeworkers and homework employers have been plagued by systematic problems. In a 1935 report, the Women's Bureau of the U.S. Department of Labor concluded that "all statements of numbers employed at home work are rough guesses" (U.S. Dept. of Labor 1935, 15). Citing census data that counted "the number of homes in which the home maker is gainfully employed in the home," the report concluded that in "at least 77,000 homes, scattered over 48 states, the home maker, assisted by members of her family, was employed with some regularity by industry in 1930." This figure was seen by the Women's Bureau as a minimum number since "not all the women doing dressmaking or laundering are in business for themselves in the home," and because the census counted the number of homes where work is done but not the number of homeworkers employed. According to the report, it is difficult to get an accurate count of homeworkers because there is no way to determine if family members assist homeworkers whose work is recorded through the employer. In addition "[w]hen the work is handled by contractors, records are not available concerning home-worker personnel." Finally, it was pointed out in the report that in states that require the registration or licensing of any homes where work is done, employers can overcount homeworkers by listing those they may give work to rather than those to whom work is actually given (U.S. Dept. of Labor 1935, 15).

Another basis for estimates of homework during the 1930s were the Federal Wage and Hour Division's records of firms requesting handbooks for homeworkers. Between March 1939 and September 1940, 1477 firms in 38 states requested handbooks for recordkeeping, reporting 45,470 homeworkers. Based on the fact that approximately 47 percent of these firms were from New York State (accounting for 50 percent of the homeworkers reported), Miller (1941) concluded that these figures were underestimates. In her view, the fact that most states did not require employers to report homeworkers to state authorities was an underlying factor in the difficulty of compiling accurate national statistics at the time. Moreover, even states with reporting systems had problems keeping an accurate count of homeworkers since

> many factors inherent in the home work system operate against the compiliation of accurate and complete data. The seasonal nature of homework industries, the constant shifting of home workers from firm to firm and from industry to industry, the fact that home work is a family occupation with an unknown number of persons employed in each household, the concealment of child labour, the presence of manufacturers who operate without permits, the influx of home work from other States, the recognised deficiencies in the employers' reports, all tend to reduce the value of available data. (47)

Serious questions about the accuracy of government statistics on homework during the 1930s are raised by Benson's (1989) analysis of the raw data collected for a 1935 Women's Bureau Report on Industrial Homework in Rhode Island (Byrne and Blair 1935). According to Benson, the raw data "offer an unusually vivid picture of the competing agendas of reformers, industrialists, and homeworkers during this critical period." The report was written as a response to the failure of the lace industry's NRA code to outlaw homework. In addition to the lace industry, four industries that had NRA codes banning homework—artificial flowers, tags, garters, and jewelry—were also covered in the report. Although prohibitions were not yet in effect for the first three when data were being collected for the Women's Bureau study, the homework ban for jewelry was in operation. While homework in the jewelry industry was found by the researchers despite the prohibition, no mention of it appeared in the final report.

Although the raw data contain interviews with ten jewelry homeworkers, Byrne and Blair maintained in the published report that they had found no jewelry homework and ignored that industry—whether to highlight the lace industry, to protect the homeworkers, or to give the impression that homework could be successfully outlawed. Margaret Ackroyd and Anna Tucker, who administered the state regulation of homework after the NRA was declared unconstitutional, affirmed that jewelry homework thrived despite its extralegal status, so that the focus on the lace industry and the omission of the jewelry industry seriously distorts the overall picture of homework in Rhode Island. (Benson 1989, 56)

While there was little systematic data collection on homework during the 1940s and '50s, the 1960s saw an improvement with the decennial census' enumeration of people who "work at home." Analyzing census data as well as recent data from other government sources such as the Bureau of Labor Statistics, Silver (1989) points out that official statistics show that homework "is declining over time, both absolutely and relatively. The data from the 1960, 1970, and 1980 censuses indicate that the number of those who worked primarily at home fell from 4.7 million to 2.2 million over the two decades. If farmers are excluded, the total fell from 2.3 million in 1960 to 1.5 million twenty years later" (Silver 1989, 109).

In assessing the validity of census data with regard to homework, a number of limitations become apparent. As Silver points out, when people answer the question about means of transportation to work (with work at home as a possible response), they refer "only to their principal place of work in their primary job during the week surveyed." Accordingly, the census' tabulation of those who work at home excludes moonlighters and those who may bring work home from the office or factory intermittently. In addition, those who work less than 15 hours a week are not counted (Silver 1989, 109).

Furthermore, census data have been criticized for their omission of illegal homeworkers. In response to this shortcoming, there is a growing literature that incorporates information from a variety of sources to estimate how much these statistics miss. Though such evidence is sketchy, it reveals important discrepancies between national data and known realities about homework.

In the context of the Reagan Administration's effort to eliminate federal homework bans in seven "traditional" homework industries, estimates of illegal homework emerged from special state investigations, labor unions, journalists and other interested groups to challenge census and Bureau of Labor Statistics figures. In testimony given before the House of Representatives Subcommittee on Labor Standards in 1986, Susan Meisinger, the U.S. Department of Labor's Deputy Under Secretary for Employment Standards, compared 1980 census data and Bureau of Labor Statistics data for homework in the six industries for which FLSA homework bans were still in place at the time. While the 1980 census reported 8,711 homeworkers in these industries, a 1985 BLS study revealed an upper limit of 122,000 homeworkers (Horvath 1986). Meisinger reported that the Department of Labor took the position that "the actual number of homeworkers currently employed in the six restricted industries is closer to the lower of the cited figures (8,711) since that figure was derived from the much larger sample universe used in the decennial census" (U.S. House of Representatives 1987, 35). The Department of Labor settled on an estimate of 10,000 homeworkers nationwide in the six industries.

Such discrepancies in estimates demonstrate the Department of Labor's inability to accurately pinpoint the actual number of people engaged in homework. Estimates from other sources reveal the likelihood that the census undercounts homework by a wide margin and that the Labor Department based its decision to rescind six of the homework bans on erroneous assumptions.[20] For example, at the 1986 hearings, testimony from state officials, employers' associations, labor unions, and journalists revealed significantly higher estimates than the federal government's figure of 10,000 homeworkers overall in the six restricted industries. New York State enforcement personnel involved in a special apparel unit estimated that there are 15,000 homeworkers annually in the apparel industry in New York City alone (U.S. House of Representatives 1987, 64). In addition, the Florida Needle Trades Association estimated between 4,000 and 7,000 homeworkers in their state, based on research that involved computer searches and blind newspaper ads. With regard to the jewelry industry, the Service Employees International Union testified that homework is prevalent in the costume jewelry industry in New England states such as Rhode Island. It was claimed that aside from the 10,000 jewelry workers who are unionized, 40,000 to 50,000, many of whom work in small shops where homework is often given out, are unorganized (U.S. House of Representatives

1987, 244). These assertions received support in earlier estimates
of jewelry homework. After a 1981 investigation, the *Providence
Journal* concluded that there were between 1,000 and 2,000
homeworkers in Rhode Island supplementing the work done by
30,000 jewelry factory workers. This estimate did not take account
of factory workers who take work home (U.S. House of Representatives 1987, 246).

Putting each of these estimates together reveals a much larger
number of homeworkers in the six restricted industries than the
Labor Department's estimate of 10,000. Jay Mazur, president of
the International Ladies' Garment Workers Union, claimed that
homeworkers in these industries probably number between
75,000 and 100,000 (U.S. House of Representatives 1987, 65).

In sum, government estimates have given us, at best, a minimum accounting of homework nationwide. The systematic under-
estimation of homework characteristic of both state-level and
federal statistics has contributed to the marginalization of the
"homework problem" and, in recent years, has served as a justification for the rollback of New Deal homework legislation.

Conclusion

In this chapter I have tried to show that the state has been a key
actor in the shaping of homework as a production option in the
twentieth century economy. In particular, the form and content
of government regulation have influenced the spatial distribution
of homework as well as the way homework production has been
organized. State intervention in the homework controversy derives from the state's need to mediate conflicts between labor and
capital with a view toward its conflicting interests—the maintenance of adequate levels of production and consumption. As the
struggle between capital and labor over homework developed,
class interests became organized and expressed at the level of the
state. At the same time, state interests in production, consumption, and its own political legitimacy were injected into the arena
of class conflict. The result has been an uneven and largely
ineffective system of government regulation that has succeeded
in minimizing the homework problem by institutionalizing a split
between legal and illegal homework operations and, in effect,
limiting regulation to a relatively small number of industries.

The case of electronics industry homework in central New
York illustrates the contradictory elements of state policy. As a

"nontraditional" homework industry, it raises questions about the applicability of existing homework statutes. In addition, recent court cases involving electronics homeworkers have illustrated the conflict among various government agencies over the legal status of home-based workers.

7

Conclusion

One of the most challenging aspects of my research has been to understand what makes homeworkers in central New York unique as well as to identify the common thread that joins their lives to the lives of homeworkers throughout the world-economy. As a starting point in my effort to meet this challenge, I set out to reveal the historical and theoretical dimensions of homework's role in modern capitalism. My objective was to counter the conventional view that homework is an anomaly in the modern world-economy and to demonstrate instead that it is an integral and growing part of contemporary capitalism. I argued that the origins of homework—its emergence out of previous forms of domestic labor such as putting-out and its coexistence with centralized factory production since the mid-ninteenth century—reveal its place in the historical development of capitalism and its viable use in a range of industries across time and geographical space. In theoretical terms, homework's compatibility with modern capitalism is demonstrated through reassessment of Marxian labor process theory and analysis of the persistence of diverse production relations in the world-economy, such as those described within the framework of informal sector analysis. In addition, homework's structural (as opposed to conjunctural) nature is revealed by the sustained pattern of its use over time. The recurrence of conditions that support its use and the persistent use of female labor for homework operations across time, geographical space, and industries testify to the permanence of its status as a production option for capitalist enterprise. These factors lend support to the view that homework is a structural feature of capitalism that derives from the confluence of women's contradictory role as laborers in the sphere of paid production and unpaid workers in the sphere of reproduction.

The implications of this view are relevant to an understanding of the lives of central New York homeworkers. An analysis of their role in a system of global production and the structural basis of the capital-labor relation of which they are a part is necessary for an understanding of the objective constraints they face on the labor market and the parameters of their "choice" to do homework. Furthermore, the political implications of the two dichotomous views of contemporary homework (anomalous versus integral) differ markedly. Conservative policy prescriptions, which call for the elimination of homework regulations and the expansion of government certification of legal homework, have been advanced in the context of a consistent effort to minimize the homework problem in terms of the number of workers and the range of industries involved. On the other side of the debate, opponents of homework recognize the deep-rootedness of the homework problem and see it as a permanent feature of modern capitalism, capable of expansion.

Key Actors in the Homework Debate

During the initial stages of my research, it became apparent that capital, organized labor, the state, and homeworkers themselves each played a significant role in forming the contours of the homework system in the United States. I have tried to elucidate the interplay of these "actors" by examining their differing interests and the contradictory outcomes of their pursuit of those interests.

From capital's point of view homework is a production option used to lower labor and overhead costs, increase flexibility, and avoid unions. At the same time, homework is a creative strategy used by workers to expand their employment options and meet the difficult task of combining paid work with household responsibilities and childcare. Accordingly, the relationship of the recent expansion of homework to crisis conditions in the world-economy can be understood in the following way. Capital's search for cheaper and more flexible forms of labor since the mid-1960s has led to industrial restructuring that often involves the adoption of decentralized production arrangements such as homework. At the same time, as crisis conditions reduce employment opportunities for workers, further constraints are placed on women in the home and on the labor market. The set of accumulation processes that operate during crisis create homework and the need for women to accept it. Thus, homework can be understood as deriving from the interplay of the responses of both capital and labor to crisis conditions. Neither exclusively motivated by capital nor exclusively motivated by labor, the recent expansion of homework is best explained by certain features of the contemporary world-economy that have given rise to conditions that make homework an attractive option for both.

While the impetus behind the spread of homework in the modern economy can be traced to the intersection of capital's and labor's needs, the state plays an important role in defining the institutional bounds for the realization of those needs. I argued in chapter 6 that the state has played a key role in shaping the organization of homework in the United States. The form and content of government regulation has influenced the spatial distribution of homework and the organization of production in homework industries. At the same time, the unevenness of homework legislation across states, its focus on specific industries, and its inadequate enforcement provisions have influenced the pattern of homework's use. The state's role in the development of homework emerges as class interests become organized and expressed at the level of the state and as the latter's own interests are injected into the arena of class conflict.

For homeworkers, the contradictory aspects of state intervention highlight their dilemma as workers who need work but also need to have their basic rights safeguarded. The state, however, has failed to act according the the real needs and interests of homeworkers. Accepting the parameters of the existing gender division of labor, and acting more in tune with the interests of capital, organized labor, and social reformers (at least at one particular period), state action has sidestepped the homework problem at best. This is clearly illustrated by the fact that the thrust of state efforts to "protect" homeworkers (in response to pressure from organized labor) has centered on eliminating homework jobs without proposing alternatives for the displaced workers. The latter, of course, would require a fundamental rethinking of state policy as it affects the gender division of labor in and out of the home.

Political Implications

While the actions of capital, organized labor, and the state with regard to homework reveal a sustained logic based on the interests of each, the limitations of their policy proposals are reflected in their continued failure to confront the inherent contradictions of home-based work, namely the conflict between production and reproduction and waged and nonwaged work in capitalist society. Until there is a fundamental change in the relations between home and work, conventional solutions to the homework problem continue to miss the point of the true dilemma facing women homeworkers.

Serious efforts to bring an end to exploitative homework must inevitably reach beyond policy prescriptions that take for granted the continued subordination of women in the household and the external economy. Accordingly, a solution to the homework problem depends on the transformation of both gender and labor-capital relations. As Boris and Daniels aptly put it, "the solution to the homework problem will not be simple: like the achievement of gender equality, it will require the transformation of both the workplace and the home and an end to the devaluation of 'women's work.' Until we redefine the terms of the debate on homework, there will be no easy answers" (9). While the kind of transformation Boris and Daniels propose is not within our immediate grasp, we can evaluate policy suggestions regarding homework with an eye toward whether or not they hamper or further our ultimate goal to restructure the gender division of labor and the organization of work in capitalist society.

The debate over homework in the United States has been framed primarily in terms of polarized views. One, associated with the political right, calls for the elimination of legislative restrictions on homework while the other, associated with organized labor, seeks to prohibit homework by expanding legislative controls. Analysis of the policy suggestions advanced by each reveals that this debate misses the point of the homework problem.

The conservative agenda of the Reagan Administration was invoked in the successful effort to repeal six of the Fair Labor Standards Act Prohibitory Orders, which had banned homework in specific industries since the 1940s. That effort, spearheaded by noted antilabor politicians such as Republican Senator Orin Hatch, was supported by conservative organizations such as the Center on National Labor Policy (a public-interest law firm and coalition of business groups) and the National Right-to-Work Committee. The activities of these organizations included an aggressive mail campaign aimed to convince the Department of Labor to remove federal homework restrictions. For example, of

500 letters received by the DOL in 1986, 305 (or 64 percent) "could by letterhead or language be directly attributed to these two organizations" (U.S. House of Representatives, 1987 312). This is significant in view of the fact that the Department of Labor justified its removal of homework restrictions in terms of "enormous public interest," demonstrated by the receipt of these unsolicited letters.

The crux of the Reagan Administration's position on homework was the contention that rescinding homework bans would bring this type of work out from "underground," thereby encouraging employees to report labor law violations. The absurdity of this position, demonstrated in the Labor Department's failure to safeguard labor standards in legal homework operations since the 1940s, reveals the relationship of this policy to the broader effort to cheapen labor and inhibit unionization. In addition, in its rationale for deregulating homework, the Reagan Administration implicitly advocated a return to the home for working mothers, focusing on homeworkers' "preference" to remain at home. In the words of Susan Meisinger, Department of Labor Deputy Under Secretary for Employment Standards under Reagan, many people prefer homework to factory work for a variety of personal reasons:

> These reasons include the desire to be at home to care for their children; a desire to avoid the costs of employment outside the home including child care, clothing, transportation, and meals; a lack of transportation or difficulty in commuting to a factory; a desire to work part time and/or to be able to set their own work schedules, or simply a lack of suitable jobs in the area. These individuals not only prefer to work at home, but consider the ability to work at home their right. (U.S. House of Representatives 1987, 8)

This summary of the reasons women prefer homework accepts as given the gender division of labor in the home, the absence of adequate childcare, and a limited labor market for women workers. Thus, in addition to creating the conditions for an increase in exploitative homework, the federal government's right-to-work policy for homeworkers leaves the root of the homework problem firmly planted.

The political right's effort to encourage the spread of homework has received support from those who see home-based work as part of an economic trend which favors self-help, entrepreneurship, and individualism. For example, organizations such as the

National Alliance for Home-based Businesswomen and Women Working Home, Inc. promote homework as an alternative for people who no longer want to participate in large organizations or whose employment options are limited. They see homework legislation as inhibiting the individual's right to work where and how he or she chooses.

> Modern industrial society has reached a point where many people no longer want to participate in large organizations. They have realized that individual effort is what built this country and will continue to maintain its greatness in a changing world.
>
> The true voice of the new work force is not the plea for Big Brother's smothering blanket of protection; it is the voice of free Americans just wanting the chance to work as they please and where they please, whether as employees or entrepreneurs. (Behr and Behr 1984)

Missing from the analysis offered by Behr and Behr is a recognition of the realities of exploitative homework. While they acknowledge that there are problems ("secret, illegal alien workers," for example) they offer simplistic solutions ("we will have to have Federal immigration laws to deal with that"). More to the point, however, the entrepreneurialism they offer is little more than an empty promise for most workers. As Karen Nussbaum, president of 9 to 5, the National Association of Working Women, points out, it is difficult to define what an entrepreneur is:

> ultimately, entrepreneurialism is a class distinction. Home work is a completely different story depending on your income. For the prefessionals who, by the nature of their work, make good money, it's a boon. But for the low-paid, lower-level worker, primarily the female clerical worker who is now being slated for home work, entrepreneurialism is just a fancy word for the kind of working conditions we tried to get away from a hundred years ago—piecework in the home. One of the reasons people choose to do home work is that they can't afford good child care; and this means that many women are doing two jobs at home, their regular work plus child care. (quoted in Louv 1983, 211)

Accordingly, the perception of homework as a reflection of successful entrepreneurialism fails to acknowledge the realities of most home-based work and the oppressive conditions that create it.

At the other end of the spectrum, organized labor has called for the complete elimination of homework through the extension of anti-homework legislation. Labor leaders see homework as exploitative because it leads to the widespread violation of labor laws and is often used to weaken or bust unions. For the most part, unions in the United States see homeworkers as unorganizable, and see elimination of homework through legislation as the only solution to the homework problem. Here too, the proposed remedy evades the root of the problem. As Daniels points out,

> history shows that attempts to prohibit homework entirely do not address the reasons why women engage in homework in the first place. Now, as in the past, homeworkers often side with the conservative manufacturers and legislators who defend their right to remain at home. Social advocates and union organizers meet with hostility from homeworkers whose options are limited by a workplace incompatible with the needs of working mothers.(1989, 13)

More innovative policy suggestions focus on the need to transform the objective conditions that limit women's options in the home and the workplace. For example, Christensen (1988) argues that "any federal approach to home-based work would be well-served to situate homework within the broader health, family, and business issues rather than focusing on it as an isolated, unique work phenomenon" (1988, 204). She focuses on policy that could improve the position of all workers on the labor market and of women in the home. Among her suggestions to bolster the former are a clarification of employee versus self-employed status and an extension of health coverage to all workers (through mandatory health benefits for part-timers and state or federally sponsored health care plans), which would eliminate one of the reasons employers seek to hire self-employed subcontractors and part-timers without benefits. In order to improve the position of women in the home and on the labor market, childcare and eldercare provisions are essential. Christensen's suggestions speak to the need for structural changes that would allow women to participate in fuller and more meaningful work experiences, whether their paid work takes place in or outside of the home (Christensen, 1993). Such changes would include alterations in the gender division of labor in the household, an end to discrimination against women in the labor market, establishment of flexible work time for all workers, and provision of high-quality, low-cost childcare.

The effort to develop a new approach to solving the homework problem would surely benefit from innovative research that recognizes the centrality of gender to the political struggles underlying the homework debate. In much of the homework literature, with the notable exception of some work (Boris, 1987), the importance of gender is recognized but no concise analysis of gender as politics is offered. For example, the centrality of gender to political struggle could be more effectively integrated into an analysis of the interplay among capital, labor, and the state in the struggle over homework legislation. Such an approach could uncover the deep-rooted obstacles to transformation of the relation between production and reproduction in capitalist society.

In short, we are still left with a large gap between the ideal of transforming the relation between waged and nonwaged work and a concrete agenda for implementing steps to realize that goal. Because homework is a particularly acute expression of this dilemma, its study offers much to the quest for a truly liberating organization of work.

Notes

Preface

1. I use the terms home-based work and homework inter-changeably, to refer generally to paid work in the home. In drawing distinctions among different types of homework I will use other, more specific terms such as waged homework, which includes industrial homework and service homework, home-based self-employment, and home-based work among salaried professionals. I use the term waged homework specifically to draw a distinction between the home-based work of employees versus the home-based work of the self-employed or independent con-tractors. The precise meaning of each will be discussed in the last section of the Introduction (chapter 1).

2. In 1984 the Reagan Administration lifted the ban on indus-trial homework in the knitted outerwear industry. In 1988 the bans on homework for gloves and mittens, embroidery, buttons and buckles, handkerchiefs, and jewelry were lifted. The prohibi-tion of homework in these industries was put into place in the 1940s under the Fair Labor Standards Act.

3. Quoted from an interview conducted in 1983 with an attorney representing a homework distributor cited for violation of New York State's homework law.

4. In addition to the 39 completed interviews, I conducted short telephone interviews with another 25 homeworkers. Nine others I contacted refused to participate in the study. The data presented in subsequent chapters are based only on the informa-tion obtained from the 39 in depth interviews.

5. I interviewed a co-owner (who was also vice-president)

and a materials manager from one firm and the owner (and president) of another. I was unable to secure an interview with a representative from the third firm, though one of the distributors I spoke to formerly worked for that firm and provided information about its homework operations.

6. The Industrial Board of Appeals is the legal body in New York State that reviews all actions of the industrial commissioner. In cases involving application of industrial homework law to the electronics industry, it is the responsibility of the Industrial Board of Appeals to decide if the commissioner has legal grounds to declare electronics industry homework illegal.

1. Introduction

1. See Baden 1981; Boris 1987; Keller 1984; *The Post Standard*, Sept. 25, 1986; U.S. House of Representatives 1982, 157–58.

2. A notable exception to the predominant union policy on homework is a formal contract to allow home-based work adopted by a local union affiliated with the American Federation of State, County, and Municipal Employees (AFSCME). In 1984, Local 2412 of the Wisconsin State Employees Union negotiated a contract with the University of Wisconsin Hospital in Madison to allow a small number of word processors to work in their homes. See Christensen (1993) for a detailed description and analysis of the agreement.

3. Boris makes this argument in her critique of liberal strategies to eliminate homework through legal prohibition. For example, she argues that ILGWU President Jay Mazur, in his focus on banning homework, failed "to address the social and cultural conditions affecting all women that make homework a solution to some women's double day. By maintaining a separation between home and work, antihomework liberals keep the home free from homework but not from the unwaged labor that is the cornerstone of power inequities between men and women" (Boris 1987, 101).

4. Other discussions of nontraditional homeworkers include Beach (1989) and Boris (1987).

5. In the chapters that follow I adhere to a distinction between the "truly self-employed" and the "disguised self-employed." The difference between the two is discussed in more detail further on in this chapter.

6. According to Silver (1989), 1980 census data show that self-employed home-based workers tend to be concentrated in agriculture, forestry and fisheries, real estate, daycare services, nonmedical professional services, business and repair services, and personal services. "Ten percent of the self-employed working at home are writers and artists, compared to only one percent of the entire labor force. They are also more likely to have executive, administrative, and managerial positions, sales jobs, and service occupations than the average American worker. They are under-represented among manual occupations, except in farming and forestry. Thus, with the exception of the nonartistic professions, home-based businesspersons are more likely to work in occupations that offer scope for initiative, creativity, and personally tailored service. Yet, they are also labor-intensive, which would account for the extraordinary work effort detected among some of the self-employed" (Silver 1989, 122).

7. As Silver (1989) points out, "the mythical nature of labor-only independent contracting has long been recognized." She summarizes the conclusions drawn in recent debates on the status of contractors in the United States and Britain: "Independent contractors are deemed to be employees if they cannot hire others, set their own hours and deadlines, profit or lose money, risk some investment, take initiative, or turn to different clients or customers. Thus, the main issues are the degree of control over the labor process and the extent of dependence on one employer who contracts only for labor, rather than on numerous clients or customers in commodity markets" (Silver 1989, 108).

2. Electronics Industry Homeworkers in Central New York

1. As mentioned briefly in the Preface, I came upon the information that led me to the network of homeworkers in central New York by chance. An organizer from the ILGWU was working in the town where I lived, Cortland, New York, during a strike at a local garment factory. He happened to write a letter to the editor in the local newspaper in response to an editorial supporting the Reagan Administration's efforts to repeal the ban on home knitting under the Fair Labor Standards Act. He mentioned the fact that he had discovered people doing electronics homework during his stay in Cortland. I contacted him and he was able to put me in touch with some of the homeworkers he had met. Through his help I gained access to the network of people doing homework for three electronics firms in the Syracuse area.

2. The small towns represented in the sample and their populations are as follows: from Madison County, Bouckville (204), Cazenovia (5,880), Clockville (182), DeRuyter (1,349), Eaton (5,182), and Morrisville (2,707); from Cortland County, Cincinnatus (1,151), Cuyler (846), and Homer (3,635); from Chenango County, Pitcher (735) and South Otselic (230); and from Onondaga County, Skaneatelus (2,789) and Spafford (1,596). The suburban areas were Liverpool (2,849) and North Syracuse (7,970), both in Onondaga County. The cities were Cortland (20,138) in Cortland County and Utica (75,632) in Oneida County (Shupe et al. 1987).

3. In seven of the 26 cases homeworkers did not reveal their incomes, but I was able to arrive at estimates based on going wage rates in their husbands' occupations. Three were production workers in local factories, one was employed by a county highway department, and one was an accountant for a local firm. In two cases where husbands were receiving social security disability benefits but exact amounts were not disclosed, I calculated their income from this source based on average monthly benefits for New York State as reported in *Statistical Abstract of the United States*, 1988, Table 566, "Social Security (OASDI)—Beneficiaries, Benefit Payments, and Average Monthly Benefits By States and Other Areas," p. 343. There were other cases where husband's occupation was given, but since I could not estimate income I did not include them in data tabulation for this section. Such cases included self-employed farmers and carpenters.

4. The following calculations are based on the yearly income of respondents in their peak years of homework activity. For example, in cases where the amount of homework done fluctuated considerably from year to year, I focused on the year/years during which it contributed most significantly to household income.

5. Seven respondents reported that their husbands had experienced long periods of being laid off. The shortest lay off period reported was four months, while the rest ranged from one to three years. Two reported that their husbands got laid off intermittently during the five years prior to the interview. Each husband totaled well over one year of time laid off.

6. In questioning homeworkers about the importance of their homework earnings, I used the exact phraseology used here. They were asked specifically whether homework was 1) the major income; 2) one of two supplementary incomes—both are essen-

tial; 3) marginal—to earn extra money. It is important to note that I am not using the word "supplementary" in such a way as to imply that this is income above some level of "necessary" income. As used here, supplementary implies that both incomes (homework and nonhomework) are equally essential to the survival of the family.

7. One respondent used part of her homework earnings to pay tuition for her children to attend a Christian Day School, while another was saving to pay her child's college tuition.

8. In her study of British homeworkers, Allen (1983) also found that homework pay was used predominantly for essential budgetary items such as food, heat, lighting, rent or mortgage, food, and clothes. Only three out of 90 respondents she interviewed said their homework earnings were used for "extras."

9. The homeworkers employed by one particular distributor reported that they were required to complete a minimum number of transformers within each two week period. They all agreed, however, that the minimum number set by the distributor was so low as to constitute a reasonable expectation of them.

10. It is important to note the high probability that the snowball sampling technique led me to homeworkers who were likely to feel satisfied with their work rather than those who were not. In fact, many of those who declined to participate in the study did so because they felt they would not have much to contribute since they didn't like the work and/or didn't stay with it very long. In addition, homeworkers I interviewed were probably more likely to give me the names of people they knew who were committed to this type of work rather than those who disliked it. Only two homeworkers in the sample indicated that they did not like the work at all and quit because they couldn't make enough money for the time they put into it.

11. It is probable that I never interviewed anyone with bad experiences with distributors because I never tapped into the subnetwork of such individuals.

12. Child labor is also a common feature of homework operations in developing countries. See Beneria and Roldan (1987, 127–30) and Rao and Hussain, (1984).

13. Since most homeworkers were aware that child labor was an important concern for the state, they might not have admitted

that their children helped them occasionally. In fact, one woman claimed to have known many people in her area who made "a lot of money doing homework" but who had family members, especially children, helping them.

14. The existence of such abusive practices has been documented by Carey and Malone (1980) and Morales (1983) for electronics industry homeworkers in Silicon Valley. For a discussion of similar practices affecting homeworkers in the developing world, see Pineda-Ofreneo (1983).

15. As mentioned earlier, homework distributors in central New York were generally viewed as trusted members of the community and usually allowed considerable flexibility in their dealings with homeworkers. For example, the homeworkers typically decided how much work they wanted to do in a given week. (Thus there were no forced quotas.) In addition, workers reported that during slack periods distributors would often go out of their way to distribute the available work evenly so no one would be without employment.

16. All homeworkers mentioned below have been given fictitious names in order to protect their anonymity.

3. Restructuring of Global Capital: An Impetus for the Spread of Homework

1. I am indebted to Joan Smith for pointing this out to me at an early stage of my research. Her insights helped me develop an understanding of the complex relationship between women's labor and capitalist accumulation strategies.

2. Some states have specified conditons that allow for the legal employment of homeworkers. For example, in New York State employers can obtain special permits for homeworkers who meet certain hardship criteria based on age, physical or mental handicap, or the need to care for an invalid at home.

3. The legal status of home-based workers has been the subject of considerable controversy. In fact, definitions of self-employment, contractor, and employee often vary among state agencies. This dilemma will be discussed more fully in chapter 6.

4. It is important to note that many subcontractors and homeworkers are not officially counted among the self-employed. Thus,

examination of data on self-employment gives us a partial picture of subcontracting trends, at best.

5. For a detailed analysis of measurement problems and available data on self employment, see the appendix, "Counting the Self-Employed" in Aronson (1991).

6. According to Fain (1980), those who are not officially counted as self-employed because their businesses are incorporated increased from 850,000 in 1967 (when first reclassified out of the self-employed category) to more than two million in 1979. Those who are self-employed in their second jobs rose by more than 28 percent between 1972 and 1980.

7. The Department of Commerce predicted in 1987 that with the closing of gasoline service stations there would be steady increases in the number of franchises that specialize in automotive repairs and services—for example, "specialized automotive centers providing service in tune-up, quick lube, muffler, transmission, brake, painting, tires, electric repairs, and general car care" (U.S. Dept. of Commerce 1987, 6).

8. This quote is from an interview I conducted on August 30, 1984.

9. Each transformer had to have the wire wrapped around the core a certain number of times and the ends of the wires had to be left a certain length. Some cores had two wires of different color, which had to be wrapped around the core together in a particular pattern. Though most workers reported that after developing sufficient skill they rarely had products rejected, many of them went through an initial period of time, which varied among respondents from a few days to a week or two, when they could not work at a steady pace without making mistakes on some of their transformers. Thus, for many homeworkers, the time spent during this "training period" was largely unremunerated.

10. This phrase is borrowed from Goldsmith (1984), who used it in reference to the effect of enterprise zones on labor standards in the United States. Goldsmith's imagery is relevant for a discussion of homework since the latter, like enterprise zones, lowers labor standards for workers in the core and puts wage rates and working conditions on a more even par with conditions in many developing countries. While researchers have documented the use of homeworkers by electronics firms in Italy, Japan, Canada, and Britain (Mattera 1980; Murray 1981; Lipsig-Mumme 1983), the

discussion below focuses on the United States because of the availability of detailed information about electronics homework operations in this country.

11. Moxon (1974) provides another way of conceptualizing what is included in the electronics industry in his delineation of three kinds of electronics products. These are consumer electronics products (televisions, radios, and so on), industrial and government electronics products, and components (resistors, tubes, semiconductors, and so on).

12. All information on the three firms discussed in this section was obtained through interviews with company managers and homework distributors.

13. Pseudonyms are used to refer to the three firms I studied.

14. Neither of the two managers I spoke to from this firm could give me an accurate count of the number of homeworkers they used, possibly because they did not deal with them directly. They simply requested a certain amount of work from their distributors, who hired as many homeworkers as needed to fill the order on a monthly basis. I arrived at an estimate of 40 based on a formula given to me by a distributor from another firm. He explained that the average homeworker could assemble, at most, 2,000 transformers a week if working on a full-time basis. In the early 1980s, the firm in question had approximately 300,000 transformers a month supplied by homeworkers. If each homeworker assembled 2,000 a week, or 8,000 a month, it would take 37.5 people to fill the company's order. Since many homeworkers did not work full-time, however, and probably did less than 2,000 per week, this is likely to be an underestimate of the number of homeworkers actually employed to meet the company's needs.

15. Benton's discussion of productive decentralization in Italy draws on the work of Brusco (1982), Sabel (1982), Capecchi (1989), and Saba (1981).

16. I obtained the following information through personal interviews with the owners of the two smaller firms discussed.

4. *Waged Homework: A Structural Feature of the Capitalist World Economy*

1. For the most part, this chapter will focus on industrial homework since it is most relevant for a historical discussion of the role of waged homework in capitalist production.

2. Benton provides a useful summary and critique of the theoretical perspectives that have emerged in recent years in an attempt to explain the coexistence of various forms of production in modern capitalism. These include scholars in "development circles" who searched for theories to account for the exclusion of vast numbers of producers from the modern industrial sector, dependency theorists, informal sector analysts, dual economy and dual labor market theorists, and those who have studied the dynamism of small firms in the context of regional economies (Benton 1990, 4–6).

3. The following discussion of Carl Bucher's work is a condensed version of a portion of my previous article in *Contemporary Crisis* (Dangler 1986, 259–62).

4. One qualification must be made here. During the nineteenth and twentieth centuries some domestic workers under the industrial homework system have owned their own tools. They include nineteenth century weavers who sometimes owned their looms, nineteenth and twentieth century garment industry homeworkers who owned sewing machines, and twentieth century knitters who purchase their own knitting machines. In fact, in twentieth century industrial and service homework operations, this practice has been interpreted as part of the reason why homework may be cost-effective for employers. Clerical telecommuters who buy their own computers, knitters who buy their own knitting machines, and sewers who buy their own sewing machines absorb the equipment costs employers would be forced to absorb for in-house operations.

5. The terms "outwork" and "homework" are often used interchangeably in the literature. Outwork is a more inclusive term, however, since it refers to any work contracted "out of" the factory, though not necessarily done in the home (Rubery and Wilkinson 1981). Workers in small workshops and other factories, as well as individual homeworkers, can be the recipients of a firm's outwork. Thus, homework is a subset of outwork; it is "outwork in domestic premises." For further clarification of the terminology typically used in writings on the subject of outwork and homework (domestic production, home production, cottage industry), see my previous article (Dangler 1986, 258).

6. According to Marx, the relative surplus population takes these forms: the floating, the latent, and the stagnant. The portion he designates as floating includes laborers in the "centres of

modern industry—factories, manufactures, ironworks, mines, etc." who are "sometimes repelled, sometimes attracted again in greater masses, the number of those employed increasing on the whole, although in a constantly decreasing proportion to the scale of production" (Marx 1967, 641). The latent surplus population emerges "as capitalist production takes possession of agriculture. . . . Part of the agricultural population is therefore constantly on the point of passing over into an urban or manufacturing proletariat, and on the look-out for circumstances favourable to this transformation. (Manufacture is used here in the sense of all non-agricultural industries.) This source of relative surplus-population is thus constantly flowing. But the constant flow towards the towns presupposes, in the country itself, a constant latent surplus-population, the extent of which becomes evident only when its channels of outlet open to exceptional width" (Marx 1967, 642).

7. Bythell recognizes that outwork is not always done on domestic premises. Still, he uses the term "outwork" when he refers specifically to domestic outwork. I prefer to substitute the term "industrial homework" for outwork, but I will use his terminology when quoting or paraphrasing his work. I believe the "outwork" Bythell describes corresponds to "industrial homework" as I have defined it. For a more extension discussion of Bythell's work, see my previous article (Dangler 1986).

8. In 1907, for example, a total of 105,633 homeworkers were registered in England and Wales, the majority of whom were employed in the wearing apparel, lace, and paper bags and boxes industries (Bythell 1978, 147).

9. Hakim and Dennis (1982) report that the British population censuses of 1901, 1911, and 1921 included questions to identify people working in their homes and that between 1901 and 1921 the number of homeworkers recorded by the census declined from 540,000 to 250,000 (from 3.8 percent to 1.4 percent of the labor force) (9).

10. See the National Board for Prices and Income (1969), Commission on Industrial Relations (1974), Commission on Industrial Relations (1973), Advisory, Conciliation and Arbitration Service (1978), and Cragg and Dawson (1981).

11. See the Advisory, Conciliation and Arbitration Service (1978), Allen (1983), Australia-Asia Worker Links (1982), Baud (1984) and (1987), Beach (1989a, 1989b), Beneria and Roldan

(1987), Benson (1989), Brown (1974), Carey and Malone (1980), Commission on Industrial Relations (1973) and (1974), Cragg and Dawson (1981), Dangler (1989), Derber (1959), Edwards and Founders (1976), Fernandez-Kelly and Garcia (1989), Hakim (1980), Hakim and Dennis (1982), International Ladies' Garment Workers Union (1981), Lipsig-Mumme (1983) and (1987), Katz and Kemnitzer (1983), Leichter (1979) and (1981), Lozano (1989), Maken (1959), Mattera (1980), Mitter (1984) and (1986), Morales (1983), Murray (1981), National Board for Prices and and Income (1969), *Newsletter of International Labour Studies* (1984), Pennington and Westover (1989), Pineda-Ofreneo (1982), Rao and Husain (1984), Roldan (1985), Sayin (1945), Silver (1989), Singh and Kelles-Vutanen (1987), Van Luijken (1984), Webb (1982), Weiner and Green (1984).

12. Shoemaking in Spain provides a good example of an industry that used homework, abandoned it for a period as conditions changed, and then reintroduced it under new circumstances. According to Benton (1990), unregulated homework was common during the 1940s and 50s when many large, family-run firms were founded. With an expansion of production during the following decade, however, homework declined as firms found it beneficial to bring workers into the factory in order to ensure steadier, high-volume production. Then, economic changes in the 1970s led to decentralization of production that included a resurgence of homework as a way to cut costs and take advantage of weakening labor organization (Benton 1990, 114).

13. The term "informal productive structures" is used by Pinnaro and Pugliese (1985).

14. According to Bromley and Gerry (1979), commission sellers are also "disguised wage-workers." They point out that manufacturing firms, wholesalers, and insurance companies often retail through commission sellers—vendors who receive an agreed upon sum as their commission for each sale and who only sell the products of one firm or a few related firms. Both homeworkers and commission sellers select their own working hours, but need to obtain a subsistence income and keep a good relationship with the firm they sell for. Such workers are often supplied with equipment, credit, raw materials, and even premises "as a means to increase their production and to tie (subordinate) them more securely to the firm" (6).

15. In drawing a distinction between the informal sector and

petty commodity production, Portes and Walton make the important point that informal sector activities are an integral part of modern capitalist production. They argue that the concept of petty commodity production (as derived from the classic Marxist analysis of different modes of production) "suggests either pre-existing modes of production, transformed by the arrival of capitalism, or transitional ones, giving way in time to fully commodified relations. . . . [I]nformal sector activities are neither traditional nor transitional but very 'modern' features of the system of capitalist accumulation and, as such, continuously reproduced by the operations of this system" (Portes and Walton 1981, 86).

5. Gender as Agency in the Shaping of Household and Labor Market Relations

1. The historical development and consequences of this ideology are discussed by Bernard 1981; Degler 1980, ch. 2; and Kessler-Harris 1982, ch.3.

2. Silver's (1983) recent analysis of the 1977 Quality of Employment Survey (QES) data, which provide information on men and women who work at home, offers new insights on the integration of paid work and domestic work for working-class and professional workers. She found that working-class homeworkers in particular tend to combine their paid work with household tasks. For example, female homeworkers in working-class occupations spend more time on childcare and household tasks than comparable on-site workers, but report having as much free time as their on-site counterparts. Silver concludes that "[h]omeworkers may accomplish more domestic work per hour of paid work without diminishing their leisure time because their families, especially older children, help with their paid jobs" (199). She points out that, in effect, having children assist them allows homeworkers to accomplish two things at once—child-minding and paid work tasks.

3. For an analysis of the origin and impact of the ideological construction of the male breadwinner and female homemaker roles, see Bernard's (1981) discussion of the rise and fall of the male "good-provider" role.

4. A chief distinction between the two tiers within the primary sector lies in the nature of the tasks performed in each. In

subordinate primary sector employment, workers are required to perform routine, repetitive tasks and often are confined strictly to machine pacing. The production process, which is usually governed by formal work rules, is presided over by general supervisors whose job it is to see that each worker performs his or her task adequately thus contributing to the smooth functioning of the process as a whole. Workers in this sector perform specific skills learned on the job and advancement depends primarily on seniority. In contrast, the professional, managerial, and technical jobs of the independent primary sector are less firm-specific and involve generalized skills acquired in advanced or specialized schooling. Since occupational or professional standards govern performance, workers rely on independent initiative and self-pacing to regulate their activity. To the extent that career ladders offer clear paths for upward mobility within specific firms, workers tend to internalize the formal objectives of their organizations and are guided accordingly in their day-to-day performance on the job. Thus, while the two tiers in the primary sector are distinguished by their differing characteristics with regard to tasks, work rules, supervision, and career advancement, the basic distinction between subordinate primary and secondary employment, which have much in common regarding the nature of tasks performed, is that workers in the former enjoy more protection through unionization and its accompanying benefits.

5. The World War II experience of women is especially significant for an understanding of the sex-typing of occupations and its consequences. During the war years when women were recruited to replace the formerly male labor supply, they were not randomly incorporated into "men's jobs." Instead, new patterns of occupational segregation were established "for the duration" that shifted the boundaries between men's and women's work but did not eliminate them. For example, job descriptions were rewritten until they seemed more suited to what were thought to be feminine attributes. The central reference point for the idiom of sex-typing in manufacturing jobs became rooted in real or imagined biological characteristics and ideas about manual dexterity, attention to detail, ability to tolerate monotony, and women's relative lack of physical strength. In this way, jobs that were previously described in terms of perceived male attributes took on new characteristics, which emphasized their suitability for women. For example, media campaigns designed to attract women to work in war industries often relied on the use of metaphors

that likened the operation of machinery in the workplace to the operation of household appliances. Sex-typing in this way thus reinforced the notion that women's "primary" commitment remained devotion to home and family, whether or not they worked for pay. Accordingly, Milkman (1982) concludes that the World War II experience reveals the "resilience of the structure of job segregation by sex and of the general ideology of sexual divisions which legitimates it, but also renders completely transparent the specific idiom of sex typing, which is flexibly applied to whatever jobs women and men happen to be doing" (Milkman 1982, 341).

6. Hakim (1980) explains that those who reported that homework provided nonessential income tended to be employed in white-collar occupations, while those for whom homework income was significant tended to be employed in blue-collar occupations.

7. Most of the homeworkers' husbands were blue-collar workers. Many worked in various area factories. Some of the other jobs held included that of custodian, gas mechanic, bus driver, carpenter, trucker, sheriff's officer, and salesman. A few were part-time or full-time farmers.

8. Sayin's 1945 study of Pennsylvania homeworkers in the knitted outerwear and women's apparel industries poses a challenge to the view that immigrants were the primary source of homework labor before the late 1970s. He reveals that most of the 125 homeworkers he interviewed, who worked under the Fair Labor Standards Act Prohibitory Orders, were white, lower middle-and working-class women.

9. The elderly, the sick, and the handicapped are other groups from which homeworkers are drawn.

10. The scarcity and high cost of childcare in the United States is documented in a 1983 U.S. Commission on Civil Rights Report. The report concluded that while there was only one daycare position open for every ten children in need, the average cost of daycare for two children was approximately $4,000 per year (Applebaum 1987, 283).

11. The typical jobs held by homeworkers in the past were assembly line worker, cleaner, waitress, cashier, secretary/typist, and telephone operator. Most of the women had more than one previous job before doing homework. In fact, most had moved from job to job, spending an average of a few years at each.

12. It is important to note that in this case the fact that people could earn more in "take-home" pay doing homework than if they worked outside at minimum wage was not due to the fact that they failed to pay taxes on their homework income, as many might assume. Of those interviewed, only four reported that they neglected to pay income tax on their earnings. Seven, however, reported that they did not pay social security taxes. Nevertheless, in claiming that homework yielded more spendable income, those interviewed did not consider the cost of overhead expenses they may have incurred, such as heating and lighting.

13. It is possible, however, that some men see home-based work as enhancing the quality of their family lives and increasing the time available for their spouses and children (by eliminating time wasted on long commutes or allowing them to be more readily available for family emergencies). Still, studies show that even among dual career, professional couples wives retain primary responsibility for household and childcare demands (Hertz 1986). Accordingly, it is probably safe to assume that most men are not choosing home-based work because they face a "double burden" that traditional work arrangements can't accomodate.

6. State Regulation of Homework: Historical and Contemporary Perspectives

1. In the final analysis, Mann expands on the concept of the state as an arena. In contrast to Poulantzas, however, he sees this as an *active* role. For Mann, the fact that the state is an "arena" "is precisely the origin and mechanism of its autonomous powers." Principal power actors of civil society "entrust power resources to state elites which they are incapable of fully recovering, precisely because their own socio-spatial basis of organization is not centralized and territorial. State power resources, and the autonomy to which they lead, may not amount to much. If, however, the state's use of the conferred resources generates further power resources—as was, indeed, intended by the civil society groups themselves—these will normally flow through the state's hands and thus lead to a significant degree of power autonomy" (Mann 1988, 29).

2. Boris (1985) explains the meaning of the term "social feminists" as follows: "Contrasting themselves to the self-proclaimed feminists of the National Women's Party, the New Deal women rejected the label 'feminist' and called themselves social

reformers. Historians, however, have renamed them 'social feminists,' because their fight for women's rights focused on improving the living and working conditions of the majority of labor women rather than on an abstract legal equality."

3. While the relatively high level of unionization in the needle trades is, in one sense, an indicator of union strength, Boris (1993) points out that the history of union efforts to secure government regulation of homework reveals a significant weakness: their inability to organize the entire industry and consequent reliance on the state to regulate conditions.

4. Though the precise stipulations of these laws varied from state to state, they generally included provisions to ensure that shops were not set up in living quarters, nonliving quarters in tenements and dwelling houses classed as factories conformed to general factory laws and sanitary and health provisions of antisweating acts, and living quarters of homeworkers conformed to sanitary and health regulations. (Thus homework could be done by families residing in the place where work was being done.)

5. New Jersey's homework law differs from Illinois' in its exclusion of prohibition for sanitary napkins, cotton batting and metal springs and its addition of infants' and children's wearing apparel and doll clothing as prohibited industries.

6. The prohibitory order for men's and boys' outerwear was enacted in 1936, followed by ones for men's and boys' neckwear in 1937 and gloves in 1941 (New York State Dept. of Labor 1982b, 4).

7. Section 351, "Powers of the industrial commissioner and exceptions" reads as follows:
"1. The industrial commissioner shall, after proper study and consideration, determine within what industries conditions may permit of industrial homework as hereinbefore defined without unduly jeopardizing the factory workers in such industries as to both wages and working conditions and without unduly injuring the health and welfare of the industrial homeworker himself. The commissioner may then restrict the granting of permits and licenses for industrial homework as herein defined to such industries and may further issue rules and regulations designed to control and regulate industrial homework in the said permitted industries. In all other industries industrial homework is forbidden unless expressly permitted in writing by the industrial com-

missioner.

2. a. Exception to this article shall be made by the industrial commissioner in respect of clerical work done in a home. 'Clerical work' shall mean typing, stenciling, transcribing, copying, bookkeeping and stenographic work. Clerical work shall not mean inserting, collating, labeling, nesting, sorting, stamping or similar work.

b. Exception to this article may be made by the industrial commissioner in respect of such other provisions consonant with the general purpose of this article as the commissioner may on study determine to be warranted by conditions.

8. The comments from the New York State Labor Department attorney and the attorney from the Industrial Board of Appeals were made at a joint interview I conducted in November 1983. The third attorney mentioned, who was interviewed separately in November 1983, represented homework distributors in four different cases.

9. In 1935 the Women's Bureau of the U.S. Department of Labor made enquiries about the effectiveness of the NRA codes. From information gathered from code authorities, organized labor, and state labor departments, the bureau concluded that homework was eliminated in 22 industries, while some plants were reportedly not complying to codes in 31 other industries where homework was prohibited. The effectiveness of the codes depended on the voluntary cooperation of employers and successful pressure from organized labor. Problems in enforcing the codes were also widely acknowledged. For example, Miller (1941) points out that there was almost complete compliance with NRA codes in the men's clothing industry, where workers were strongly unionized. In the Rhode Island jewelry industry, where employers proved to be extremely cooperative, code provisions prohibiting homework were similarly obeyed. In contrast, there was general evasion of homework provisions in the artificial flower industry, where workers lacked union representation and employers failed to acknowledge NRA codes.

10. In 1934 the U.S. Department of Labor investigated 1,473 homework families in seven states, working for 24 industries not protected by NRA codes regulating homework. The study revealed that 56 percent of the main homeworkers made less than ten cents an hour, while 5 percent earned as much as 35 cents (the usual minimum required under NRA codes). Most of the homeworkers

studied worked more than 40 hours a week, with nearly 40 percent working 40 hours or more and eight working 70 hours or more (Miller 1941, 31).

11. After the invalidation of the NIRA in May of 1935, several states (including New York, Pennsylvania, and Rhode Island) reported an increase in homework and a general breakdown in labor standards. Homework was revived even in industries where it had been largely eliminated, such as the jewelry industry in Rhode Island. The interstate aspect of the problem intensified with the abolition of the NIRA, as work was increasingly sent from states with homework laws to those without such laws. A U.S. Department of Labor report on the interstate shipment of homework, published in 1936, showed that in New York alone, 171 manufacturers were sending work to 1,451 homeworkers and contractors in 16 other states and Puerto Rico. Seven of the states had no homework laws (Miller 1941, 33).

12. This shift in the focus of anti-homework laws first occurred in California between 1914 and 1929. Instead of emphasizing the health hazards endemic to the sweating system, California regulations implemented during this time attacked low wages by setting minimum piece rates, mandating that earnings records be kept, and requiring manufacturers to obtain permits before giving out homework. Wisconsin followed this same line of attack with its 1921 Home Work Law. These new laws mark the beginning of a general shift from regulation aimed at protecting the consumer from the health hazards of purchasing goods made under unsanitary conditions to regulation aimed at protecting the homeworker from low pay, long hours, and poor working conditions.

13. In a letter to the director of the state's Labor Standards Division, Industrial Commissioner Lillian Roberts stated that uninvestigated complaint backlogs statewide approached 4,500 in 1984.

14. Telephone interview conducted in November, 1988 with Hugh McDaid, Chief Labor Standards Investigator, New York State Department of Labor, Division of Labor Standards, Brooklyn.

15. This increase occurred because state and local government employees are now covered by the FLSA as a result of a Supreme Court ruling (*Garcia v. San Antonio Metro Transit Authority*).

16. Interview with Hugh McDaid, November 1988.

17. The methods used during this investigation to identify where homework was being done were quite interesting. Department of Labor officials contacted building inspectors, plumbing inspectors, electrical inspectors, construction offices, building and electrical permit offices, health offices, fire and police departments, labor unions, and employers who would be affected by unfair competition from illegal homework in an effort to locate homeworkers. In addition, it was discovered that illegal homeworkers were being advised that they needed a registered trade name to avoid legal repercussions. Many homeworkers then applied for registered trade names with the county. In Hudson County, more than 90 percent of the trade names registered belonged to illegal homeworkers.

18. Under the Unemployment Insurance Law industrial homeworkers are employees and not independent contractors. This was supported in the case of *Commodore Knitting Mills v. the Industrial Commissioner* (1939) and *Bailey v. the Commissioner of Labor* (1987). The latter was a case about eligibility for unemployment insurance coverage and involved homework in the electronics industry. A summary of the decision describes an operation that was the same as those I learned of through my interviews. It reads as follows: "Claimant, who was engaged by manufacturer of wire and cable to work at her home cutting wires and placing conductors on each end, who picked up wire, conductors and storage boxes at employer's premises, and upon completion of each task at her home would return items to employer, was 'industrial homeworker,' presumed to be employee, and not independent contractor, where employer provided specific written and oral instructions with each order, each order had quota and some had deadline, claimant provided employer with record of work performed and was paid on piecework basis at rate set by employer, and if work proved unsatisfactory, claimant was required to correct it at her own expense" (*McKinney's Consolidated Laws of New York, Annotated,* Book 30, *Labor Law,* Sections 1 to 499, Cumulative Annual Additions, 1993).

19. Sayin compares his research on Pennsylvania homework with data collected by Agnes Byrn during the 1920s.

20. Altogether, six of the seven FLSA prohibitory orders have been lifted to date. The ban on homework in knitted outerwear

was lifted in 1984, followed by the lifting of bans for gloves and mittens, embroideries, buttons and buckles, handkerchiefs, and jewelry in 1988. Only the ban on homework in women's apparel remains in place.

Bibliography

Advisory, Conciliation, and Arbitration Service. *Toy Manufacturing Wages Council.* Report No. 13. London: ACAS, 1978a.

————. *Report on Button Manufacturing Wages Council.* Report No. 11. London: ACAS, 1978b.

Albrecht, Sandra L. "Industrial Home Work in the U.S.: Historical Dimension andContemporary Perspective." *Economic and Industrial Democracy* 3, no. 4 (1982): 413–30.

Alexander, Suzanne. "More Working Mothers Opt for Flexibility of Operating a Franchise from Home." *Wall Street Journal*, 31 January 1991, B1–2.

Allen, Sheila. "Domestic Production and Organising for Change." *Economic and Industrial Democracy* 3, no. 4 (1982): 381–411.

————. "Production and Reproduction: the Lives of Women Homeworkers." *Sociological Review* 31, no. 4 (Nov. 1983): 649–65.

Allen, Sheila and Carol Wolkowitz. "The Control of Women's Labour: The Case of Homeworking." *Feminist Review* 22 (February 1986).

Applebaum, Eileen. "Restructuring Work: Temporary, Part-Time, and At-Home Employment." In *Computer Chips and Paper Clips: Technology and Women's Employment*, edited by Heidi I. Hartmann. National Research Council, Case Studies and Policy Perspectives, vol. 2. Washington, D.C.: National Academy Press, 1987.

Arden, Lynie. *The Work-at-Home Sourcebook.* Boulder, Colorado: Live Oak Publications, 1992.

Aronson, Robert L. *Self-Employment: A Labor Market Perspective.* Ithaca, N.Y.: ILR Press, 1991.

Arrighi, Giovanni. *Semiperipheral Development: The Politics of Southern Europe in the Twentieth Century.* Beverly Hills, London, and New Delhi: Sage Publications, 1985.

Ashton, Thomas Southcliffe. *The Industrial Revolution, 1760–1830.* New York and London: Oxford University Press, 1948.

Associated Press. "Cuomo Proposes Sweatshop Crackdown." *Cortland Standard,* December 1987.

Australia Asia Worker Links (AAWL). *Outwork: Undermining Union Gains or an Alternative Way of Working?* Case Study No. 6, December 1982.

Averitt, Robert T. *The Dual Economy.* New York: W. W. Norton, 1968.

Baden, Tom. "State Spotlights Firm, Then Alleges Labor Law Violations." *The Post-Standard,* Syracuse, N.Y., 30 November 1981: A 6.

Bane, Mary Jo. "Politics and Policies of the Feminization of Poverty." In *The Politics of Social Policy in the United States,* edited by Margaret Weir, Ann Shola Orloff, Theda Skocpol, 383–96. New Jersey: Princeton University Press, 1988.

Baud, Isa. "Housewifisation of Production: A New Phase in the International Gender Division of Labour." *Newsletter of International Labour Studies* 21 (April 1984): 2–5.

———. "Industrial Subcontracting: The Effects of the Putting-Out System on Poor Working Women in India." In *Invisible Hands: Women in Home-Based Production,* edited by Andrea Menefee Singh and Anita Kelles-Vutanen. California: Sage Publications, 1987.

Beach, Betty. *Integrating Work and Family Life.* Albany: State University of New York Press, 1989.

———. "The Family Context of Home Shoe Work." In *Homework: Historical and Contemporary Perspectives on Paid Labor at Home,* edited by Eileen Boris and Cynthia Daniels, 130–46. Urbana and Chicago: University of Illinois Press, 1989.

Behr, Marion and Omri M. Behr. "Working at Home is a Blow for Freedom." Letter. *New York Times,* 10 December 1984.

Behr, Marion and Wendy Lazar. *Women Working Home: The Homebased Business Guide and Directory*, first edition. New Jersey: Women Working Home, Inc. (WWH Press), 1981.

———. *Women Working Home: The Homebased Business Guide and Directory*, second edition. New Jersey: WWH Press, 1983.

Belsie, Laurent. "Home-Based Industries Take Root in Rural America." *Christian Science Monitor*. 25 August 1986, 3.

Beneria, Lourdes and Martha Roldan. *The Crossroads of Class and Gender: Industrial Homework, Subcontracting, and Household Dynamics in Mexico City*. Chicago: University of Chicago Press, 1987.

Bennett, K. "Dawning of a New Age of Electronics." *Iron Age* 209 (1972): 40–41.

Benson, Susan Porter. "Women, Work, and the Family: Industrial Homework in Rhode Island." In *Homework: Historical and Contemporary Perspectives on Paid Labor at Home*, edited by Eileen Boris and Cynthia R. Daniels. Chicago: University of Illinois Press, 1989.

Benston, Margaret Lowe. "For Women, the Chips are Down." In *The Technological Woman*, edited by Jan Zimmerman, 44–54. New York: Praeger Publishers, 1983.

Benton, Lauren. *Invisible Factories: The Informal Economy and Industrial Development in Spain*. Albany: State University of New York Press, 1990.

Berch, Bettina. "The Resurrection of Out-Work." *Monthly Review* 37, no. 6 (November 1985): 37–46.

Berger, Suzanne. "The Uses of the Traditional Sector in Italy: Why the Declining Classes Survive." In *The Petty Bourgeoisie* edited by F. Bechhofer and B. Elliot. London: Macmillan, 1980a.

———. "The Traditional Sector in France and Italy." In *Dualism and Discontinuity in Industrial Societies*, edited by S. Berger and M. Piore, 88–131. Cambridge: Cambridge University Press, 1980b.

———. "Discontinuity in the Politics of Industrial Society." In *Dualism and Discontinuity in Industrial Societies*, edited by S. Berger and M. Piore. Cambridge: Cambridge University Press, 1980c.

Bernard, Jessie. "The Good-Provider Role: Its Rise and Fall." *American Psychologist* 36, no. 1 (January 1981): 1–12.

Bhatt, Ela. "The Invisibility of Home-Based Work: The Case of Piece Rate Workers in India." In *Invisible Hands: Women in Home-Based Production*, edited by A. M. Singh and A. Kelles-Vutanen. California: Sage Publications, 1987.

Bhatty, Zarina. "Economic Contribution of Women to the Household Budget: A Case Study of the Beedi Industry." In *Invisible Hands: Women in Home-Based Production*, edited by A. M. Singh and A. Kelles-Vutanen. California: Sage Publications, 1987.

Black, Clementina. *Sweated Industry*. London: Duckworth and Co., 1907.

Blackwelder, Julia Kirk. "Texas Homeworkers in the 1930s." In *Homework: Historical and Contemporary Perspectives on Paid Labor at Home*, edited by E. Boris and C. R. Daniels, 75–90. Chicago: University of Illinois Press, 1989.

Blewett, Mary H. "Work, Gender and the Artisan Tradition in New England Shoemaking, 1780–1860." *Journal of Social History* (Winter 1983): 221–48.

Block, Fred. "The Ruling Class Does Not Rule." *Socialist Review* 7 (1977): 6–28.

Blumberg, Paul. *Inequality in an Age of Decline*. New York: Oxford University Press, 1980.

Boris, Eileen. "Regulating Industrial Homework: The Triumph of 'Sacred Motherhood'." *The Journal of American History* 71, no. 4 (March 1985): 745–63.

———. "Homework and Women's Rights: The Case of the Vermont Knitters, 1980–1985." *Signs* 13 no. 1 (Autumn 1987): 98–120.

———. "Homework in the Past, Its Meaning for the Future." In *The New Era of Home-Based Work*, edited by K. E. Christensen, 15–29. Boulder and London: Westview Press, 1988.

———. "Organization or Prohibition: A Historical Perspective on Trade Unions and Homework." In *Women and Unions: Forging a Partnership*, edited by D. S. Cobble, 207–25. Ithaca, N.Y.: ILR Press, 1993.

———. *Home to Work: Motherhood and the Politics of Industrial*

Homework in the U.S.. New York: Cambridge University Press, 1994.

Boris, Eileen and Cynthia R. Daniels. *Homework: Historical and Contemporary Perspectives on Paid Labor at Home*. Urbana and Chicago: University of Illinois Press, 1989.

Bose, Christine. "Technology and Changes in the Division of Labor in the American Home." *Women's Studies International Quarterly* 2 (1979): 295–304.

Boxer, Marilyn J. "Protective Legislation and Home Industry: The Marginalization of Women Workers in Late Nineteenth–Early Twentieth-Century France." *Journal of Social History* 20, no. 1 (Fall 1986): 45–65.

Braverman, Harry. *Labor and Monopoly Capital*. New York: Monthly Review Press, 1974.

Bromley, Ray. "The Urban Informal Sector: Why is it Worth Discussing?" *World Development* 6, no. 9–10 (1978).

Bromley, Ray and Chris Gerry. "Who are the Casual Poor?" In *Casual Work and Poverty in Third World Cities*, edited by R. Bromley and C. Gerry. New York: John Wiley and Sons, 1979.

Brooke, James. "The Pros and Cons of 'Computer Commuting'." *New York Times*, 23 September 1984, F15.

Brooke, M. "The Growth of Labor Law in the United States." Washington, D.C.: U.S. Department of Labor, 1967, 265–72.

Brookman, D. "People Crunch Drives Firms to New Methods of Recruitment." *Electronic Business* (July 1979): 109–10.

Brown, Marie. *Sweated Labour*. London: Low Pay Unit, 1974.

Brusco, Sebastiano and Charles Sabel. "Artisan Production and Economic Growth." In *The Dynamics of Labour Market Segmentation*, edited by F. Wilkinson. New York: Academic Press, 1981.

Brusco, Sebastiano. "The Emilian Model: Productive Decentralization and Social Integration." *Cambridge Journal of Economics* 6 (1982): 167–84.

Bucher, Carl. *Industrial Evolution*, second printing. New York: Augustus M. Kelley Publishers, 1968 (First English translation, New York: Henry Holt, 1901.)

Burg, Robert. " 'Toggler Bolt' Inventor Fights Ruling." *Patent Trader*, 14 February 1986.

Burgess, Robert G. *Field Research: a Source and Field Manual.* London: George, Allen, and Unwin, 1982.

Byrne, Harriet and Bertha Blair. *Industrial Home Work in Rhode Island, with Special Reference to the Lace Industry* Bulletin of the Women's Bureau, No. 131. Washington D.C.: U.S. Government Printing Office, 1935.

Bythell, Duncan. *The Sweated Trades.* New York: St. Martin's Press, 1978.

"Can Semiconductors Survive Big Business?" *Business Week,* 3 December 1979, 66.

Capecchi, Vitoria. "The Informal Economy and the Development of Flexible Specialization in Emilia Romagna." In *The Informal Economy*, edited by A. Portes, M. Castells, and L. Benton. Baltimore: Johns Hopkins University Press, 1989, 189–215.

Carey, Pete and Michael Malone. "Black Market in Silicon Valley." *San Jose Mercury News*, 31 August 1980, 1A.

Carney, Larry S. and Charlotte G. O'Kelly. "Women's Work and Women's Place in the Japanese Economic Miracle." In *Women Workers and Global Restructuring*, edited by Kathryn Ward. Ithaca, N.Y.: ILR Press, 1990, 111–45.

Cawthon, Brenda. "Crackdown on Industrial Homework Operations Overturned." *The Post-Standard*, Syracuse, N.Y., 15 June 1983, 1.

Chamot, Dennis. "Blue Collar, White Collar: Homeworker Problems." In *The New Era of Home-Based Work*, edited by K. E. Christensen, 168–76. Boulder and London: Westview Press, 1988.

Christensen, Kathleen E. "Independent Contracting." In *The New Era of Home-Based Work*, edited by K. E. Christensen, 79–91. Boulder and London: Westview Press, 1988.

———. "Reevaluating Union Policy Toward White-Collar Home-Based Work." In *Women and Unions: Forging a New Partnership*, edited by D. S. Cobble, 246–59. Ithaca: ILR Press, 1993.

Clark, Christopher. "Household Economy, Market Exchange and

the Rise of Capitalism in the Connecticut Valley, 1800–1860." *Journal of Social History* 13, no. 2 (Winter 1979): 169–89.

Clark, Edie. "It's Against the Law to Knit a Hat at Home." *Yankee Magazine*, June 1981.

Coates, Vary T. "Office Automation Technology and Home-Based Work." In *The New Era of Home-Based Work*, edited by K. E. Christensen, 114–25.

Collins, Jane L. and Martha Gimenez, eds. *Work Without Wages: Domestic Labor and Self-Employment Within Capitalism*. Albany: State University of New York Press, 1990.

Commission on Industrial Relations (CIR). *Pin, Hook and Eye, and Snap Fastener Wages Council*. Report No. 49. London: Her Majesty's Stationery Office (HMSO), 1973.

———. *Clothing Wages Council*. Report No. 77. London: HMSO, 1974.

"A Company that Works at Home." *Business Week*, 26 January 1981a, 98.

Costello, Cynthia B. "The Clerical Homework Program at the Wisconsin Physicians Service Insurance Corporation." In *Homework: Historical and Contemporary Perspectives on Paid Labor at Home*, edited by E. Boris and C. R. Daniels, 198–214. Urbana and Chicago: University of Illinois Press, 1989.

Coyle, Angela. "Sex and Skill in the Organization of the Clothing Industry." In *Work, Women, and the Labour Market*, edited by J. West, 10–26. London: Routledge and Kegan Paul, 1982.

Cragg, Arnold and Tim Dawson. *Qualitative Research Among Homeworkers*. Department of Employment, Research Paper No. 21. London: May 1981.

Craig, C., J. Rubery, R. Tarling, and F. Wilkinson. *Labour Market Structure, Industrial Organization and Low Pay*. University of Cambridge Department of Economics, Occasional Paper 54. Cambridge: Cambridge University Press, 1982.

CSE Microelectronics Group. *Microelectronics: Capitalist Technology and the Working Class*. London: Blackrose Press, 1980.

Czernek, A. "Delco to Begin Subassembly of Board in Singapore." *Electronic News*, 7 August 1978, 47.

Dangler, Jamie Faricellia. "Industrial Homework in the Modern World-Economy." *Contemporary Crises* 10 (1986) 257–79.

———. "Electronics Subassemblers in Central New York: Nontraditional Homeworkers in a Nontraditional Homework Industry." In *Homework: Historical and Contemporary Perspectives on Paid Labor at Home*, edited by E. Boris and C. R. Daniels, 147–64. Urbana and Chicago: University of Illinois Press, 1989.

Daniels, Cynthia R. "There's No Place Like Home: The Politics of Home-based Work." *Dollars and Sense*, (December 1986): 16–22.

———. "Between Home and Factory: Homeworkers and the State." In *Homework: Historical and Contemporary Perspectives on Paid Labor at Home*, edited by E. Boris and C. R. Daniels. Urbana and Chicago: University of Illinois Press, 1989.

Davin, Anna. Unpublished notes on Homework in Britain, 1981.

Degler, Carl. *At Odds: Women and the Family in America from the Revolution to the Present*. New York: Oxford University Press, 1980.

DeGrazia, Raffaele. *Clandestine Employment*. Geneva: International Labour Office, 1984.

Derber, Milton. "Industrial Homework, Part I: An Old Problem Lingers On." New York State Department of Labor *Industrial Bulletin*. March 1959, 8–11.

Doeringer, Peter and Michael Piore. *International Labor Markets and Manpower Analysis*. Massachusetts: Heath Lexington Books, 1971.

Drucker, Peter F. *Innovation and Entrepreneurship*. New York: Harper and Row, 1985.

Dublin, Thomas. "Women and Outwork in a Nineteenth-Century New England Town." In *The Countryside in an Age of Capitalist Transformation*, edited by S. Hahn and J. Prude, 51–69. Chapel Hill and London: University of North Carolina Press, 1985.

Eberts, Paul R. *Socioeconomic Trends in Rural New York State: Toward the 21st Century*. Albany: New York Legislative Commission on Rural Resources, 1991.

Eder, Peter F. "Telecommuters: The Stay-At-Home Work Force of the Future." In *The Computerized Society: Living and Working in an Electronic Age*, edited by Edward Cornish. Maryland: World Future Society, 1985.

Edwards, P. and E. Flounders. "The Lace Outworkers of Nottingham." In *Are Low Wages Inevitable?*, edited by F. Field, 47–53. London: Spokesman Books, 1977.

Eisencher, Michael. *Silicon Valley: A Digest of Electronics Data.* San Jose: Silicon Valley Digest, August 1984.

Eisenstein, Zillah. *Feminism and Sexual Equality: Crisis in Liberal America.* New York: Monthly Review Press, 1984.

Elling, Monica. "Remote Work/Telecommuting." *Economic and Industrial Democracy* 6, no. 2 (May 1985): 239–49.

Everett, Jana and Mira Savara. "Institutional Credit as a Strategy Toward Self-Reliance for Petty Commodity Producers in India: A Critical Evaluation." In *Invisible Hands: Women in Home-Based Production*, edited by A. Singh an A. Kelles-Vutanen, 207–28. California: Sage Publications, 1987.

Ewing, K. D. "Homeworking: A Framework for Reform." *Industrial Law Journal* 11, no. 2 (June 1982): 94–110.

Fain, T. Scott. "Self-Employed Americans: Their Number Has Increased," *Monthly Labor Review* 103, no. 11 (November 1980): 3–8.

Feige, Edgar L. *The Underground Economies.* New York: Cambridge University Press, 1989.

Fernandez-Kelly, Maria Patricia. "Gender and Industry on Mexico's New Frontier." In *The Technological Woman*, edited by J. Zimmerman. New York: Praeger Publishers, 1983.

Fernandez-Kelly, M. Patricia and Anna M. Garcia. "Informalization at the Core: Hispanic Women, Homework, and the Advanced Capitalist State." In *The Informal Economy*, edited by A. Portes, M. Castells, and L. A. Benton. Baltimore and London: The Johns Hopkins University Press, 1989.

Fessler, Pamela. "Congress Weighs Tax Status of Independent Contractors." *Congressional Quarterly*, 8 May 1982, 1064–65.

Fitchen, Janet. *Endangered Spaces, Enduring Places: Change,*

Identity, and Survival in Rural America. Boulder: Westview Press, 1991.

Flaim, Paul O. "Work Schedules of Americans: An Overview of New Findings." *Monthly Labor Review* 109, no. 11 (November 1986): 3–6.

Friedman, Andrew L. *Industry and Labour: Class Struggle at Work and Monopoly Capitalism.* London and Basingstoke: Macmillan, 1977.

Frobel, Folker, Jurgen Heinricks and Otto Kreye. "The Tendency Towards a New International Division of Labor." *Review* 1, no. 1 (Summer 1977): 73–88.

"Future of Homework." *Social and Labor Bulletin* 3 (1981a): 306–08.

Gabriel, Jurgen and Fabian Holzapfl. "Entrepreneurial Strategies of Adjustment and Internal Labour Markets." In *The Dynamics of Labour Market Segmentation,* edited by F. Wilkinson. New York: Academic Press, 1981.

Garnsey, Elizabeth. "Women's Work and Theories of Class Stratification." In *Classes, Power, and Conflict,* edited by A. Giddens and D. Held. Berkeley: University of California Press, 1982.

Gerry, Chris. "Small-Scale Manufacturing and Repairs in Dakar: A Survey of Market Relations Within the Urban Economy." In *Casual Work and Poverty in Third World Cities,* edited by R. Bromley and C. Gerry. New York: John Wiley and Sons, 1979.

Gershuny, Jonathan. *Social Innovation and the Division of Labor.* New York: Oxford University Press, 1983.

Gerson, J. "Clerical Homeworkers: Are they Organizable?" In *Women and Unions: Forging a New Partnership,* edited by D. S. Cobble, 226–45. Ithaca: ILR Press, 1993.

Giddens, Anthony. *A Contemporary Critique of Historical Materialism.* Berkeley and Los Angeles: University of California Press, 1981.

Goldberg, Marilyn Power. "The Economic Exploitation of Women." In *The Capitalist System,* edited by R. Edwards, M. Reich, and T. Weisskopf. Englewood Cliffs, N.J.: Prentice-Hall, 1972.

Goldsmith, William. "Bringing the Third World Home: Enterprise Zones for America?" In *Sunbelt/Snowbelt: Urban Development and Regional Restructuring*, edited by L. Sawyers and W. K. Tabb. New York: Oxford University Press, 1984.

Gordon, Gil. "Corporate Hiring Practices for Telecommuting Homeworkers." In *The New Era of Home-Based Work*, edited by K. E. Christensen. Boulder and London: Westview Press, 1988.

Gordon, David M., Richard C. Edwards, Michael Reich. *Labor Market Segmentation*. Massachusetts: D.C., Heath and Co., 1975.

"Government Report on Homeworkers," *Social and Labour Bulletin* 3 (1981b): 313.

Green, Hardy and Elizabeth Weiner. "Bringing It All Back Home." *In These Times*, 11–17 March 1981, 8–9.

Green, Susan S. "Silicon Valley's Women Workers: A Theoretical Analysis of Sex Segregation in the Electronics Industry Labor Market." In *Women, Men, and the International Division of Labor*, edited by J. Nash and M. P. Fernandez-Kelly, 273–331. Albany: State University of New York Press, 1983.

Greenberger, Robert S. "Florid Press Release on a Sweatshop Raid Draws Cries of 'Foul'." *Wall Street Journal*, 20 May 1981, 1.

Greengard, Samuel. "Businesses: No Place Like Home." *Los Angeles Times*, 19 October 1984, 5.

Grieves, Robert T. "Telecommuting from a Flexiplace." *Time Magazine*, 30 January 1984, 63.

Grossman, Rachael. "Women's Place in the Integrated Circuit." *Southeast Asia Chronicle* 66 (January–February 1979): 2–17.

Haggberg, Marie. "Changing Patterns in the Garment Industry." *New York Affairs* 6, no. 2 (1980).

Hakim, Catherine. "Homeworking: Some New Evidence." Department of Employment Gazette. London: HMSO, October 1980.

Hakim, Catherine and Roger Dennis. "Homeworking In Wages Council Industries: A Study Based on Wages Inspectorate Records of Pay and Earnings." Department of Employment, Research Paper No. 37. London: September 1982.

Harrington, Michael. *The New American Poverty*. New York: Penguin Books, 1984.

Herteaux, Michel. "Taking Work Home." *World Press Review* (January 1985): 38–39.

Hertz, Rosanna. *More Equal Than Others: Women and Men in Dual-Career Marriages*. Berkeley and Los Angeles: University of California Press, 1986.

Hewes, Jeremy Joan. *Worksteads: Living and Working in the Same Place*. New York: Doubleday and Co., 1981.

High Tech Research Group. *Whatever Happened to Job Security? The 1985 Slow Down in the Massachusetts High Tech Industry*. Boston: The High Tech Research Group, January 1986.

Holder, A. "Subcontracting: the Economic Principle Underlying Female Labour for Wages." *Berkeley Journal of Sociology* 26 (1981): 3–25.

"Homeworking on a World Scale." Special Issue. *Newsletter of International Labour Studies* 21 (April 1984).

Horvath, Francis. "Work at Home: New Findings From the Current Population Survey." *Monthly Labor Review* 109, no. 11 (1986): 31–35.

Hosenball, Mark. "Supply-Side Sweatshops." *The New Republic*, 16 May 1981, 19–21.

Hossain, Hameeda. "Capitalist Penetration into Handi-Crafts Manufacture: An Historical Review of Women's Work for the Market in Bangladesh." In *Invisible Hands: Women in Home-Based Production*, edited by A. M. Singh and A. Kelles-Vutanen. California: Sage Publications, 1987.

Howard, R. "Second Class in Silicon Valley." *Working Papers* 9 (September/October 1981): 21–31.

Huws, Ursula. "New Technology and Homeworking: New Opportunities for Low Pay?" *Newsletter of International Labour Studies* 21 (April 1984): 5–7.

Illinois Department of Labor. Annual Reports, 1977–1981, Chicago, Illinois.

International Ladies' Garment Workers Union. "Statement Of ILGWU in Opposition to the Removal of Restrictions on Industrial Homework." 1 July 1981.

Jacobs, Sanford L. "Federal 'Help' for these Workers Could Cost Them Their Incomes." *Wall Street Journal*, 30 June 1980, 17.

"Japan: the World's Biggest Cottage Industry." *The Economist*, 26 July 1980, 65.

Jensen, Leif. "Rural-Urban Differences in the Utilization and Ameliorative Effects of Welfare Programs." In "Symposium: Rural Versus Urban Poverty," *Policy Studies Review* 7, no. 4 (1988): 782–94.

Jessop, Bob. "Recent Theories of the Capitalist State." *Cambridge Journal of Economics* 1 no. 4 (December 1977): 353–73.

Johnson, Laura C. and Robert E. Johnson. *The Seam Allowance: Industrial Home Sewing in Canada.* Toronto: Women's Educational Press, 1982.

Jordon, David. "The Wages of Uncertainty: A Critique of Wages Council Orders." Pamphlet No. 6. London: Low Pay Unit, 1977.

Katz, Naomi and David S. Kemnitzer. "Fast Forward: The Internationalization of Silicon Valley." In *Women, Men, and the International Division of Labor*, edited by J. Nash and M. P. Fernandez-Kelly, 332–45. Albany: State University of New York Press, 1983.

Kawakami, Steven S. "Electronic Homework: Problems and Prospects from a Human Resources Perspective." Report for tutorial seminar LIR 494, Institute of Labor and Industrial Relations, University of Illinois at Urbana-Champaign, 7 September 1983.

Keller, Bill. "U.S. Ends Ban on Home Knitting for Sale." *New York Times*, 6 November 1984a, A18.

———. "Of Hearth and Home and the Right to Work." *New York Times* 11 November 1984b, E8.

———. "At the Center of New Fight: Home Work." *New York Times*, 20 May 1984c, 1.

Keller, John F. "The Division of Labor in Electronics." In *Women, Men, and the International Division of Labor*, edited by J. Nash and M. P. Fernandez-Kelly, 346–73. Albany: State University of New York Press, 1983.

Kenrick, Jane. "Politics and the Construction of Women As Second-Class Workers." In *The Dynamics of Labour Market Segmentation*, edited by F. Wilkinson. New York: Academic Press, 1981.

Kessler-Harris, Alice. "Stratifying By Sex: Understanding the History of Working Women." In *Labor Market Segmentation*, edited by D. M. Gordon, R. C. Edwards, and M. Reich. Massachusetts: D. C., Heath and Co., 1975.

———. *Out to Work*. New York: Oxford University Press, 1982.

Ketchum, R. "Letter from the Country." *Blair and Ketchums Country Journal* 7 (1980): 18–19.

Kinsman, Francis. *The Telecommuters*. New York: John Wiley and Sons, 1987.

Korte, W. B., S. Robinson, and W. J. Steinle, eds., *Telework: Present Situation and Future Development of a New Form of Work Organization*. New York: Elsevier Science Publishing Co., 1988.

Kraut, Robert E. and Patricia Grambsch. "Home-Based White Collar Employment: Lessons from the 1980 Census." *Social Forces* 66, no. 2 (December 1987): 410–26.

Kriedte, Peter, Hans Medick, and Jurgen Schlumbohn. *Industrialization Before Industrialization*. New York: Cambridge University Press, 1981.

"Labor Dept. Wants to End Curbs On Work at Home." *Wall Street Journal*. 4 May 1981, 10.

Landes, David. *The Unbound Prometheus*. London: Cambridge University Press, 1969.

Larson, Erik. "Working at Home: Is It Freedom or a Life of Flabby Loneliness." *Wall Street Journal*, 13 February 1985, 33.

Lawson, Tony. "Paternalism and Labour Market Segmentation Theory." In *The Dynamics of Labour Market Segmentation*, edited by F. Wilkinson, 47–66. New York: Academic Press, 1981.

Lazonick, William. "The Subjection of Labour to Capital: The Rise of the Capitalist System." *The Review of Radical Political Economics* 10, no. 1 (Spring 1978): 1–31.

Leichter, Franz S. *The Return of the Sweatshop: A Call for State Action*. New York State Senate Report. October 1979.

———. *The Return of the Sweatshop: Part II.* New York State Senate Report. 26 February 1981.

———. *Sweatshops to Shakedowns: Organized Crime in New York's Garment Industry.* New York State Senate Report. March 1982.

Lipsig-Mumme, Carla. "The Renaissance of Homeworking in Developed Economies." *Relations Industrielles* 38, no. 3 (1983): 545–66.

———. "Organizing Women in the Clothing Trades: Homework and the 1983 Garment Strike in Canada." *Studies in Political Economy* 22 (1987): 41–71.

Louv, Richard. *America II.* Boston: Houghton Mifflin Co., 1983.

Lozano, Beverly. "Informal Sector Workers: Walking Out the System's Front Door?" *International Journal of Urban and Regional Research* 7, no. 3 (September 1983): 340–61.

———. *The Invisible Workforce.* New York: Free Press, 1989.

Macrae, Norman. "The Coming Entrepreneurial Revolution: A Survey." *The Economist* 41–44, 25 December 1976, 53–65.

Maken, Morris. "Industrial Homework: The Bell Tolls for New York." *Industrial Bulletin.* New York State Department of Labor, March 1959, 12–16.

Mann, Michael. *States, War and Capitalism.* New York: Basil Blackwell, 1988.

Marglin, Stephen A. "What Do the Bosses Do? The Origins and Functions of Hierarchy in Capitalist Production." Discussion Paper No. 222, Harvard Institute of Economic Research, Cambridge, Massachusetts, May 1971.

Markoff, John. "The Sweatshop Returns: A New Subterranean Labor Market in Silicon Valley." Unpublished Paper, Pacific Studies Center, Mountain View, California, 1980.

Marsh, Barbara. "Franchisees See Home as Place to Set Up Shop." *Wall Street Journal,* 12 February 1990, B1.

Martinez, Sue and Alan Ramo. "In the Valley of the Shadow of Death." *In These Times* 8–14 October 1980, 12–13.

Marx, Karl. *Capital, Vol. 1.* New York: International Publishers, 1967.

Mattera, Philip. "Small is Not Beautiful: Decentralized Production and the Underground Economy in Italy." *Radical America* 14, no. 5 (September–October 1980): 67–76.

———. "Home Computer Sweatshops." *The Nation* 2 April 1983, 390–92.

———. *Off the Books: The Rise of the Underground Economy.* New York: St. Martin's Press, 1985.

McKay, Roberta V. "International Competition: Its Impact on Employment." In *The New Era of Home-Based Work*, edited by K. E. Christensen, 95–113. Boulder and London: Westview Press, 1988.

Michon, Francois. "Dualism and the French Labour Market: Business Strategy, Non-Standard Job Forms and Secondary Jobs." In *The Dynamics of Labour Market Segmentation*, edited by F. Wilkinson. New York: Academic Press, 1981.

Miliband, Ralph. *Marxism and Politics.* New York: Oxford University Press, 1977.

Milkman, Ruth. "Organizing the Sexual Division of Labor: Historical Perspectives on 'Women's Work' and the American Labor Movement." *Socialist Review* 10, no. 49 (January–February 1980).

———. "Redefining 'Women's Work': The Sexual Division of Labor in the Auto Industry During World War II." *Feminist Studies* 8, no. 2 (Summer 1982).

Miller, Frieda S. "Industrial Home Work in the United States." *International Labor Review* 43, no. 1 (January–June 1941): 1–50.

Mingione, Enzo. "Social Reproduction of the Surplus Labour Force: The Case of Southern Italy." In *Beyond Employment: Household, Gender, and Subsistence*, edited by N. Redlift and E. Mingione. Oxford: Basil Blackwell, 1985.

———. *Fragmented Societies.* Cambridge: Basil Blackwell, 1991.

Mitter, Swasti. "Rise of a Semi-Proletariat: Bangladeshi Female Homeworkers in the London Rag Trade." *Newsletter of International Labour Studies* 21 (April 1984): 7–9.

———. "Industrial Restructuring and Manufacturing Homework:

Immigrant Women in the U.K. Clothing Industry." *Capital and Class* 27 (Winter 1986): 37–80.

Morales, Rebecca. "Cold Solder on a Hot Stove." In *The Technological Woman*, edited by J. Zimmerman. New York: Praeger Publishers, 1983.

Moskowitz, Daniel B. "IRS Sharpens Definitions of Who is an Employee." *Washington Post*, 2 September 1991, WB15.

Moxon, Richard W. "Offshore Production In the Less Developed Countries—A Case Study of Multinationality in the Electronics Industry." *The Bulletin.* New York University Graduate School of Business Administration, Institute of Finance, Nos. 98–99, July 1974.

Murray, Geoffrey. "Japan's Cottage Workers—Vital Cogs in Big Machine." *Christian Science Monitor*, 23 June 1981, 2.

Narotzky, Susana. " 'Not to Be a Burden': Ideologies of the Domestic Group and Women's Work in Rural Catalonia." In *Work Without Wages: Domestic Labor and Self-Employment Within Capitalism*, edited by J. Collins and M. Gimenez, 70–88. Albany: State University of New York Press, 1990.

National Board for Prices and Income. "Pay and Conditions in the Clothing Manufacturing Industries." Report No. 110. London: HMSO, 1969.

New Jersey Department of Labor. "Study on Industrial Homework." Division of Workplace Standards, 1982.

"New Regulations on Homeworkers." *Social and Labour Bulletin* 2 (1982b): 216–17.

New York State Department of Labor. Public Hearing on Industrial Homework, 2 April 1981. Transcript.

———. Division of Labor Standards. "Report to the Governor and the Legislature on the Garment Manufacturing Industry and Industrial Homework." Albany, February 1982a.

———. Division of Labor Standards. "Study of State-Federal Employment Standards for Industrial Homeworkers in New York City." Albany 1982b.

New York State Statistical Yearbook. The Nelson A Rockefeller Institute of Government. New York, N.Y.: Science Press, 1980–1990.

Noble, Kenneth B. "U.S. Weighs End to Ban on Factory Homework." *New York Times*, 20 August 1986.

Norwood, Allen. "Caught in the Threads of Bureaucracy." *Charlotte Observer*, 2 March 1986, C1.

O'Connor, David. "Global Trends in Electronics: Implications for Developing Countries." Unpublished paper, 1984.

O'Connor, James. *The Fiscal Crisis of the State*. New York: St. Martin's Press, 1973.

Office Workstations in the Home. Washington: National Academy Press, 1985.

Olson, Margrethe H. "Corporate Culture and the Homeworker." In *The New Era of Home-Based Work*, edited by K. E. Christensen, 126–34. Boulder and London: Westview Press, 1988.

Oppenheimer, Valerie Kincade. *The Female Labor Force in the United States*. Population Monograph Series, no. 5. Berkeley: Institute of International Studies, University of California, 1970.

Pahl, R. E. and Claire Wallace. "Household Work Strategies in Economic Recession." In *Beyond Employment: Household, Gender, and Subsistence*, edited by N. Redclift and E. Mingione, 189–227. New York: Basic Blackwell, 1985.

Paulin, Valentine. "Home Work in France: Its Origin, Evolution, and Future." *International Labour Review* 37 (January–June 1938): 192–225.

Pennington, Shelley and Belinda Westover. *A Hidden Workforce: Homeworkers in England, 1850–1985*. London: Macmillan Education, 1989.

Pineda-Ofreneo, R. "Philippine Domestic Outwork: Subcontracting for Export-Oriented Industries." *Journal of Contemporary Asia* 12, no. 3 (1983): 281–93.

Pinnaro, Gabriella and Enrico Pugliese. "Informalization and Social Resistance: The Case of Naples." In *Beyond Employment: Household, Gender, and Subsistence*, edited by N. Redclift and E. Mingione. New York: Basil Blackwell, 1985.

Piore, Michael. "Dualism as a Response to Flux and Uncertainty." In *Dualism and Discontinuity in Industrial Societies*, edited by S. Berger and M. Piore, 23–54. Cambridge: Cambridge University Press, 1980a.

———. "The Technological Foundations of Dualism and Discontinuity." In *Dualism and Discontinuity in Industrial Societies*, edited by S. Berger and M. Piore, 55–81. Cambridge: Cambridge University Press, 1980b.

Piore, Michael and Charles Sabel. "Italian Small Business Development: Lessons for U.S. Industrial Policy." In *American Industry in International Competition*, edited by L. Tyson and J. Zysman. Ithaca: Cornell University Press, 1983.

Piore, Michael J. and Charles F. Sabel. *The Second Industrial Divide*. New York: Basic Books, 1984.

"Plan to Lift Ban on Hiring Individuals to Work at Home Meets Stiff Criticism." *Wall Street Journal*, 20 May 1981, 22.

Portes, Alejandro and John Walton. *Labor, Class, and the International System*. New York: Academic Press, 1981.

Portes, Alejandro, Manuel Castells and Lauren Benton, eds. *The Informal Economy*. Baltimore: Johns Hopkins University Press, 1989.

Portes, Alejandro and Saskia Sassen-Koob. "Making It Underground: Comparative Material on the Informal Sector in Western Market Economies." *American Journal of Sociology* 93, no. 1 (July 1987): 30–61.

"The Potential for Telecommuting." *Business Week*, 26 January 1981b, 94.

Potter, Ray. "This Businessman Hopes to Profit from the Midas Touch." *San Jose Mercury News*, 26 December 1982.

Poulantzas, Nicos. *Political Power and Social Classes*. London: New Left Books, 1973.

"Printed Circuits." *Global Electronics Information Newsletter* 46 (September 1984).

Probert, Belinda and Judy Wajcman. "Technological Change and the Future of Work." *Journal of Industrial Relations* 30, no. 3 (September 1988): 432–48.

"Protection of Homeworkers." *Social and Labour Bulletin* 3 (1981c): 311–12.

Rao, Rukmini and Sahba Husain. "Women Workers in the Delhi Garment Export Industry." *Newsletter of International Labour Studies* 21 (April 1984): 11–12.

Rauch, Johathan. "Anatomy of a Regulatory Proposal—The Battle Over Industrial Homework." *National Journal* 13, no. 23 (6 June 1981): 1013–16.

Risseeuw, Carla. "Organisation and Disorganisation: A Case Study of Women Coir Workers in Sri Lanka." In *Invisible Threads: Women in Home-Based Production*, edited by A. M. Singh and A. Kelles-Vutanen, 177–205. California: Sage Publications, 1987.

———. "Invisible Hands: Women in Home-Based Production in the Garment Export Industry in Delhi." In *Invisible Threads: Women in Home-Based Production*, edited by A. M. Singh and A. Kelles-Vutanen, 51–67. California: Sage Publications, 1987.

Rohini, P. R., S. V. Sujata, C. Neelam. "Strategies for Mobilising Women Workers." *Newsletter of Interational Labour Studies* 21 (April 1984): 22–25.

Roldan, Martha. "Industrial Outworking, Struggles for the Reproduction of Working-Class Families and Gender Subordination." In *Beyond Employment: Household, Gender, and Subsistence*, edited by N. Redclift and E. Mingione. New York: Basil Blackwell, Inc., 1985.

Rubery, Jill and Frank Wilkinson. "Outwork and Segmented Labour Markets." In *The Dynamics of Labour Market Segmentation*, edited by F. Wilkinson. New York: Academic Press, 1981.

Russell, Raymond. "Using Ownership to Control: Making Workers Owners in the Contemporary United States." *Politics and Society* 13, no. 3 (1984): 239–52.

Saba, A. *La Industria Subterranea: Un Nuevo Modelo de Desarollo.* Institut Alfons el Magnanim, 1981.

Sabel, Charles. *Work and Politics: The Division of Labor in Industry.* Cambridge: Cambridge University Press, 1982.

Sayer, A. "Postfordism in Question," *International Journal of Urban and Regional Research* 13, no. 4 (1989): 666–95.

Sayin, Afife Fevzi. *Industrial Home Work in Pennsylvania.* Ph.D. diss., Bryn Mawr College, 1945.

Schlein, Lisa. "Los Angeles' Garment District Sews a Cloak of Shame." *Los Angeles Times,* 5 March 1978, V3.

Schwartz, John. "Three Views of Working At Home." *Personal Computing,* February 1987, 87–95.

Schmiechen, James A. *Sweated Industries and Sweated Labor: The London Clothing Trades, 1860–1914.* Urbana and Chicago: The University of Illinois Press, 1984.

Scott, A. J. "Industrial Organization and the Logic of Intra-Metropolital Location II: A Case Study of the Printed Circuits Industry in the Greater Los Angeles Region." *Economic Geography* 59, no. 4 (October 1983): 343–67.

———. "Industrial Organization and the Logic of Metropolitan Location III: A Case Study of the Women's Dress Industry in the Greater Los Angeles Region." *Economic Geography* 60, no. 1 (January 1984): 3–27.

Scott, Joan Wallach. "The Mechanization of Women's Work." *Scientific American,* September 1982.

"See No Quick Return of Offshore Work." *Electronic News.* 16 February 1976, 70.

Serrin, William. "Part-time Work New Labor Trend." *New York Times,* 9 July 1986, A1.

"Sewers Support Unraveling of Garment Homework Rules." *The Post-Standard.* Syracuse, N.Y. 25 September 1986, B9.

Shabecoff, Philip. "Donovan Seeks to End Ban on Jobs at Home in Apparel Industries." *New York Times,* 2 May 1981b, 1.

———. "U.S. Eases Ban On Knitting By Workers in Their Homes." *New York Times,* 9 October 1981a, A12.

Shallcross, Ruth Enalda. *Industrial Homework: An Analysis of Homework Regulation, Here and Abroad.* New York: Industrial Affairs Publishing Co., 1939.

Sharp, Hugh. "Working in a Wages Council Industry." *Department of Employment Gazette* 86, no. 11 (November 1978): 1259–62.

Sharpston, Michael. "International Sub-contracting." *Oxford Economic Papers* 27, no. 1 (March 1975): 94–135.

Shirley, Steve. "A Company Without Offices." *Harvard Business Review* 64, no. 1 (January–February 1986): 127–36.

Shupe, Barbara, Janet Steins, and Jyoti Pandit. *New York State Population.* New York: Neal-Schuman Publishers, 1987.

Silver, Hilary. "The Demand for Homework." In *Homework: Historical and Contemporary Perspectives on Paid Labor at Home*, edited by E. Boris and C. R. Daniels, 103–29. Urbana and Chicago: University of Illinois Press, 1989.

———. "Homework and Domestic Work." *Sociological Forum* 8, no. 2 (1993): 181–204.

Simonson, Joy R. "Protection of Clerical Homeworkers: From What, by Whom?" In *The New Era of Home-Based Work*, edited by K. E. Christensen, 157–67. Boulder and London: Westview Press, 1988.

Singh, Andrea Menefee and Anita Kelles-Vutanen, eds., *Invisible Hands: Women in Home-Based Production.* California: Sage Publications, 1987.

Skocpol, Theda. *States and Social Revolutions.* New York: Cambridge University Press, 1979.

———. "Political Response to Capitalist Crisis: Neo-Marxist Theories of the State and the Case of the New Deal." *Politics and Society* 10, no. 2 (1980): 155–201.

Slade, Margot. "Working At Home: The Pitfalls." *New York Times*, 21 October 1985, B8.

Sleeper, David. "The Electronic Homestead is Coming." *Blair and Ketchums Country Journal* 9 (1982): 77–80.

Smith, Joan. "The Way We Were: Women and Work." *Feminist Studies* 8, no. 2 (Summer 1982).

———. "The Paradox of Women's Poverty: Wage Earning Women and Economic Transformation." *Signs* 10 (Winter 1984): 291–310.

Snow, Robert T. "The New International Division of Labor and the U.S. Work Force: The Case of the Electronics Industry." In *Women, Men, and the International Division of Labor*, edited by J. Nash and M. P. Fernandez-Kelly. Albany: State University of New York Press, 1983.

Stansell, Christine. "The Origins of the Sweatshop: Women and

Early Industrialization in New York City." In *Working-Class America*, edited by M. Frisch and D. J. Walkowitz, 78–103. Urbana and Chicago: University of Illinois Press, 1983.

Statistical Abstracts of the United States, 1992.

"Tangled Yarn." Editorial. *Wall Street Journal* 6 December 1983.

Tanzi, Vito. *The Underground Economy in the United States and Abroad*. Massachusetts: D.C. Heath and Co., 1982.

"Tending to Knitting." Editorial. *Wall Street Journal* 16 September 1981, 26.

Teper, Lazare and Nathan Weinberg. "Aspects of Industrial Homework in Apparel Trades." International Ladies' Garment Workers Union Research Department, July 1941. (Reprinted in U.S. House of Representatives, "The Reemergence of Sweatshops and the Enforcement of Wage and Hour Standards." Hearings before the Subcommittee on Labor Standards of the Committee on Education and Labor. Washington, D.C.: U.S. Government Printing Office, 1982.)

"Terminal Crossroads: Office Automation and the Future of Clerical Work." *Dollars and Sense*, June 1986, 12–14.

Thompson, E. P. *The Making of the English Working Class*. New York: Vintage Books, 1963.

Trades Union Congress. "Homeworking: A TUC Statement." London: Victoria House Printing Company, not dated.

"Tripartite Enquiry on Homework." *Social and Labour Bulletin* 1 (1982a): 78.

"Uncle Sam Nitpicks the Knitters." *Newsweek*. 9 February 1981, 71.

U.S. Department of Commerce. Bureau of Industrial Economics. "Franchising in the Economy—1982–84." Washington D.C.: U.S. Government Printing Office, 1984.

U.S. Department of Commerce. Bureau of Industrial Economics. "Franchising in the Economy—1985–1987." Washington, D.C.: U.S. Government Printing Office, 1987.

U.S. Department of Labor. "Hours and Earnings in the Leather-Glove Industry." Women's Bureau Bulletin, no. 119. Washington, D.C.: U.S. Government Printing Office, 1934.

U.S. Department of Labor. Children's Bureau. "Child Labor and the Work of Mothers in Oyster and Shrimp Canning Communities on the Gulf Coast." Bureau Publication no. 98, 1922. Reprinted in *Suffer the Little Children*. New York: Arno Press, 1977.

———. Children's Bureau. "Industrial Home Work of Children: A Study Made in Providence, Pawtucket, and Central Falls, R.I." Bureau Publication no. 100, 1922. Reprinted in *Suffer the Little Children*. New York: Arno Press, 1977.

———. *The Commercialization of the Home Through Industrial Home Work*. Women's Bureau Bulletin no. 135. Washington D.C.: U.S. Government Printing Office, 1935.

———. *Employment and Earnings*. Bureau of Labor Statistics Monthly Reports. Washington D.C.: U.S. Government Printing Office.

U.S. Congress. House. House Committee on Ways and Means. "Independent Contractors: Hearings Before the Subcommittee on Select Revenue Measures on H.R. 3245, 20 June, 16–17 July 1979. Washington, D.C.: U.S. Government Printing Office, 1979.

———. "The Reemergence of Sweatshops and the Enforcement of Wage and Hour Standards." Hearings before the Subcommittee on Labor Standards of the Committee on Education and Labor. Washington D.C.: U.S. Government Printing Office, 1982.

———. Subcommittee on Labor Standards of the Committee on Education and Labor. "Oversight Hearings on the Dept. of Labor's Proposal to Lift the Ban on Industrial Homework." Washington D.C.: U.S. Government Printing Office, 1987.

Van Kleeck, Mary. "Child Labor in Home Industries." Supplement to the Annals of the American Academy of Political and Social Science, no. 26, March, Child Employing Industries. Proceedings of the Sixth Annual Meeting of the National Child Labor Committee. 1910, 145–49.

van Luijken, Anneke. "Homework in the Tilburg Region of the Netherlands." *Newsletter of International Labour Studies* 21 (April 1984): 9–11.

"VDT Law." *Technology Review* 91 (August/September 1988): 16.

Walsh, Joan. "Is Homework the Answer?" *MS.* (July/August 1987).

Webb, Marilyn. "Sweatshops for One: The Rise in Industrial Homework." *Village Voice*, 10–16 February 1982, 24–27.

Weiner, Elizabeth and Hardy Green. "A Stitch in Our Time: New York's Hispanic Garment Workers in the 1980's." In *A Needle, A Bobbin, A Strike: Women Needleworkers in America*, edited by J. M. Jensen and S. Davidson, 278–96. Philadelphia: Temple University Press, 1984.

Weir, Margaret, Ann Shola Orloff, Theda Skocpol. *The Politics of Social Policy in the United States.* New Jersey: Princeton University Press, 1988.

West, Jackie, ed. *Work, Women and the Labour Market.* London: Routledge and Kegan Paul, 1982.

Wilkinson, Frank, ed. *The Dynamics of Labour Market Segmentation.* New York Academic Press, 1981.

Index

215

47, 150, 151; benefits of for
workers, 21, 22, 36, 41, 46, 117,
119, 120; in central New York,
xiii–xvi, 6, 17–45, 59, 60, 63–
69, 70, 74, 91, 136, 138, 148,
149, 160, 161; depictions of, 1,
15, 112, 113; disadvantages for
employers, 92; distributors of,
xv, 19, 30, 32, 33, 64–66, 174n;
in electronics, xiv, 1, 14, 17–45,
54, 58–69, 72, 73, 87, 90, 91;
and family economy, 99, 117;
and gender division of labor, 2,
3, 10, 47, 74, 80–82, 97, 99–101,
107, 108, 120–122; geographical
distribution of, 123, 134, 151,
158, 162; government investigations of, 132–134, 141–147, 153,
155, 185n, 186n, 187n; illegal
operations, xiv, 10, 19, 69, 88,
89, 92, 109, 110, 148, 152, 153,
156, 158; impetus behind spread
of, 6, 17, 18, 46, 47, 123, 162;
importance of income from, 27–
29, 34, 39–43; 112–115, 173n,
182n; inaccuracy of statistics on,
88, 89, 154–158; industrial, 8,
15, 46, 74–76, 101, 132; industries using, xiv, 1, 14, 15, 17–45,
46, 54, 55, 58–69, 71–73, 88, 90,
91, 113, 128, 145, 153, 155,
184n, 186n; labor process for
waged, 14, 30; origins of industrial, 8, 76, 78–83, 160; and labor market, 10, 12, 13, 35, 36,
74, 118, 121, 122; and labor
shortages, 91; laws in U.S., xiv,
1, 10, 20, 65, 66, 75, 109, 110,
123–159; liberal views on, 3, 4,
11, 163, 170n; and multinational
corporations, 7, 19, 48, 53, 64;
necessary conditions for, 89–92;
organization of production in,
11, 152, 158; permits issued, 18,
48, 134–136, 140, 141, 146, 153,
155, 161, 174n; political debates
about, xv, 11, 127, 163–165;

politics of, 3, 4, 12, 162, 163;
productivity of, 111, 112; public
perceptions of, 2, 15, 153; role
in development of production
process, 107, 108; in rural areas,
10, 21, 33, 38, 43, 45, 91, 113;
119, 120, 151; and salaried
professionals, 1, 12, 13, 15, 91,
121; in service occupations, 15,
75, 92; in shoe industry, 71, 72;
in service occupatuons, 15, 75,
92; in shoe industry, 71, 72; social relations underlying, 92, 97;
structural nature of, 6, 8, 18, 74,
87–89, 97, 98, 160; supervision
of operations in, 14; and subcontracting, 54, 56, 68, 69, 90,
91; as unfair competition, 129;
and union-busting, 55, 92, 166;
unpaid labor in, 59, 60, 175n; in
urban areas, 10, 33, 34; working
conditions of, 14, 31, 47, 58–61,
132, 153. See also telecommuters.

homeworkers: as agents of change,
4; attitudes about work, 109–
112; in Britain, 110–112; in central New York, xiv, xv, 6, 17–45,
109, 110, 114, 115, 117–120;
characteristics of, xv, 6, 20, 21;
class divisions among, 6, 33,
116, 120–122; controversy over
legal status of, 110–112; in electronics, xiv, xv, 17–45, 109;
enumeration of, 154, 156, 157;
feelings about homework, 1, 11,
17, 36, 43, 109; in Los Angeles,
xv, 34; men as, xv, 20, 36, 121,
183n; in Mexico City, 7; in New
York City, 34; political views of,
3; poverty among, 22–27, 34, 38,
40–43; race and ethnicity of, 6;
reasons for doing homework,
35–37, 43, 44, 116–120; in Silicon Valley, 34, 113; social networks among, 32, 33; views on
unions, 109

Rao, Rukmini, 113, 173n
Rauch, Jonathan, xiii, 129
Reagan Administration, 1, 142,
  143, 146, 154, 156, 157, 163,
  164, 169n, 171n
refugees, 59
restructuring: of capital and industry, 48, 52, 57, 70–74, 76, 97,
  104, 161; effects of on labor
  market, 104, 105; of electronics
  industry, 61–69, 70, 72–74; and
  franchising, 52; and homework,
  7, 46, 48, 52, 53, 70, 72; of shoe
  industry, 71, 72; and subcontracting, 52, 53. See also decentralization of production
Rhode Island, 75, 152, 155–158,
  185n, 186n
Right, the. See conservatives
Risseeuw, Carla, 113
Roberts, Lillian, 136, 186n
Rochester, N.Y., 132
Roldan, Martha, 7, 52, 59, 61, 96,
  117, 173n
Roosevelt, Eleanor, 128
Rubery, Jill, 85, 91, 177n
Russell, Raymond, 49, 50, 52

Saba, A., 176n
Sabel, Charles, 49, 56, 86, 176n
Sayin, Afife Fevzi, 114, 123, 124,
  153, 182n, 187n
Schmiechen, James, A., 86
Schwartz, John, 59
Scott, A. J., xiii, 56, 69, 90
self-employment, 48–50, 166; and
  decentralization of production,
  51, 52; differences between men
  and women in, 121; as disguised
  wage work, 95, 110, 111, 170n;
  and franchises, 49, 50, 52;
  home-based, 12–15, 47, 50,
  171n; measurement problems
  with, 50, 174n; of men, 13; in
  service sector, 13; and subcon-

tracting, 49–51, 175n; trends in,
  50–52, 56; of women, 13.
semiconductors, 87. See also electronics components; electronics
  industry
Service Employees International
  Union, 92, 157
service sector, 58, 105; self-employment in, 13
sewing machine, 86, 87
Sheinkman, Jack, 143
shoe industry: family labor system
  in, 80, 81; homework in, 71, 72,
  80, 81, 88, 90, 91, 179n; homework's effect on organization of
  production in, 107; in Spain, 71,
  179n
Silicon Valley, xiii, 34, 55, 58, 63,
  69, 113, 120
Silver, Hilary, 13, 14, 58, 121, 129,
  153, 156, 171n, 180n
Skaneatelus, N.Y., 172n
Skocpol, Theda, 125
Sleeper, David, xiii
Snow, Robert T., 62, 64
snowball sampling, 18, 19, 173n
social reformers, 124, 127–130,
  132, 183–184n
Social Security, 50
South Otselic, N.Y., 172n
Spafford, N.Y., 172n
Spain, 7, 70–73
Sri Lanka, 66, 113, 152
Stansell, Christine, 78, 86, 101,
  107
state, the: and class conflict, 6,
  125, 126, 131, 158; contradictory interests of, 11, 124–127,
  131, 158, 162; effect on homework, 5, 10, 11, 109, 123, 124,
  126, 127, 132, 149–159, 162;
  and gender ideology, 125, 128–
  131; interaction with capital and
  labor, xvi, 5, 10, 11, 124–127,
  129, 136, 147, 149, 158, 167; investigations of homework by,

Wisconsin State Employees Union, 170n
women. *See* gender division of labor; gender ideology; homework; self-employment
Women Working Home, Inc., 165
women's apparel, 114; homework ban in, xiv, 140
Women's Bureau. *See* United States
Women's, Infant's and Children's Program (WIC), 23, 38, 42
Women's Trade Union League, 128
work: casualization of, 47, 48, 56–58, 73, 111; conditions of for homeworkers, 14, 31, 47, 58–61, 132, 153; deskilling of, 49, 73; disguised wage work, 94, 95, 179n; part-time, 56, 57; supervision of and control by capitalists, 83–85; temporary, 56–58; variations in patterns of, 8, 70–74, 93, 97, 104, 105; unpaid, xvi, 5, 59, 60, 101–103, 131, 160, 170n. *See also* gender ideology
working conditions. *See* work

zoning laws, 147